'A raw, honest story that needs to be heard. Sharon Pincott gives a passionate and moving voice to a species in peril; the silent, innocent victims of man's greed.'

Tony Park, bestselling author of *An Empty Coast*

'A woman on a passionate mission. Her astonishing adventure. Political intrigue. A book to take the reader into another world.'

Caroline Jones AO, presenter, *Australian Story*

'This mesmerizing book is not just about a love of elephants, it is also about the indomitable spirit of someone who followed her passion. Sharon Pincott is one of the bravest women I have ever known. She has risked so much for elephants and it is a gift to us that we can now read this moving account of her thirteen years in Zimbabwe fighting to save a population of elephants she came to know intimately.'

Cynthia Moss, world-renowned elephant specialist, celebrated in BBC's *Echo of the Elephants*

# SHARON PINCOTT

# ELEPHANT DAWN

The inspirational story of thirteen years living
with elephants in the African wilderness

ALLEN&UNWIN
SYDNEY•MELBOURNE•AUCKLAND•LONDON

First published in 2016

Allen & Unwin
83 Alexander Street
Crows Nest NSW 2065
Australia
Phone:  (61 2) 8425 0100
Email:  info@allenandunwin.com
Web:  www.allenandunwin.com

Cataloguing-in-Publication details are available
from the National Library of Australia
www.trove.nla.gov.au

ISBN 978 1 76029 033 7

Maps by Janet Hunt
Set in 11/17 pt Minion Pro by Midland Typesetters, Australia
Printed and bound in Australia by Griffin Press

10 9 8 7 6 5 4 3 2

*In memory of Lady*

Some names in this book have been changed to protect identities.

# CONTENTS

'The greatness of a nation and its moral progress can be judged by the way its animals are treated.'

— Mahatma Gandhi

'You have enemies? Good. That means you've stood up for something, sometime in your life.'

— Winston Churchill

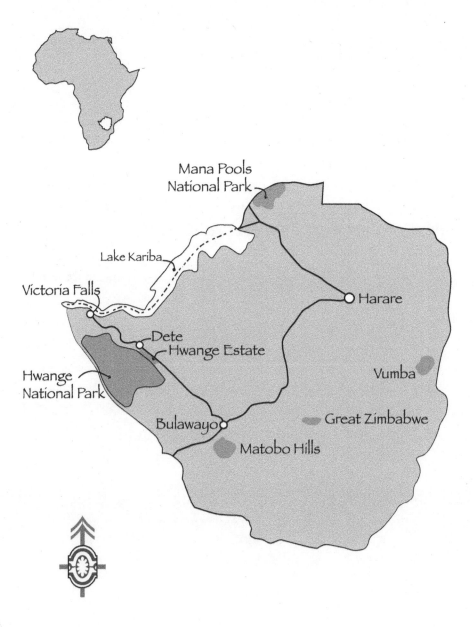

Mana Pools
National Park

Lake Kariba

Victoria Falls

Harare

Dete
Hwange Estate

Hwange
National Park

Vumba

Great Zimbabwe

Bulawayo

Matobo Hills

# PROLOGUE

I am sitting at a desk in a high-rise office block in Brisbane when an email arrives in my inbox. Contracted to Telstra as an information technology consultant, there is nothing unusual about this. Even my colleagues sitting only a few metres away send me emails with documents to review. I sigh under the weight of more apparent work and choose to delay the inevitable. How important can it be?

On this warm autumn day in the year 2000 I learn that my friend Andy Searle, a wildlife warden in Zimbabwe's Hwange National Park, is dead. He was 38. I am one year younger. He was alone, heading home to his wife, Lol, and young son, Drew, after a rhino tracking outing inside the national park when his helicopter went down.

Hwange National Park in Zimbabwe's west is a place that I have come to know well. Now I'm travelling there unexpectedly for the funeral of my friend. Only last year, Andy and Lol had been my guests on Fraser Island, the world's largest sand island off the coast of Queensland where I'd spent many childhood holidays. Fond memories of them holding hands, splashing through waves with seagulls flitting around them, brings tears to my eyes.

As I jet over the ocean, a deep rectangular hole is being dug in the earth by Andy's friends, as is the African way. He will be buried at the edge of the vast 14,600 square kilometre tract of land that is the national park. For some it might seem a lonely place to be laid to rest, but not so for Andy. He will be at one with the wildlife that he dedicated his life to: creatures such as the rhino, lion, giraffe and zebra. And the magnificent elephant.

It was in a nearby area, during 1999, that Andy first introduced me to the Presidential Elephants of Zimbabwe. He had taken me with him on a lion-collaring exercise and we'd stopped off at a waterhole to observe the comings and goings of some of these wild elephants. Andy believed that I belonged in the African bush. But neither of us realised how profoundly these magnificent animals would become the centre of my life.

I am present at Andy's funeral held under a clear blue sky, in attractive bush surroundings beside his grave. I am among friends. A week passes, just another week for some but a particularly sorrowful one for me. I decide that I need to visit the site where the crash occurred, to see it with my own eyes. We're soon on our way, escorted by a National Parks scout, driving past enchanting wildflowers and trees, animals and waterholes. Then we are off the tourist roads and into the bush. As I step down from our vehicle I catch sight through the bushes of the helicopter on the ground, lying broken. I pick a handful of bright yellow wildflowers and place them where Andy's body had been found. I speak to him. I feel close to him. I make a silent promise to return.

Two days before I fly back to Australia, we have a *braai* (as the locals call a barbeque) and a sing-along accompanied by guitar beside Andy's grave. It's time for me to say goodbye. We arrive to herds of antelope keeping Andy company. United once again in grief, we watch in silence as an elephant wanders by in the sunset. The John Denver song 'Leaving on a Jet Plane' that we later sing under a vivid full moon, holds real meaning; I have no idea when I'll be back again. Words from Kuki Gallmann's book *I Dreamed of Africa* come to mind, bringing some comfort:

They had loved him, shared in fun, mischief, adventures. Now they shared the same anguish ... contemplating their memories and their loss. This experience would forever live with them, and make them grow, and make them better, wiser.

I fly back to Australia and never quite settle into my First World life again.

A decade earlier, I'd been happily immersed in my career as an information technology executive, which peaked with my role as national director of information technology for Ernst & Young. I had loved my work with this accountancy giant, together with the memorable camaraderie and lasting friendships that accompanied it, happily putting in exceptionally long hours. But it was time for a change. In 1993 I resigned from this last permanent position that I would ever hold and, at the age of 31, I moved across the Tasman to Auckland and began a series of IT contracts, including an enduring one with Air New Zealand.

I enjoyed a high-flying life with a harbour-view apartment, luxury cars and frequent first-class trips around the globe for business and pleasure. Somewhat surprisingly, Africa—and most notably a fascination with its wildlife—began to feature prominently in my life. Its great expanses of wilderness, replete with stunning fauna and flora, had become my garden of Eden. After five years based in New Zealand, I'd found myself back in Australia, living in a beautiful suburban Brisbane home and enjoying the comforts of being mortgage free. I continued to travel to the wilds of Africa as often as I could in between IT contracts that financed this growing obsession.

A few months after Andy's death, while still contracted to Telstra, I'm invited to join a leadership seminar in Victoria's Dandenong Ranges. It's all rather New Age. I'm in a room filled with IT professionals lying on the floor, surrounded by candles, relaxation music and soft voices. Feeling cosy and warm with duvets and pillows amid snowy mountainous surrounds, we listen for three days to a man telling stories. Every story has a message. It's up to us to find that message, confront it, and if we choose to, incorporate its lessons into our personal and professional lives. These few days help me to realise what is really important in my life: to believe in my own abilities, to look out for my own welfare, to find a balance between my personal and professional lives and not to worry unduly about the small stuff. My time here helps me to accept the things I can't change and to leave life's unnecessary baggage behind.

It is here too that I learn about a survey carried out among a group of 95 year olds. If they could do it all again, these wise elders were asked, what would they do differently? They would take more risks. They would take more time for reflection. And they would leave a legacy.

I head off from this seminar, having grown in mind and spirit, enjoying the warmth of new friendships and feeling ready to move my life forwards in a totally different direction. It is not what Telstra was hoping for when it invited me along. This is the last time that I work in information technology. I throw caution to the wind, resolving to embark on an entirely new and impossibly different life.

In Zimbabwe.

*Zimbabwe? Who in their right mind would voluntarily go and live in Robert Mugabe's Zimbabwe?*

# PLAIN CRAZY

## 2001

'Tell me again why I'm learning to do this,' I plead.

'They're killing white farmers over there, under the pretext of land reform,' I'm told matter-of-factly. 'It's the wrong time for anybody white to be going to live in that crazy country. Learning how to at least handle a weapon is a good idea.'

So I spend the early months of 2001 undergoing weapons training in Brisbane. I do this only because caring friends insist that it is wise. My neighbour is a security guard and he enthusiastically accompanies me to an indoor firing range where my shooting prowess is soon evident. With a revolver in hand I am lethal. He stands beside me shouting streams of mock abuse, trying to intimidate, to undermine my concentration and determination as I scramble to reload and fire. He doesn't succeed in unsettling me. In one swift movement I shoot my would-be attacker right between the eyes.

At the same time, my white Zimbabwean friend Val has me making phone calls to Australian government agencies in search of the necessary forms that she will need to complete in order to get herself and her son *out* of Zimbabwe. Hundreds of thousands of others are doing the same thing, diving into the diaspora away from the madness of their president and his regime. Yet here I am, excited at the prospect of going in the opposite direction. Maybe I'm dangerously naïve—or perhaps just plain crazy.

Certainly, others seem to know much more about Zimbabwe than I. Many, though, don't seem to know anything about this country at all. 'Zaire?' my father questions. We are siting on the patio of the family home where I grew up, the third of his four daughters, in the sleepy country town of Grantham in Queensland's Lockyer Valley.

'No, no, Dad,' I sigh. '*Zimbabwe.*'

I dig out an old school atlas and flick through the pages until I find a map of the African continent. I point to Zimbabwe, a landlocked country in the south-east, just above South Africa. It is, apparently, judging by the confused reactions of my family and friends, a rather insignificant country known only for its president. I start to call my future home 'Robert Mugabe's Zimbabwe' so that they will all remember where I've gone. Even this doesn't always help, I realise, after bumping into a couple who ask when I'll be leaving for Zanzibar.

'You're mad going to Zululand,' says my dad the next time I see him.

I roll my eyes. 'Zimbabwe, Dad,' I say again. 'I'm going to live in *Zimbabwe.*'

My ticket is booked and I will be flying into the town of Victoria Falls, home to one of the seven natural wonders of the world. The falls are flanked by the southern African nations of Zimbabwe and Zambia, on the Zambezi River. I dare not tell too many people this. More 'Z' words would only serve to confuse them further.

I haven't yet decided whether I will sell my Brisbane home, or rent it out. For now I will leave it locked up, with kind friends happy to keep an eye on things and tend to my garden. I still have to plough through the messy web of visa approvals and paperwork needed to allow me to legally stay in Zimbabwe on a full-time basis. I leave everything as it is, packing just one suitcase, while remembering a promise I once made. Someone very close to my heart will accompany me on this journey—my nearly eighteen-year-old white toy poodle, Chloe, who took her last breaths just six months ago. She will travel with me in her little ceramic pot, and I will sprinkle her ashes in this country that I am soon to call home. For years I had promised her that, one day, she would come with me to Africa.

On 5 March 2001, 364 days after receiving that heartbreaking email, I gaze down on what looks like smoke, but is in fact the thick misty spray of the Victoria Falls. I disembark at a quiet, ramshackle airport in Robert Mugabe's Zimbabwe. Flight arrival and departure information is scrawled in white chalk on blackboards, and immigration agents with rubber stamps sit behind rickety wooden desks like school children. There is not a computer in sight.

I breathe deeply. This is *exactly* where I want to be. It's not that I'm worn out by my First World life. It's simply that I believe I can make a bigger difference here.

There are few tourists arriving these days, a sign that international travellers are prudently heeding travel warnings to stay away. As I collect my bag from a line of luggage neatly assembled on the floor, I can see the beaming faces of Val and others as they smile at me through a gap in the wall, waving frantically. They're my African family. We're already bonded by a common choice of life in the African bush and an acute awareness of sharing this privilege with each other.

'You made it,' Val gushes as she hugs me tightly. 'Your cottage renovations are just about complete, but first let's go for lunch and a celebratory drink in town.'

We stop to marvel briefly at the falls, and to listen to the continuous thundering roar of the huge volumes of water plunging over its cliffs, appreciating its African name *'Mosi-oa-Tunya'* ('the smoke that thunders'). Vervet monkeys with powder-blue balls bound around in the treetops. At a safari lodge looking out over the spectacular Zambezi

National Park we spot magnificent elephants, and excitedly raise our glasses in a toast.

'Cheers!' we all grin, clinking our glasses together and savouring this new beginning.

# GREEN EGGS AND HAM

# 2001

When I was just 24 years old I worked as an instructor for Wang Australia. Power-dressed to disguise my young age, I tutored executives and veteran secretaries in computer literacy and word processing, way back when most of the world knew little about either. My trainees were not always enthusiastic. In desperation, I turned to one of Dr Seuss' legendary children's books in an attempt to persuade them to try something new and different. I began each class—'*I am Sam, Sam I am . . . Do you like Green Eggs and Ham?*' But not even I imagined that my own 'new and different', some fifteen years later, would turn out to be *quite* so out of the ordinary. I've ditched it all and stepped outside my routine life. I'm about to start working with wild free-roaming elephants!

I saw my first wild elephant in South Africa's Kruger National Park in 1993. I was instantly enthralled: his sheer size and magnificence took my breath away. Now I'm about to start up my very own project, working with the Presidential Elephants of Zimbabwe.

They're a group of several hundred elephants who roam on a 140 square kilometre slice of land just outside the Main Camp entrance to Hwange National Park. This land is known locally as the Hwange Estate. Their special status was bestowed back in 1990, when a white Zimbabwean safari operator, who had close ties to the Ruling Party and an exclusive grip on this land, requested from President Mugabe a 'special protection decree' for the elephants that spend the majority of their time here. They were never to be hunted or culled and were supposed to symbolise Zimbabwe's commitment to responsible wildlife management. President Mugabe issued the decree, and that's how they acquired their name. Up until the year 2000, when farm invasions started and Zimbabwe began its downward spiral into violence, lawlessness and economic collapse, this name had no particularly negative connotations for most people. President Robert Mugabe was considered to be a liberation hero for his part in ending white rule a decade earlier.

But there had never been anything special implemented on the ground to give weight to the decree and there'd been no notable government interest in them since early publicity about their naming. The day that Andy first introduced me to some of the Presidential Elephants, he told me the man who'd obtained the decree had already sold up and was gone from the area. No one was currently monitoring these elephants or actively promoting their existence.

I later learn that numerous people within Zimbabwe believe the notion of this herd to have been little more than a clever publicity stunt that had financially benefited only a handful of people. Others think that these elephants no longer exist; that they've been shot out by poachers. Most international tourists, and quite a lot of locals too, have never even heard of them.

No one knows exactly how many there are. They're said to currently number around three hundred, but this has to be a stab in the dark at best since all of the family structures are not yet accurately known, although some prior identification work had taken place years earlier. So my planned day-to-day work is to properly understand the social structure, and ultimately the population dynamics, of this particular clan of elephants—by first getting to know them all as individuals as well as members of their cohesive families. The vast Hwange National Park and this adjoining estate are unfenced and so elephants (and other animals) roam freely between the two, simply by walking across the railway line which separates them. This will make figuring out what constitutes a *Presidential* Elephant family, as opposed to a general national park one, not easy at first.

Andy had taken me to meet Lionel Reynolds, a conservation-minded man on the ground, who at the time had jurisdiction over this land. After Andy died, my friend Val helped me get back in touch with Lionel, carrying a letter requesting that I be permitted to work on a full-time, voluntary basis with these elephants. I understood that committing anything less than three to five years full-time would be inconsequential. This was approved on the basis that I would be unpaid, and would have to find my own accommodation, and organise and fund everything myself. As we drive past one of the entrances to the Hwange Estate, I can still hardly believe that I'll be living and working here, among these elephants. It's such a far cry from information technology.

My planned work is not revolutionary, although it certainly is an exciting prospect for me: world-renowned and respected pioneers Iain Douglas-Hamilton, Cynthia Moss and Joyce Poole have been living among elephants in East Africa since the 1960s and 70s and all learnt to know their study groups intimately. I've been a follower and admirer of their work for years, fantasising that I might one day follow in their footsteps. They've already had lifetimes of adventures with elephants, and now here I am to begin my own.

While I'm certainly inspired by these three elephant pioneers, I have no interest in becoming an academic and working towards a degree—despite knowing that many of these folk with letters after their names contribute enormously to the knowledge pool. But scientific papers often sit in piles gathering dust on high shelves of academic libraries, read by relatively few. Increased public awareness and long-term comprehensive monitoring is what's really important to these particular elephants right now.

My mission is to concentrate on what will benefit them. Unpaid and self-funded, my own reward will be the wellbeing of the elephants themselves.

I remind myself of Dr Louis Leakey's early view of Jane Goodall's work with the chimpanzees of Gombe. What Dr Leakey considered most important was 'a mind uncluttered and unbiased by theory, a real desire for knowledge and a sympathetic love and understanding of animals'. It's a view that I share.

I'm incredibly fortunate to have been given a chance to work with these elephants, who have already been habituated to the presence of people in vehicles. What I want most is for them to be safe and cared for, with access to sufficient water and with help available to deal with the human-inflicted injuries that Andy used to attend to. Over time, I'd love to see them grow to become a true flagship herd for Zimbabwe, to be genuinely well-understood and well-respected around the world.

# IS THAT A DUCK OR A FROG?

# 2001

Dete, a small railway community about 180 kilometres south-east of Victoria Falls, is not your most enticing African township—Zimbabwean author Alexandra Fuller memorably wrote that the word Dete means 'Narrow Passage: *Shithole*'—but the Main Camp entrance to Hwange National Park is close by, and that's why I love this region so much. Val co-owns a small rustic safari lodge in the area and it is in these grounds that I will live.

Things have changed in the area since I was last here. Several white faces are gone as racial tensions in the country escalate. (Use of the words 'white' and 'black' is standard practice in Zimbabwe. Although not conventional today elsewhere in the world, it's the language of President Mugabe, and therefore the usual way to speak of the different races.) Lionel is no longer in Hwange. Andy's wife, Lol, is gone too, having been required to leave their national parks home.

What's more, there's a saying now that you're more likely to see an elephant in Zimbabwe than a white person! All around the country people are fleeing the violence and general lawlessness associated with Zimbabwe's fast-track 'land reform' program, in which white-owned farms are being forcibly seized. Whites are literally being thrown off, not only losing their land but their homes and sometimes their farm equipment and furniture too, with no monetary compensation.

In spite of this havoc, some people are staying put. John, a grey bearded old-timer Zimbabwean, is somebody I already know well. He's a spider-loving man, always with a knife on his belt, and renowned for once having been caught stark naked on the roof of his dilapidated home, and for having been seriously gored by a buffalo. There's a waterhole nearby fondly named after him.

'Howzit,' John exclaims, embracing me with his trademark stiff hug. Without waiting for an answer, he adds: 'The elephants have been waiting for you.'

Over the past few years, John and I have shared extraordinary wildlife adventures—with elephants, rhinos, lions and more. Although he's some-what of a hermit, I plan to cajole him into getting out and about with me a little more.

There are also academic researchers in the area who I've known for several years. Julia and Marion work with hyenas, and Greg works with painted dogs. Along with Val and John, we were all together at Andy's funeral.

As my little thatched-roof cottage is not quite ready for habitation, some of us opt to sleep for a few nights on wildlife viewing platforms inside Hwange National Park. These tall, sturdy, wooden structures overlook busy pans. In wild Africa a pan is so much more than a mere waterhole. It's an oasis where animals quench their thirst, a place where birdlife abounds. There is always a quiet beauty, a cooling of the air, a magical feeling at sunset and sunrise. Right now, the moon is exquisitely full, a fabulous time to be out with the wildlife. The unmistakeable laugh of hyenas, the deep throaty call of lions, and exhilarating rumbles from elephants are constant companions throughout these nights. The rains are almost over, but the musical voices of throngs of frogs rise from reeds in the pans, some tinkling like wind chimes in the night, others sounding like champagne bubbles bursting.

I'm now living in Africa, the world's largest animal sanctuary. I have to constantly pinch myself to test that I'm awake; that it's really true. All around me, there are sounds that I'm having trouble identifying, despite having visited often. 'Is that a duck or a frog?' I ask, bewildered.

'It's a baboon,' Julia declares with confidence.

Well, that was embarrassing. I have plenty to learn. Then I'm confused once again. 'And that? What is *that*?'

'It's a distant train.' And I realise that, try as one might, it's never easy to escape all trappings of civilisation.

In the grounds of Val's lodge, my cottage renovations are finally complete. But *other* species have already moved in.

Coming from Australia, I'm all too familiar with snakes and spiders. Coming from Australia is perhaps the reason why I *loathe* snakes and spiders. They're really the only two 'bite-y' things that I've grown up with. In Africa they seem to be even more prevalent—and much bigger and more inclined to bite. It's not long before I discover a Mozambique spitting cobra inside my home. And baboon spiders, the size of . . . well, baboons! Not quite, I must admit, but awfully big and hairy. So, while there are footsteps and all sorts of other sounds around my cottage at night that never seem to quieten, indicating creatures that can quite literally eat you alive, it is the silent snakes and spiders that trouble me the most.

When John appears at my doorstep one morning I blurt out, 'Come in, my friend. I still have no furniture, but hey, sit back, relax. Go ahead, pull up a spider!'

Spider-loving John just chuckles. But he soon redeems himself by helping me sprinkle ash, from nightly campfires, around the perimeter of my cottage. 'It's a deterrent against snakes,' he tells me.

'What about spiders?' I ask, hopefully.

'Perhaps spiders too,' he winks.

I ask John if he'll help me select a suitable 4x4 to buy. Until I have one of my own, my work with the elephants can't begin in earnest. I don't want to spend too much money, since I have no idea, really, how this will all work out for me. I need something cheap, but most importantly it must be reliable. There's no radio network here, no mobile phone network either, and I'll be alone in my vehicle most of the time. And living by myself, there's no guarantee that anyone will notice if I happen not to arrive home one day.

With Julia in tow, we squeeze into John's old ute and travel almost three hundred kilometres south-east to Bulawayo, Zimbabwe's second largest city. It's a little like a First World country town. Once a handsome city, with wide streets and reasonably modern buildings, it is now grubby and littered with rubbish. Everything looks tired and run down. We are all desperate to get back to the bush as quickly as we can.

Scouting the second-hand car dealerships, and after much rolling of eyes, I eventually settle on a 1980 Range Rover. This model was manufactured in the same year Zimbabwe gained independence from Britain, and so is as old as the country itself. It costs me only a few thousand dollars, and although it's going to be a gas-guzzler, fuel is currently subsidised by the government and with my foreign currency is cheap to buy. It is a permanent four-wheel drive with a black leather roof I can slide back, enabling me to stand up through the top when out among the elephants. It's hardly reminiscent of the shiny red MX5 convertible I used to drive Down Under, but John is convinced that, after a bit of work, it will be a dependable vehicle. Given that he drives an ancient Isuzu that's often off the road, I'm not sure I should trust his idea of dependable, but I take a chance and celebrate by buying some second-hand furniture at an auction house. Because so many people, both white and black, are fleeing the country, bargains are easy to find. I also buy myself a miniature fridge and some kitchen, bedroom and bathroom necessities.

John is determined to ensure that I never get stuck alone in the bush, and so once we're back in Hwange he instructs me in the art of tyre changing and the use of a high-lift jack. He makes me take off a tyre, and put it back on. Over and over and over again.

'This contraption could knock your head off,' I cry.

'That's why you'll do it again, to be very sure you know exactly how to handle it,' John insists.

I would desperately love to call roadside assistance, but that is out of the question. I don't think there's even such a thing in the cities, let alone here in the bush. So I huff and puff with the heavy tyres and a hollow metal pipe that John bequeaths me to help loosen tight wheel nuts.

'Well, they wouldn't be so tight if you'd stop tightening them so much behind my back,' I whine. I should have kept my mouth shut. John picks up the wheel spanner and makes the nuts on the next wheel really, really, *really* tight. By now I'm laughing so much I can barely even *lift* a tyre.

'Do it again,' John commands.

There are long *Acacia erioloba* thorns everywhere in the bush, and frequently hidden in elephant dung too, so I know that I'll have to be able to cope with endless flat tyres. Right now though, all I really know for certain is why that buffalo gored this man. If I had horns, I'd be tempted to do the same.

'Come on, John! Let's go,' I shout. 'I need you to show me some of the bush roads.' With permission to ignore the NO ENTRY signs, we drive into the estate in my Range Rover with the top open, delighting in a deep sense of freedom. 'Yesss!' I yell, punching the air, while John chuckles beside me, sharing in my excitement.

My work with elephants has begun.

# ELEPHANT RUMBLES

# 2001

'I have absolutely no idea where I am,' I admit, rather sheepishly.

We're on the estate, at a fork in a sandy road. 'It's time to head back home,' John declares. 'Are you going to turn left or right?'

I seriously have no idea. 'Right,' I say, hesitantly, while peering at him out of the corner of my eye for some hint as to whether or not I'm heading in the correct direction—but he just lets me turn that way, without a twitch or a word.

And now I am completely lost. I have no idea if the tyre tread on the track in front of me belongs to my vehicle or another, but I fear that I've not been here before. All of the bushes along the roadside look exactly alike.

'Getting lost is the best way for you to learn,' John eventually announces, after I've driven around aimlessly for a further 10 minutes. I glance over at him, and feel a sudden urge to find a buffalo . . .

I'm already well aware of my feeble sense of direction. While on a three-month stint surveying a remote uninhabited island in Lake Victoria, Uganda, in 1997 (in preparation for the release of captive and abused chimpanzees), I became renowned for repeatedly getting lost, despite carrying a compass. Even so, I feel a sudden need to defend myself. 'I don't always want to know where I'm going anyway,' I declare.

A few days later John agrees to come out with me again. I have admitted to him that I'm having difficulty telling male and female elephants apart. 'Oh, really?' John is clearly surprised. 'A male elephant's pecker can be well over one metre long. It shouldn't be too difficult.'

Until you know what you're looking for, it can indeed be challenging. Big males often wander alone, or with other big males, so that makes them pretty simple to identify and sex correctly. And if they appear five-legged I can be very sure! Those who are leading family groups will be female, so that's not too difficult either. But the smaller fellas all look the same. We laugh at ourselves after having recorded one as being female, only to later watch 'her' pee.

It's not easy, either, working out all of the mother–calf relationships. The link between a mother and her youngest calf seems simple enough, since the youngest never wanders far from mum. That's until I notice one with a ripped ear, easily identifiable, now suckling from a different female than it was before. 'Okay, so this isn't going to be as easy as I first thought,' I lament to John. But he barely hears me. He's staring at the genitals of the largest land mammals on earth. Of those huge males, I suspect, he's a tad envious.

By day's end, the only elephants we've seen mounting each other are male; teenage male on male. 'Imagine that,' John utters with a smirk. 'Our president is one of the most notoriously homophobic people in the world. He'd have a heart attack if he saw that going on in his herd.'

John is fascinated by all things wild. 'So, do you see different animals together like this in Australia?' he asks. At that moment we're surrounded by elephants, giraffes, zebras, impalas, kudus, waterbucks, warthogs and jackals.

'I lived most of my life in the cities,' I reflect. 'The only time I saw koalas, kangaroos, wombats and the like was in captivity—or dead on the side of the road.' Then, looking around at the gathering of animals on all sides of us, I say, 'There are stunningly beautiful places in Australia, but you don't see sights like this.' And I'm reminded again that I am, indeed, somewhere very different.

Four years earlier, John had been involved in a project that I participated in for a few weeks, investigating the role of elephants in dispersing seeds inside Hwange National Park. One day we'd painstakingly counted an astonishing 5689 *Acacia erioloba* seeds in just one dung pile. Another day we came across a bull elephant, who'd recently feasted on the sweet fruit of a manketti tree, busily defecating. He'd swallowed the nut-like seeds inside the fruit whole, and their hard woody shell ensured they remained untouched by his digestive system, passing through him completely intact. We dutifully collected them. The next day we enjoyed freshly baked 'manketti nut cake', the key ingredient of which came out of a pile of pachyderm poo.

In the days and months ahead, I spend countless hours working on an elephant identification library. Without the luxury of a digital camera, I have hundreds and hundreds of rolls of film developed in Bulawayo. Making sense of thousands of notations and photographs is a time-consuming task, to say the least, but it's worthwhile when I no longer see a photograph of an elephant, but rather now see a photograph of a *particular* elephant.

I study the tusks. Is the elephant left or right-tusked? Just as we are left or right-handed, elephants also favour the use of one tusk. This master tusk becomes more worn, often shorter than the other, with a groove in its tip where the constant action of pulling branches across it wears a furrow in the ivory. I look at the length and circumference of these oversized incisor teeth, marvelling at this quirk of nature. I also study the elephants' massive ears, noting all of the holes, the nicks and the rips. Even more than the tusks, the ears of the adults are uniquely identifiable. Or at least they're supposed to be. I roll my eyes at those elephants who seem to have walked into the same thorny bush, sustaining almost identical ear injuries, and at those who don't have any injuries at all.

I organise my photographs into family groups. Who are the great matriarchs? Who belongs to which family? Who is the mother of whom? Who is a sister? Brother? Aunt? Grandmother? In order to be able to understand their social structure and population dynamics, I need to get to know the elephants both individually and in a family context, before ultimately recording such things as births, deaths, oestrus and musth periods (when females and males respectively are in heat), matings, calving intervals and sex ratios. All of these are important inputs to understanding what is really going on within an elephant family.

To aid identification, I use the same naming convention that was devised in East Africa: I assign a specific letter to each family group and then give each elephant in the family a name beginning with that letter. There is the L family, for example. I name the matriarch of this family Lady, and I dig out my baby names book and assign L names to all of her family members. So now there's Leanne, Lucky, Louise, Leroy, Lesley, Levi, Loopy and others.

My data collection becomes increasingly meaningful as I become more and more familiar with the elephant families. I note changes in group size and composition, and I construct family trees. I become familiar with individual interactions, both within the family groups and between different families. There's an awful lot to learn and understand, so I dedicate eight hours to field work each day, and work on photographs and notes long into the night.

The elephants fast become like family to me. I look forward to encountering them on the estate and am thrilled when I easily recognise members of a particular family. They're no longer just great lumps of endearing grey. They're individuals as well as members of close-knit families—and I look forward, in time, to getting to know them intimately. Curious, they move close to my 4x4. Rarely threatening in any way, they simply wander casually by. I revel in my close-up view of their finer details—eyelashes to die for, a hairy lower lip that you wouldn't wish on your worst enemy and huge tough-looking toenails. Some of them pass by close enough for me to count tail hairs.

At times, though, they get a little too close for comfort. When one cheeky teenager momentarily puts his huge foot on my front bumper, John urges me to put my foot on the accelerator and get out of there. But in fact, as I learn in due course, this elephant was just being friendly.

I become fascinated with elephant language. Through a symphony of rumbles elephants greet, call, comfort, coordinate and converse. There are long soft rumbles, loud throaty rumbles, slow deep rumbles, low purring rumbles, short gurgling rumbles—and these are just the ones that are audible to my ears. Many, I know from studies undertaken in Kenya, are below the level of human hearing. This infrasound ability is so effective they can communicate with each other over distances as great as 10 kilometres. I get a kick out of the discovery that female elephants use many more and varied vocalisations than males do. So, it seems the ladies like to natter! And even more typical, the males are known to talk primarily of supremacy and sex.

Not all elephant noises indicate a conversation in progress, mind you. 'Was *that* an elephant rumble?' I'm asked one day.

'Actually that was elephant flatulence,' I reply.

Just like any toddler, baby elephants seek constant attention. And like human families, close bonds between family members are strikingly evident. Resorting to a temper tantrum when his mother doesn't stand still long enough to allow him to suckle, a young elephant screams in protest. I find it incredible that one so comparatively small can make so much noise. His chilling high-pitched scream has the desired effect, stopping his mother in her tracks. Another youngster, standing alone, bellows a call of distress. He has lost his mother—or at least he believes he has. He bellows relentlessly; a loud, harsh call that echoes around the *veld*. The calf's mother runs towards him and upon reaching him, wraps her trunk around his belly, caressing and comforting.

One day I'm observing a small family group when two more families arrive, and soon there are over fifty elephants surrounding me. Everything is peaceful until a dominant bull approaches, his rumbles audible. Excited by his arrival, the members of the family groups jostle. One huge female finds herself pushed up against the side of my 4x4, which I'd stupidly parked on a slight incline.

'Holy shit,' I mumble in fright, as several tonnes of elephant threaten to topple my vehicle. Thankfully, she manages to regain her balance and right herself pretty quickly, leaving three small dents and no side mirror as a lasting reminder of this memorable day.

The elephants love to play in the deep excavations that they make while seeking minerals in the open calcrete areas. Using their tusks—heads deep in the excavations and huge bums in the air—the adult elephants break off large chunks of salty earth, which then crumble to the ground. The youngsters steal what they can. It certainly doesn't look particularly appetising, but for the elephants—and indeed for pregnant local women who often crave it as a calcium and potassium packed dietary supplement—these chunks of sand are clearly a special treat.

Sitting on the rooftop of my 4x4 as the twilight deepens, I watch the elephants disappear into darkness. For a short time, before the moon and stars shed enough light, I'm unable to see anything around me. During these moments I'm intensely aware of the sound of leather against bark as the elephants scratch themselves against tree trunks, and the gasp of mineral dust being inhaled. Playful screams echo in the still night. When the moon is full it rises like a gigantic single hot coal, resplendent in the night sky, fully illuminating the elephant families surrounding me.

I'm out in the field doing what I love most—unravelling the secret lives of the Presidential Elephants of Zimbabwe.

# CUTTING THE WIRE

# 2001

'Stop! I want to check this herd of zebras for snares,' John demands, bringing a pair of binoculars to his face. I do as I'm told, but I actually wonder if he's showing off a bit in front of me. Is it really necessary to check every single animal for a snare? These are wire trapping devices set by both commercial and subsistence poachers. They consist of a noose, often with the wire twisted into multiple strands for strength, and are set in the bush at variable heights depending on what type of animal the poacher is trying to catch. Trapped animals sometimes escape from them, often seriously injured with the strangling wire embedded in a part of their body.

It doesn't take long for me to understand that John is entirely correct. There are all sorts of animals, elephants included, walking around with wire snare injuries that will eventually kill them if nothing is done. Although snares aren't usually set with the intention of catching an elephant, they walk into these traps nonetheless.

And it turns out that I'm the first person in years to dedicate entire days, every day, to observing the wildlife on this land. I see first-hand that poaching is on the increase in Zimbabwe and animals are suffering. Of course there are the safari guides who drive tourists around for a couple of hours every day. However their focus is understandably on the beauty and wonder and they tend to spend only a minute or two with a group of animals before moving off to find their next great sighting. Now, with Zimbabwe in such decline, there are fewer game-drive vehicles around and therefore even fewer eyes than there would normally be in the field. Parks personnel concentrate their efforts inside the national park and rarely venture here.

Thankfully, just like Andy before them, there are a few trained and licenced men around who I can call in to 'dart'—that is, to immobilise the animal with a tranquiliser dart fired from a rifle, remove the wire and treat the wound. Before I left Australia, I helped secure a dart rifle for one of them. But without radio or mobile phone contact, I need to leave the injured animal temporarily, race to find the closest landline, and hope the animal is still there when I return. It's certainly not ideal, but this is the only way we can work for now. John, Val and I attend various snare removals together. We're all keen to help, and to learn more.

I sight a zebra with a wire clearly visible around her neck. Thankfully it hasn't yet cut into her skin, but it needs to be removed since it could easily tighten further. As soon as she's darted, she gallops off. We drive off too, through thick bush, searching for her. She has collapsed with her head caught in the fork of a small tree. She hasn't hurt herself however, and within seconds of the wire being cut she bolts off at high speed, now freed from the deadly trap.

An adult sable bull, noble with massive curved horns, is suffering the debilitating effect of a tight wire snare around his leg. He also flees into dense bush immediately after the dart hits his rump. This time, it's not possible to drive in after him, leaving us with no choice but to walk into the thick bush, relying on the impressive skills of an indigenous tracker. The ground is hard in places, and covered with leaf litter, yet the tracker expertly follows the indistinct spoor (footprints) and manages to locate the sable. It takes time however and the drug is already wearing off. Three men are needed to hold the sable down while a top-up is administered. The tight wire around his leg is then successfully removed and another animal is spared what could have become a protracted and painful death.

Darting can be a risky business, as I come to know personally. A heavily pregnant zebra is successfully immobilised and her deadly snare removed, however she gets to her feet before all the reversal drug is administered and starts to gallop away. With a high chance that she will relapse into immobility, which would leave her vulnerable to lions, it's decided to dart her again with the remainder of the reversal drug, using a non-barbed dart this time. The drug will automatically inject on contact with her body and the dart will fall to the ground. There'll be no requirement to pull it from her rump, avoiding more distressing human contact. But something goes wrong. The dart is prepared as usual but by pure mischance it explodes and the liquid drug sprays all over us.

'Oh shit!' we gasp in unison.

We are lucky. Had it been the immobilisation drug in that dart rather than the reversal drug, our lives would have immediately hung in the balance. Without the antidote, death is only minutes away if the immobilisation drug is absorbed into the human body via cuts on the skin. The antidote is always kept close at hand, and we all know how to use it, however it's a frightening reminder of the deadly risks involved in saving an animal's life. Another non-barbed dart filled with the reversal drug soon hits the zebra, and all is well.

Not all hazards associated with snare removal are quite so life threatening. Holding no grudges following his serious goring years earlier, John takes off his shirt and places it over the head of a sedated buffalo to protect the animal's eyes from the glaring sun while its snare is being removed. The snare is soon off and the fearsome buffalo is up and running into the bush quicker than expected, shirt around his horns. John pats the pockets of his shorts. And panics. His house keys are in *that* shirt! The benevolent buffalo soon tosses the shirt off and we all chuckle with relief.

Human-inflicted suffering continues. Early one morning I'm driving with Julia on the main tar road when we come upon a painted hunting dog by the roadside. Considered vermin by some, they're one of the most endangered animals in Africa, their patterned coats and white tips of their tails a sight to behold. This particular dog had been hit by a vehicle and although we didn't know it for certain then, it had a severed spine. From a nearby lodge we get hold of an animal rescue team. They respond quickly. A blanket is thrown over the dog and it is carefully placed into the back of a vehicle. A drip is attached and it is driven the three long hours to a vet in Bulawayo. But the journey is in vain. We tried to undo the damage humans had caused but there was nothing that could be done to save this dog's life.

I have seen life-threatening snares around the trunks and legs of female elephants, but nobody is yet game to dart within an elephant family. The risk of attack by protective family members is considered high. As I get to know the elephants, their family structures, their personalities, and their rank within the family, I'm confident that, with this increased background knowledge, the risks can be minimised. For now though, only lone bull elephants are darted.

I'm already making plans to help support a dedicated anti-poaching cum snare destruction team for the Hwange Estate. These men will be employed, paid and fed by a nearby photographic safari company, which has compassionately agreed to assist. It will be my task to elicit donations of overalls, boots, hats, jackets, warm jumpers, tents, bedrolls, sleeping bags, water bottles and the like. I will also help to deploy the team into the field, in the areas where the Presidential Elephants roam. These men will not only destroy all wire snares that they come across, they will sit in ambush near trap lines, capturing poachers to hand over to the local police. It is, after all, illegal to set a snare in Zimbabwe. Or at least it's supposed to be.

I feel a deep sense of satisfaction being able to help in this way. It won't be easy, though, to get the support we need. President Mugabe's wildlife minister is Comrade (a wartime title that the Ruling Party still love to use) Francis Nhema. He makes it clear that we must not speak publicly about any snaring or other poaching problems. He fears that any public reports will discredit his government's land reform program. And in this country, if you speak out, it's at your own peril.

# RHINO SCARS

# 2001

Around the country, white farmers and their workers continue to be intimidated, tied up, abducted, tortured and murdered as the land reform program continues. The offending mobs are said to be government paid rent-a-thugs, frequently numbering several hundred travelling together. They use *pangas* (machetes), *knobkerries* (clubs), rocks, sticks, bricks, axes and iron bars when confronting farmers and their families at their homes. Some have guns. They scream and shout, *'Hondo! Hondo!'* ('War! War!')

In 2000, when the fast-track land reform program began, approximately 4500 white farmers owned close to 70 per cent of Zimbabwe's prime agricultural land. Furthermore, whites made up less than 1 per cent of the 12.5 million population. Land reform was therefore widely applauded. The way it is being implemented by President Robert Mugabe's ZANU-PF (Zimbabwe African National Union, Patriotic Front) is, however, widely condemned.

In all the chaos, photographic safari lodges around the country are now being threatened with take-over too, even though they are not on agricultural land. Lawlessness is escalating.

The locals call this madness *jambanja*. One day, when I take the opportunity to ask a man on the streets of Bulawayo what *jambanja* means, he replies shyly: 'It's a place you go to cause war . . . it is a very bad thing.' The police rarely intervene, as the invasions are deemed 'political'. Kidnappings and torture of farmers and their workers are alarmingly referred to as 're-education'. The government is forcibly removing the white farmers and their trained workers without even giving them a chance to pass on their skills to the new black land claimants. It becomes increasingly clear that the aim is to merely boost the individual power and land wealth of Ruling Party officials and their supporters, at the cost of continuing any sort of productive farming.

With no television, radio or internet access, I don't hear much about all of this violence, and am happy to be able to bury my head in the sand most of the time and simply get on with things. Like most whites, though, I have several jerrycans of fuel stowed (I have no choice but to store mine inside my cottage) as well as a 'gap bag', which is packed with my passport and other important documents, some cash, a change of clothes and a few other essentials. We have all discussed a plan, and know which way we will drive together if we need to 'gap it' and get ourselves out of the country in a hurry. I am also registered with the Australian Embassy in Harare, which issues email bulletins with need-to-know information and warnings.

I'm more worried about losing my support network after it becomes clear that Val still plans to leave the country. She has a two-year-old son to think about. And even John is now feeling he may be forced to leave as well, his Zimbabwean pension worth a pittance with the Zimbabwe dollar devaluing. John's wife, Del, is entitled to a South African pension and they may find themselves with no choice but to move across the border in order to survive.

Despite all of this, we still manage to share some wonderful times. When I'm not in the field, finding relief under the calming influence of the elephants, I'm pleased to have an added night-time diversion. Val is an accomplished singer and loves to play guitar, as does John. We have sing-alongs in my cottage, and around campfires. We share stories, so many stories. We are each other's company, something that we take great pleasure in.

I frequently think back to the days when Andy was alive. Without him I might never have found the courage to take the giant leap into this new life. John and I had flown together with Andy in the National Parks helicopter in which he died. Both of us knew him to have been a particularly cautious pilot, always double- and triple-checking everything before take-off. I'm always nervous in light aircraft, but Andy made me feel like there was absolutely nothing to fear. John and I have never quite believed he ran out of fuel, as the accident report declared, and have our own thoughts and suspicions about what might have happened. We prefer, though, to reflect on the happy times.

The story of the lion cub relocation is one that John loves to hear, especially since he was supposed to be with us on that day. He'd pulled out at the last minute—ever the hermit—to stay home alone.

It was only Andy, Lol and I together inside Hwange National Park. I was once again on holidays, in between IT contracts, and took every opportunity on offer to spend time with them. On this particular day, Andy was simply planning to do a few routine patrols inside the park.

He knew that two lion cubs were missing from their radio-collared mother, a collar that he had fitted: he'd seen the mother with only two of her four cubs just the day before. When two lone cubs unexpectedly appeared right in front of us, Andy immediately pieced the puzzle together. The cubs were weak and clearly wouldn't survive for much longer without their mother, whom he knew to be several kilometres away. He made an on-the-spot decision to capture both of them, by hand.

'Hold this,' Andy said as he walked towards me, casually carrying one of the lion cubs by the scruff of its neck.

'Hold *that*? Seriously?' I muttered in disbelief. 'Well, okay . . . ' I grabbed the cub in the same way.

And so it was that on this day when we were all simply enjoying the splendour of Hwange National Park, I suddenly found myself in the back of our 4x4, holding a truly wild lion cub. These cubs were not sedated. They were not sleeping. They were alert and feisty, although thin and vulnerable. We held on to them as one might battle with a strange, overgrown domestic cat. I tried to memorise their every detail—their whiskers, their almond-shaped eyes and the colouring of their tails.

It was an extraordinary drive across the plains towards their mother. We finally caught up with her as the sun began to set. She clearly sensed we had lions on board, well before we had stopped and dropped them to the ground. After some tense moments while we wondered together whether they *really* were her cubs, we shared overwhelming joy to see them reunited. The lioness instinctively took the weakest cub in her mouth while the other one ran by her side. They all headed away to rejoin her other two cubs, who were watching from the safety of a fallen tree.

There had been no time to tag the rescued cubs, in order to easily identify them later. Everything had happened so quickly and night would soon be upon us. I had pleaded with Andy earlier to let me take a photograph, but he quite justly would not compromise our safety. They were lions after all, with full-grown relatives, and we were in their territory. And with just a flat tray, there were no 'bite me barriers' on the back of our 4x4!

In emails after I was back in Australia, Andy referred to these cubs as *my* cubs. He continued to give me updates on their wellbeing, right up until he died and their identity was lost with him.

'I wish I had been there,' was all that John could ever say.

There is another story that is often retold, and this time John was there as a witness. It was a rhino relocation that didn't go quite as expected. It went perfectly well for the rhino, I suppose. It just didn't go quite so well for me.

Andy was in charge of this operation and had granted me permission to stand close by, alone at the base of an *Acacia erioloba*, so that I could photograph the release of a radio-collared rhino. He was already up in the helicopter, all set to monitor where the rhino wandered. His men were on the ground preparing to release this great horned creature.

I knew that when the door of the transportation crate was opened, the rhino would be free to run off in any direction. I watched him back out slowly and for a few moments he moved only his head, taking in his new surroundings. I stood admiring his ancient splendour, wondering how anyone could slaughter such a magnificent beast for its horn.

Then, as luck would have it, the rhino turned and charged. Straight towards me.

'Oh, give me a break,' I remember thinking. 'You could have run in *any* direction.'

I wasn't about to miss this opportunity though. I snapped a photograph of him in mid-stride, thundering straight towards me. Then I found myself scrambling for my life up the acacia tree. Long, sharp, white thorns ripped my arms before I managed to reach a safe height.

Trying desperately to keep hold of my camera—I wasn't about to lose that photograph now—I gazed down from my precarious position to the rhino below, his huge horn not far beneath my feet.

'Don't move! Don't move!' one of the National Parks scouts yelled at me, while everyone looked on helplessly.

*Don't move? Look at me! Where could I possibly move to?*

Luckily for me, but not so for them, a group of spectators momentarily grabbed the rhino's attention. After scattering them, he disappeared into the bush and I was free to climb down from the tree, a little shaken and nursing my bleeding 'rhino scars', which I was secretly rather proud of. When I looked up into the tree I wondered how on earth I'd actually got up there.

'Do you still have your rhino scars?' John asks me, whenever we reminisce.

Now, I sit quietly, staring into the flames of the campfire, wondering, *If both Val and John leave, will I have what it takes to remain in the Hwange bush?* Even my hyena friend Julia and her team-mate Marion seem unsure how long they might stay. If they leave, I'll have nobody to catch a chicken bus with; those old, noisy and smelly, cramped buses that hurtle along like crabs, with their rear frequently hanging out to one side. Or nobody to hitchhike with, like the time we managed a lift to Bulawayo in a passing hearse.

We refill our glasses with Amarula. This is a delicious South African cream liqueur made with the tasty fruits of the marula tree, which elephants love to eat, that we love to drink. And we toast absent friends.

# SELLING UP

# 2001

It's another glorious dawn in the African bush. Val's two-year-old son, Declan, appears at my cottage door and grabs me by the hand.

'Sharon, come! Come! I want to show you what the *ndlovus* did to the garden. They're in biiiigggg trouble!' this little white boy declares with tangible urgency, his eyes wide. An *ndlovu* is an elephant; words from the isiNdebele language—the native tongue of the local Ndebele people, who live in this province called Matabeleland—frequently pepper Declan's sentences.

I'm still rubbing sleep from my eyes as he yanks me out of my cottage and hurries me towards the lodge garden. I soon see that the *ndlovus* really are in big trouble. What was once tall, thick, green plant-life has been sheared off at ground level. There are a few—really rather large—craters where the roots were savoured too. Then, to rub salt into the wound, the *ndlovus* quenched their thirst in the swimming pool. Any guests so inclined would have to swim with huge clumps of dirt and floating banana tree roots.

'Please, can't you keep "your" elephants on a leash?' Val asks me wickedly. We can do little but laugh, and then clean up the mess.

Even Declan now knows me by the isiNdebele name '*Mandlovu*'—meaning 'Mother Elephant'—given to me by Gladys, one of Val's staff members. Gladys had first christened me '*Thandeka*', meaning much-loved. Being known as *Thandeka Mandlovu*—much-loved Mother Elephant—is an honour that I'm thrilled to accept. Beautiful wooden signs have been skilfully hand-carved by one of the safari guides, featuring elephants and my given name, to recognise this special tribute. Everywhere I go now, and despite the colour of my skin, the Ndebele people call me *Mandlo*, the shortened version. Even John is busy hand-tooling an exquisite leather book cover for me, featuring elephants and my isiNdebele name, as a special keepsake.

So when terrorists attack the United States on September 11—six months after my arrival in Zimbabwe—I'm jolted back to a reality that I have been avoiding. While deep in the bush, I feel strangely removed from this appalling tragedy while simultaneously overwhelmed by grief at the horror of it all. The events taking place around the world are shocking. Even so, some of us, I believe now more than ever before, need to stay focused on the welfare of the wildlife, particularly in troubled and seemingly insignificant places like Zimbabwe. It is a country fortunate to still have such a diverse variety of life, but for how much longer, I wonder?

I'm frequently asked, 'Why do you bother with the wildlife, in a country where so many *people* are suffering?' My answer is always the same. I try to explain that there are hordes of organisations worldwide assisting hungry and disadvantaged people. 'It doesn't mean that I don't care about the underprivileged people,' I say, 'but there's relatively few organisations assisting the wildlife—and even fewer bothering in Zimbabwe.' I emphasise that I'm one lone person who needs to focus my energy where I believe I can make the most difference. And this happens to be with the wildlife, and with a very vulnerable species. The elephants are key to attracting much-needed tourist revenue, which is crucial to this country's economy. And having compassion for another species is really what humanity is all about anyway.

A disturbing incident that I recently witnessed inside Hwange National Park, after it closed to tourists for the day, doesn't help tourist revenue, the economy, or indeed anything at all. It left me alarmed and with the impression that some people employed here are little more than poachers themselves. Just a short distance up the road from where I sat with colleagues on the tourists' favourite Nyamandlovu platform (a wildlife viewing structure not far from the main gate), Parks staff drove by and casually shot at wildebeest right beside us. Naturally the next morning, after all this commotion, there wasn't an animal in sight for tourists to see, let alone any wildebeest, which are certainly not abundant in this area. Nobody publicly questioned this authorised 'ration hunting' (which is hunting to feed Parks staff), since that would mean risking permits. That Parks staff would ration-hunt wildlife at all baffled me; that they would do it right in the middle of key tourist areas, inside a national park, was simply unfathomable. Needless to say, John and others are horrified. We all know that elephants are also ration-hunted frequently. There has to be a way, we want to believe, to positively influence attitudes and policies.

In the wake of the awfulness of September 11, I decide that I will sell my Brisbane home, even though my visa situation is still not sorted out. And I will stay on with the elephants, no matter what, and make a real go of things.

Having already spent the maximum time allowed in Zimbabwe on a tourist visa in one year, and also because I need to start to think more about my house sale, I am returning to Brisbane for just a few weeks. This is the city where Val is planning to live—simply because it's where I'm from. In fact we've discussed the possibility of her renting my home, but it's clear to me that in order to fulfil my commitment to stay with the elephants, I must sell up, since I'll need this money free to support my work.

Soon after stepping off the plane I experience a very real culture shock, even though I've been away for only six months. It feels surprisingly odd returning to the Western world. There is a regular supply of electricity and water, and there are working telephones, fax machines and photo-copiers. There are no fuel queues; no streams of people 'footing' along the roadside; no one constantly thrusting carvings and bananas under your nose. People look familiar, yet these are faces I do not know. It takes me some time to figure out that this feeling of familiarity among strangers is because I'm once again in the midst of a sea of white faces. There seems to be an incredible number of food and clothing shops, offering endless varieties of brands and styles. My own walk-in wardrobe is overflowing with clothes. Why had I ever thought that I needed so much clothing? Everywhere, there is so much 'stuff'. I walk around a little bewildered, it all seeming to me now more than a tad excessive.

Even though the materialistic world in which I'd previously lived is glaringly obvious to me now, it is still a little overwhelming to think about selling and packing up my life completely. But regardless of what the future holds, I know, with a comforting certainty, that I could never live quite like this again. Despite it once being an all-consuming and rewarding part of my life, I can't pretend to miss my former career and the lifestyle that had come with it. There have certainly been times in this past year when I've craved a more functional country and a five-star meal. But, despite everything, there is now no place in the world other than Hwange that I want to be.

I believe my decision to sell up is the right one. I make a promise to myself that if the time comes when I ask myself, 'You have six months to live and can do anything you wish with your remaining time on earth. Where will you spend your time?' and my answer is no longer 'With the elephants in Hwange', then I will leave Zimbabwe. It will be my reality check, my litmus test.

I make sure that my friends in Brisbane are happy to keep an eye on things for a couple of months longer, and decide that I'll return to Aus-tralia again in early 2002 to pack and sell up.

I fly back to Zimbabwe, happy that there are still no computers in sight at the airports. Like countless others in past years, I have no desire to pay the substantial bribe that would be necessary to facilitate my re-entry while my visa situation is being sorted out, and so I present a new passport. There is no visual evidence that I've already been here for six months this year. I breathe a sigh of relief when I hear the thump of the officer's stamp on its blank pages. I do not lie when I tell him that I'm on my way to Hwange, to see elephants.

It's wonderful to be back, and I immediately drive myself into the bush to try to find some elephant families. It's always like a box of chocolates in the field; I never quite know what I'm going to get. Thankfully, I don't get a flat tyre. The sights, sounds and smells of the Hwange bush hit me once again, squarely in the face, and I know that I am back where I belong. Others, however, don't feel quite the same way about their own situation.

When Val starts to speak with more certainty about her planned move to Brisbane, I am silent. John says, 'I want to come with you.' And I notice others consciously stopping themselves from blurting out, 'Me too.'

I have returned to Zimbabwe with thousands more elephant photographs developed in Oz. For the next few months, I work long into the night, looking closely at left ears and right ears, tusk formations and family group configurations, excitedly watching my identification booklets take shape. It is so satisfying, trying to figure this all out. Every day by 10 a.m. I'm out among the elephants, right through until the sun sets.

My three sisters and I grew up helping out on our parents' farm in Grantham: catching and throwing cabbages in a chain between cutter and packer, washing cucumbers, picking potatoes, mowing lawns. We were rarely idle. After schoolwork was complete, paint-brushes, brooms, rakes and mops were frequently thrust into our hands. My mum has a serious aversion to idle bodies. I was also granted the freedom to roam and the independence to indulge my curiosity for nature. My impressionable childhood days were not filled with loafing around. I'm more than happy to burn the midnight oil. As I learn more and more about the elephant families, they occupy an increasingly special place in my heart. The days fly by.

Soon, it's Christmas. And sadly, Val is gone. Although not my original plan, I'll be finding myself a new place to live. It's more than I can think about for now, though, and I join Julia and our mutual friend, Dinks, inside the national park for an early bush Christmas. Dinks was also a friend of Andy and Lol and once managed the Hwange Main Camp restaurant. She now lives in Bulawayo. I've already known her for several years and love her 'to the moon and back', as we so often say.

It's Mother Nature entwined with Father Christmas. Nothing beats celebrating the festive season in the African bush. We hang decorations (discarded porcupine quills, seed pods, feathers) on a broken branch of a tree, which we push into the soft earth. From the paper plates on our laps red-hatted koalas and kangaroos smile back at us.

Julia always has some memorable plan up her sleeve. Her Christmas gift to us on this day is a beauty salon in the bush, accompanied by a glass of chilled wine. With grotesquely bright masks on our faces, and our feet soaking in red plastic basins, we revel in the throaty rumbles of passing elephants. When an afternoon thunderstorm forces us to scurry across the sandy ground to shelter, we laugh and laugh, knowing just how crazy we all must look. We are alone though, except for the elephants. For now, it's still easy enough to forget that the country is crumbling around us and that people everywhere continue to flee.

I fly out once again to Australia, and sell my beautiful home.

# NO LOOKING BACK

## 2002

'*Mushi* hat,' John mutters in thanks on my return, when I present him with his very own Akubra, the legendary hat of the Australian outback. It is indeed a really nice hat. I may have chosen to live elsewhere, but my national pride and the symbols of my origin don't vanish, such as a jar of Vegemite I've squirrelled away to savour alone (here South African Marmite is preferred), and the packets of delectable Tim Tams (my favourite Aussie biscuits) that I will grudgingly share.

It took me more than three months to sell my Brisbane home, my car and a considerable portion of my belongings, and to store the rest. I had to dig deep to find the courage I needed to go through with it all. The most difficult time had been the lead-up to my decision to sell. Once I'd reached that decision, it all became easier, although I knew that I was leaping into just another level of the great unknown. A little apprehensively, I'd walked around the empty house that was no longer mine: the lush garden, the sparkling pool, and then from room to room switching off the lights. I'd gently closed the front door behind me and, without looking back, driven away from my past life.

My visa problems are finally sorted out, at least for now, and I have re-entered my homeland of choice on a two-year work permit, required despite my efforts being purely voluntary and self-funded. I dismiss suggestions that I should instead find a Zimbabwean to marry. This alternative holds no appeal for me at all. I was married—for what felt like about five minutes—when I was in my twenties and it's not something that I'm keen to do again, despite having been assured that I would be worth many *mombes* (isiNdebele for cattle).

'How many *mombes*?' I want to know.

Cattle are highly valued here as a display of prosperity. Some locals clearly hold me in high esteem and estimate my bride price to be 20 *mombes*! But whether it's 20 or only one or two, I feel quite certain that my mum and dad in Australia—the would-be parents of the bride—can do without them.

One drunken 'gentlemen' once offered the male friend who just happened to be by my side at the time three baboons for one night with me. I realise it was just for one night, but three *baboons*! This is not an animal the local people value at all. We giggle about my erratic worth.

What we don't giggle about is the documented promiscuity and associated high prevalence of HIV in Zimbabwe. While currently one in four people are known to be HIV-positive, in the younger age brackets the figure is even higher, with over 40 per cent of those in their late twenties believed to be suffering from this virus.

It's also commonplace here for a married man to have 'a small house' (a kept mistress) and 'a big house' (the marital home) along with other casual lovers on the side. That Zimbabwe has expressions like 'small house' is evidence of a polygamous culture. It's wise to be mindful.

'I think I'll pass on the three baboons,' my friend said, unnecessarily.

Baboons give me another giggle while having photographs developed in Bulawayo. Austin and Patrick, who work in the back room of Camera Centre, want to know about the animals in my country.

'Is it true that a kangaroo has a pouch here?' Austin asks me, patting his belly.

I nod. I already know what is coming next, aware of the trouble local people sometimes have with baboons in their small *mealie* (corn) fields, which they grow to help feed their families.

'Imagine if a baboon had a pouch there!' Austin exclaims. 'That would be a big problem; he would stuff *so* many stolen *mealies* into it.'

I now tell the local people that I'm married to the elephants—which only serves to confirm their suspicion that there must be something a little wrong with me. I have no children after all. This is lamented. When I go on to say that I *choose* not to have any children (a delicate decision I made when I was 30), this is clearly cause for alarm. In many ways, we are worlds apart. What's more, the gap now appears to be widening rapidly.

To date, most locals in my immediate surrounds have been friendly and welcoming. While there are those who will always try their luck, repeatedly asking for things simply because I am white and therefore perceived to be very wealthy, I'm generally made to feel that I belong. While I was away selling my house however, Robert Mugabe won another presidential election, in a vote widely reported to have been rigged. His ruling party, ZANU-PF, continues to violently seize property without payment, solely on the basis of skin colour. Just as worrying, he has begun a 'Go back to Britain' chant to the whites—many of whom are actually third and fourth generation Zimbabwean, and who have never been to Britain in their lives. These public tirades are actually directed at *all* whites, since few seem to care about the difference between white Zimbabweans, white British, white Americans . . . white Australians.

Alas, this rhetoric has succeeded in inciting increased violence and amplified white hatred in some quarters, particularly among the unscrupulous and the assorted bands of highly impressionable, aggressive and power-hungry black youths who blindly follow directives from the Ruling Party elite. Twenty-two years after racial reconciliation (following Independence in 1980), this is for many young men and women a learnt hatred, a learnt bitterness, since so many weren't yet born, or were primary school age at best, when the war ended. It is hatred taught and instilled by a ranting president and egged on by some similarly prejudiced government ministers. In televised speeches, the president now frequently utters such things as, 'To those of you who support whites, we say down with you.' And, 'Our Party must continue to strike fear into the heart of the white man who is the real enemy.' To which he gets wild applause. Great presidents guide the moral compass of a country. Understandably, President Mugabe's morality is now under fire. Such racial hatred in the 21st century is difficult to comprehend. All light-skinned folk are targeted, but white Zimbabweans are the most deeply affected. This is the country of their birth after all. Many have nowhere else to go.

I sit back and try to imagine how it must have been for the black people in this country that was once called Rhodesia (renamed Zimbabwe at Independence), who lived through the white supremacist era. They overwhelmingly outnumbered the whites, accounting for approximately 96 per cent of the 7 million-strong population at that time. I try to imagine how it must have felt to be treated as inferior, in practically every aspect of their lives. Whites who wouldn't walk with you, sit with you, eat with you. All while black people raised their kids, cleaned their houses, prepared their meals and worked in their fields. Some white employers did have genuinely devoted and caring relationships with their staff during this supremacist period, and solid friendships were formed between the races, even back then. Still, bad memories certainly linger for a lot of people.

'Mugabe is 78 years old. He won't be president for much longer,' is what I hear people saying everywhere I go.

I go out and sit among the elephants. They don't care about skin colour.

In spite of it all, I am high on my new life with elephants.

Lady, the grand matriarch of the L family, leads a small close-knit group of sixteen. I already love her and her family, and am thrilled when they're out and about in the open areas where I can easily spend time with them.

'Hey, Lady; hey, my girl,' I greet her fondly.

She is an enormous pachyderm, easily identifiable with a longer left tusk and a distinctive hole in her left ear. I estimate her to be in her mid thirties, just a few years younger than me. This is based on the ages of her offspring and also her body shape. Female elephants, unlike males, stop growing in height when they're around 25 years old and proceed to get a little longer and less round with age. I've had more sightings of this family than others, which has allowed me to piece together their family tree quickly and easily.

I talk to them constantly, and after initially giving me only sideways glances, they now observe me closely and appear to enjoy my presence. Like Lady, Leanne, her closest sister, is particularly grand. Sitting among them one day, I recall the Kenyan researcher, Joyce Poole, admitting that she used to sing to the elephants in her study group, and all of a sudden I'm singing the first verse of 'Amazing Grace', over and over and over again. And sing I definitely can't, but goose bumps spring up on my arms nonetheless. I think for many, regardless of religious persuasion, it is a song of hope and these days I really see all of the wonder around me. Standing her ground, a few metres away from my 4x4, Lady crosses her back legs and rests her trunk in an L shape on the ground, evidence that she's feeling particularly relaxed. Adults Leanne, Lucky and Louise do the same. They stay like this for several minutes but are soon bored (or perhaps can't stand my incredibly bad singing for even one second longer) and then they casually wander off. After those few minutes I feel warmed, my spirit instantly replenished, for I know that I have more and more friends in wild places.

I never wear or rarely even carry a watch, as the time it tells has lost all significance. The position of the sun in relation to the horizon tells me how much sunlight is left in the day. My elephant friends don't know or care what hour, or day, it is—and neither do I. I move from one family to the next, until the evening cries of the black-backed jackals, the roosting commotion of the guinea fowls, and the hysterical raucous cackling of the seemingly tone-deaf red-billed francolins bring a feeling of all-pervading peace to the end of my day, and I know that it will soon be dark.

The family I've called the Ws are a much larger group than the Ls. They don't always wander together as they're an 'extended family', who meet up together quite frequently, all five sub-families becoming one. Eventually they go their separate ways once more, with weeks sometimes passing before they meet again as a complete group. In the meantime, I see various combinations of the five smaller sub-families together.

I have firm favourites in this family group too. We humans choose our friends based on traits that we like and respect, finding ourselves attracted to some people more than others. There are those we opt to spend time with, a few who really brighten our world, but not everybody is the sort of person we want to hang out with. To my surprise, I find this is exactly the same when it comes to the elephants. They all have different personalities, just as people do. There are definitely some I prefer over others.

Whole is one of the matriarchs in this extended family. I named her so because of the large hole in the middle of her left ear, but of course it needed to begin with W. Although Whole is huge, I think of her as a marshmallow, a giant one for sure—all sweet and soft and gooey inside. One of her daughters is Whosit, who has small tusks that curve inward on her trunk. Whosit is an accomplished clown, always managing to make me laugh out loud at her playful antics. And then there is Willa, with a square notch that juts from the middle of her left ear, who happily lingers in the background. But she always seems to be checking to see if I'm watching her. 'Did you see that, Sharon? Did you? Did you? Did you see me do that?' I imagine Willa saying under her breath, with a longing glint in her eye.

When Whole's family meet up with the gorgeous Wilma's family, or another W sub-family, there is a big commotion, that at first I didn't understand at all. I finally realised they're greeting each other, with loud screams and open-mouth rumbles that fill the air. They urinate in excitement, back into one another with their ears waving wildly, and then affectionately rub their faces together, such is their level of jubilation at being back together once again. In the excitement of the moment, liquid streams from their temporal glands, which are located just behind their eyes. This streaming liquid indicates something different in adult males, where it's an indicator of musth: a period of heightened sexual activity that periodically grips males over 30, during which they charm oestrous females and mate. What I learn too, in time, is that it can also be an indicator of terror and distress, in both males and females.

I particularly love meeting up with Anya and Adele from the As, Belda and Brandy from the Bs, Cathy and Courtney from the Cs, Emily and Eileen from the Es, Joyce from the Js, Grace from the Gs . . . and my list goes on and on. And there's Mertle and Misty from the Ms, who I adore for different reasons. I'm drawn to Misty because she's so gentle and polite. She's a pretty elephant with unusually small ears, sad eyes and a dignified aura. Mertle, I think, is Misty's mother. Given that both are adults, it's impossible to verify this assumption even after hundreds of sightings. They may in fact be sisters. Whatever the case, they're always wandering together. Mertle has spunk. She takes no nonsense from anybody, her sheer size alone commanding respect. I make a mental note never to tussle with her.

It is already apparent to me that elephant family bonds are incredibly strong, and that female elephants do indeed, as prior research has found, stay together for life. Males, on the other hand, are forced out of their families when they're teenagers, presumably to reduce occurrences of inbreeding. They go on to form bull groups, and later to lead more solitary lives, while skilfully passing on their genes and decades of wisdom to their companions. Because the males are so transitory and can travel huge distances, often gone for long periods, I concentrate my efforts primarily on the family groups. Given how frequently I see each family, I know that they don't wander far.

When I sit with elephants in the wild, even for a short time, I always feel immensely humbled to be sharing their lives. They are the world's largest land mammal, and are remarkable in every way. When not harassed, they are incredibly calm, quiet, gentle and inquisitive, something you cannot imagine such enormous animals could be.

Just as I've learnt to know more of them by name, I've learnt to understand their individual joys and their sadnesses, their losses, their gains and their relationships. Their moods and emotions have become familiar and I've become completely intertwined in their lives. There is a downside to knowing elephants so intimately. They've already touched a place in my heart so deep that I sometimes feel almost paralysed by this passion. When tragedies occur—and it's perhaps even more inevitable in this troubled country that they will occur—I already understand how heartbreaking this will be.

I fully expect troubled times ahead.

# V FOR VICTORY

# 2002

I have moved to an even smaller abode: a one-room roundhouse with a pointy thatched roof known as a *rondavel*. It is typical of what many rural folk live in, but at least my version has been made with cement, rather than mud. It was previously used only for storage, but I decided that it would do. My bed will not fit, so I reduce my furnishings to just one sofa, which I fold out each night to reveal the thin piece of foam I sleep on, two small cupboards, a tin storage trunk, a couple of wooden coffee tables I bought from John, and not much else.

The fact that John is getting rid of furniture worries me. It certainly looks like he's going to be the next one to leave. 'This place has gone to the dogs,' he says, and I listen patiently while he lets off steam.

I've bought him a tin of his favourite mixed fruit jam, refusing his pennies that he offers to me in payment. This small tin alone costs nearly as much as his monthly pension. John is bitter and I certainly don't blame him. On top of everything else, sightings of snared animals are increasing and gunshots are heard in the night. It is, understandably, all driving John a little crazy.

I drag him to see my new little home, in the hope that he might better appreciate all that he still has. I have five by four metres in which to live.

(A concrete partition separates this space from another that is one metre wide, containing a cement shower cubicle, hand basin and toilet.) With my scattering of furniture placed around its edges, I have just three metres by two metres of free space.

Beside my fridge, I cook (now and then) on a two-burner hotplate that sits on top of one of John's coffee tables, with cardboard boxes of utensils beneath it—*my kitchen*. I eat while sitting on my sofa—*my dining room*. I sit on the floor on my grass mat with my computer on my lap and my printer on the floor beside me—*my office*. I laze on my sofa to read a book—*my living room*. Every night I unfold the sofa and make up my bed, tucking the edges of a mosquito net under the foam mattress to protect me against malaria—*my bedroom*. I hand-wash my clothes in the small hand basin on the other side of the partition—*my laundry*.

'Count your lucky stars you don't live in just three metres by two metres of space,' I urge John.

While Zimbabweans like him prepare to leave, expatriates like me still happily stay in this country, our foreign currency making life inexpensive.

I accept an invitation from Julia to travel to Mana Pools, a World Heritage wilderness in the far north of Zimbabwe, accessible from the capital Harare. This is an opportunity to make new friends and it seems to me that I'm going to need them if too many of my mates go off to greener pastures. We are with Dinks. Carol is with us too. She and her friend Miriam, also present, are American schoolteachers living and working in Harare, and with ties to wildlife projects in Hwange.

As a result of international warnings against travel to Zimbabwe, we have this huge wilderness area practically to ourselves. It is extraordinary, and a great time to be visiting these areas. If only tourists knew what they were missing out on.

On our first night we wander down to the riverbank after dark. 'I hope we don't come face-to-face with a hippo,' I mutter nervously, but apart from a few smiles, nobody takes much notice of my unease.

The next evening I dig out a spotlight to see what is making such an incredibly loud munching noise. 'Holy shit, hippo,' I squawk. The hippo is grazing less than 10 metres away from us, but my friends calmly continue chatting. 'What is wrong with you ladies?' I squawk again. 'Is this really so normal?'

Nothing too much is said either the next morning when a vervet monkey whisks away an entire loaf of our bread, although there is definitely more leering from my friends this time around. When the vervet later returns for an avocado, Carol is incensed as well as me.

'Here,' I shout, holding up the Worcestershire sauce bottle. 'You'll need some of this!'

We drown our sorrows over this loss of food rations. The G&Ts are strictly for medicinal purposes, of course. It's a sound local theory: the quinine in the tonic helps ward off malaria. There is a lot of water around Mana, and a lot of mosquitoes. We all agree that we'd better have a few.

There is a sign in the area that warns us in bold type: DRIVING OFF-ROAD IS STRICTLY PROHIBITED, ESPECIALLY UP TO LION KILLS. LEAVING YOUR VEHICLE AND WALKING IS PERMITTED.

I frown, and read it again, just in case the G&Ts are impairing my senses. But no. It still says exactly that.

'Really?' I shake my head, bewildered. 'Well, good luck with that.'

I feel like I've taken a step back in time. I do so love it, of course, every last bit of it. But I find myself wondering—on this weekday afternoon as we casually observe the herds of elephants inside this national park—what boardroom meetings are going on Down Under, what strategic plans are being written, and who is flying first-class to what part of the globe. I, on the other hand, am in a place where zebra crossings are really zebras crossing, and families of elephants form the only traffic jams.

Stopped by the roadside, looking in wonder at the long pendulous seed-pods of the sausage tree, which can grow to an incredible metre in length, I can't help but giggle at their phallic appearance. I decide that I absolutely have to have one, and collect a pristine specimen from the ground. Then, after an outing to visit Lol and her son Drew who, since Andy's death, have settled in this eastern side of the country, we drive my sausage eight hours back to my *rondavel* in Hwange. I display it proudly in my garden, a reminder of a memorable excursion.

I spend time with the small anti-poaching team of four men, now in place, dedicated to patrolling the Hwange Estate. Tall and athletic, Jabulani is a reliable and conscientious leader, with a real determination to catch poachers. He regularly appears on the doorstep of my *rondavel* to show me great handfuls of wire snares that he and his team have located and destroyed. SAVE Foundation of Australia, a wildlife conservation group based in Perth that focuses its energies primarily on assisting rhinos, has kindly donated overalls, boots and sleeping bags. This relatively small gesture makes a huge difference to the morale of the team. They are clearly proud of their new role in the community, and their new look.

Animals are still suffering from human-inflicted injuries all around me. I've already seen some of the most gruesome wounds imaginable, caused by snares. Ends of trunks ripped off, some barely long enough to reach the mouth with water. Bloodied flesh dangling on legs. A wire wrapped tightly under a chin, up past the ears, finishing in a disgusting bow of wire on top of the head. One W family member had his trunk severed to tusk length. He'd been cruelly stripped of his dexterity and didn't survive.

Snares are a despicably cruel, cowardly way to kill an animal, and I'm dismayed by what I see, particularly since I've often been powerless to help. We've still only ever darted lone bull elephants. Darting those who are part of a protective family group is still considered too great a risk; there is fear that the other elephants will rush to the darted one's aid, with ensuing danger to us. I keep finding females who are horribly injured but which none of the qualified darters are game to dart.

Over the course of a few tortured weeks I watch a little four-year-old calf from the V family, led by the adult female I've named Vee, debilitated by a tight wire embedded deep in his right back leg. He and his family have been drinking regularly at the same waterhole every day. They're a small sub-family of only eight, with three adult females. They haven't wandered far from this pan as the snared calf—as yet unnamed—is clearly unable to walk long distances.

But now Greg from the Painted Dog Conservation project has been thinking about a way to safely dart injured family members. His idea may be a little controversial, but I'm so thankful to have a way to at least try to help this injured V family calf. I've spent countless hours convincing Parks management to allow this darting to proceed. All of the red tape is more than irritating—indeed, it is infuriating. Everybody has their own agenda it seems to me, and it isn't always the same as mine and Greg's, which is simply to save this elephant. John tells me angrily that there are probably some people who just want to kill the calf and eat it. And there is indeed some tragic irony in us wanting to save it, when only a few kilometres away Parks staff are probably shooting one for rations. But we're not about to let this deter us.

Finally, after obtaining the approval needed from Parks, there is an opportunity to test out Greg's technique. There are lots of different elephant families around on this day; too many I fear, although I know that some will soon move off. From my daily observations, I know too that none have close ties to the V family. Through binoculars I find the snared calf. His horrific wound is getting worse by the day. He keeps his foot in the air and swings it backwards and forwards at every opportunity. It is awfully swollen and infected, and clearly very painful.

We thankfully now have access to a field radio network—my handset and base station kindly donated by that same Perth-based fundraising body, SAVE Foundation—so communication is simpler. Greg arrives with extra backup.

From the rear of an open 4x4 Greg takes aim with the first dart. It is a tranquilliser and it's directed at Vee, the snared calf's mother. She has a distinctive 'v' injury in her right ear and is easy to identify. Not one of the more habituated and better known Presidential Elephants, she could potentially cause us the biggest problem. The snared elephant is her youngest calf, still occasionally suckling, and she is likely to be particularly protective of him. There is little doubt, given the age of this calf, that she is also heavily pregnant, a condition sometimes surprisingly difficult to confirm for certain, since female elephants routinely appear huge around the belly. But I know that elephants typically give birth about every four years, so an advanced pregnancy is very likely.

Rather than bringing Vee completely down, Greg has decided that she will instead be tranquillised with a concoction of drugs so that she will continue to stand, albeit in a sedated state. The dart hits, and a pink-feathered needle protrudes from her rump. Shocked by the sting of the dart, she runs a few paces and then continues to move off slowly. More tranquilliser is needed. A second dart has already been prepared. It's a perfect hit once again. Vee now has two pink-feathered darts protruding from her rump. She moves off further into the bush, while we do some bush-bashing to keep up with her. The family group move with her, the snared calf at her heels.

We wait. Although she's clearly feeling the effects of the tranquilliser, a third dart is fired from ground level (with armed support standing by), just to be sure that she is properly sedated. Although she is vocalising, other family members thankfully remain a short distance away. Because she is on her feet, they do not rush to her aid. A big old bull comes to harass her, and us, but he soon moves off.

It's time now to administer the immobilising drug to the calf. Greg fires once again and it's another perfect hit. In no time at all, the calf is down.

It is a little disconcerting working on an injured calf with his mother standing just metres away, although everything continues to go smoothly. Armed rangers keep watch while Greg removes multiple strands of hideously thick twisted wire from deep in the calf's leg. He then injects large amounts of antibiotics, while I continuously spray water on and under the calf's exposed ear to keep him cool.

Working quickly, Greg administers the reversal drug to the calf. Then he *walks* up to Vee to remove the three pink darts from her rump and to administer her reversal, all on foot and by hand. This was definitely not in the original game plan. But this man is fearless. After a long deep snort, the calf scrambles to his feet and walks over to his mother's side. She is starting to regain mobility.

We feel joy, relief, pride. We smile. We hug. I brush away a tear. In the air, there is that sweet smell of success. 'I'm proud of you,' one of Greg's colleagues says to me, while giving me an extra big hug. Of course it is Greg who has saved this calf, but as always I do feel proud to have played a part.

Perhaps Greg had been lucky to get the three sedation darts into Vee without her running off. Perhaps we had been lucky too that she had not, while standing sedated, fallen over into a life-threatening position. There were moments when she leaned to one side, and then leaned heavily forwards. If she had fallen forwards onto her chest, she could have suffered severe respiratory distress. There is still plenty to learn.

I become concerned when the de-snared calf doesn't stay with his still drowsy mother, instead walking off by himself into the bush. With the deep open wound on his leg, he is particularly vulnerable to lions. The other family members are by now nowhere in sight. I stay to watch over them until nightfall, the family still split.

Back at my *rondavel* I have a restless night's sleep, wondering if the calf has eventually returned to the safety of his mother.

Early the next day, I search and wait. Finally I sight the family of eight drinking once again at the same pan. It is confirmation of success. They're all back together and the calf is already putting more weight on his injured leg. They show no signs of agitation at my close presence, despite their recent ordeal. I whisper a quiet thank you.

Weeks pass, and although I search daily, I haven't seen them again. I consider this to be a good sign, believing that the de-snared calf is no longer inhibiting the wanderings of his family, but I long to know for certain that he is still okay.

Then one evening I'm driving home after a full day in the field when I pass a small family in the bush by the roadside. I hit the brakes. Out of the corner of my eye I'd seen the big v notch in Vee's ear. I reverse quickly, feeling anxious. But I needn't have been worried. There they all are, all eight members of the family. The de-snared calf is by Vee's side. His little leg has healed so well, and it is clear there will be no permanent injury.

I name this little V family calf Victory—because a glorious victory it was.

# SOULS THAT SUFFER

## 2002

I try to learn some isiNdebele. I figure that I should know more than *ndlovu* (elephant), *Mandlovu* (mother elephant) and *mombe* (cow). Although I'm told that isiNdelebe is simple to learn in comparison to some African languages, I'm unconvinced. I'm hopeless at all languages and this one is littered with incredibly complex clicks.

Numerous people try to teach me where to place my tongue, how it should be depressed and where it should touch inside my mouth, in order to make these sounds. 'Seriously? This is just never going to happen for me,' I decide defiantly after listening intently to one of several clicks. 'It's just impossible for me to make that sound. It's like a cricket makes. And I'm not a cricket.'

I end up learning no more than a couple of the most basic words, all devoid of clicks: '*Salibonani, linjani bangane*'. I feel like I'm asking for a banana. What I'm actually saying is, 'Hello, how are you friend?' Which is about as accomplished as I'm going to get. I 'excel' with just one more word, '*Yebo*' (Yes). At least that one I can handle.

'Say something in your language,' I'm asked.

'But this *is* my language,' I try to explain.

To redeem myself, I try out a few good Aussie phrases. 'G'day mate,' I say, which just makes everyone laugh. And then, 'Fair dinkum,' which has the same effect.

I tell my kind teachers that it's time for me to leave now, that I need to get out into the bush and record the level of the pans. The dry season runs from April until November, so the last few months before the rain comes are a particularly harsh time for the wildlife and especially for the elephants, who drink large quantities of water.

'Some pans,' I say, 'are already as dry as a dead dingo's donger.' I admit it's not a phrase that I typically use, but it has the desired effect: I get another laugh. It's easy enough for me to compare a dingo to a painted dog and, if that causes confusion, to a jackal, which these women more often catch a glimpse of. But when I get to 'donger', I decide it's definitely time to leave. Interestingly, it is the word 'dead' that I should have immediately remembered would cause me a problem. It's not a word commonly used here. Once when I was told that someone was 'late', I embarrassingly asked when they would arrive. I had absolutely no idea I was being advised that this person had died.

Expressions are indeed an interesting thing, as I find out when I meet Dinks' friend Shaynie, another white Zimbabwean. Dinks has recently separated from her husband and is now sharing a flat with Shaynie in Bulawayo. They kind-heartedly offer me their couch to sleep on while I finish my supply shopping, a laborious task that I do every two months or so. As we laugh and chat, slapping at mosquitoes which buzz around us relentlessly, I can't help but notice Shaynie putting an impressive dent in a packet of cigarettes, knocking back cheap white wine (interspersed with the occasional bottle of Coca-Cola), and uttering some remarkably colourful language. *Who on earth is this person?* I wonder to myself.

I learn that Shaynie lived through some pretty violent times in the years following Independence, when her family resided on a gold mine. In those years, I was working in the prime minister's office in Canberra, my career already on fast-track with parties galore to attend, while Shaynie was across the ocean trying not to die. From 1982 to 1987, it's estimated that no fewer than 20,000 Ndebele (and some say many more) were massacred, and tens of thousands more were brutalised unspeakably at the hands of the newly elected ZANU-PF government. This is how the Ruling Party, very soon after taking power, dealt with its only political opposition of the time, those based on the Hwange National Park side of the country. This horrendous period in Zimbabwe's history became known as the Matabeleland Massacres (referred to as 'Gukurahundi' by the local people) and is now widely viewed as genocide: the Shona from the east systematically eliminating the Ndebele from the west. Caught up in all of this fear and bloodshed, there were periods when Shaynie had slept with a G3 rifle under her bed, and carried it with her everywhere she went. It was clearly an awful time.

I can't help but laugh, though, when she tells me of one evening when she was about seventeen and feeling rattled after several recent murders at the mine. Everyone aside from Shaynie was a few hundred metres away at the mine's club. Still carrying a rifle, she was lazing on the lounge-room couch watching *Dallas* on television as the saga of 'Who shot JR?' was unfolding. Getting to her feet at the end of the episode, she crazily tried to balance gun, cigarette, Coca-Cola bottle and a book in her hands.

'In a flash the rifle hit the coffee table and there was an almighty crack. Hysterically thinking that I was once again under attack, I was racing frantically out of the door towards the security of the club, covered in white dust.'

As it turned out, she had shot the television! Its frame was still intact, but the glass had been reduced to tiny slivers, there was a hole in its rear, and an impressive crater in the white plaster of the wall, where the bullet had ultimately lodged. Predictably, the family joke became: '*Who* shot JR?' . . . It was *Shaynie!*'

And this night in Bulawayo, gun-toting Shaynie becomes part of my Zimbabwean life. She'd previously been impressed when Dinks had spoken of her elephant friend (me), her hyena friend (Julia), and her froggie friend

(Lol, who adores frogs). Now she has her own 'animal friend', and in time I become especially grateful for her presence in my life.

Months pass and Carol arrives from Harare, generously bringing with her mouth-watering goodies only available in the capital. I'm living primarily on instant noodles with sweet chilli sauce and tins of preserved fruit so it's a treat to have something fresh and different to eat for a change. As a thank you, I take Carol out with me to meet some of the Presidential Elephants.

The gorgeous Wilma is a high-ranking member of the W family, a matriarch of one of the five W sub-families, just as Whole is. When I'm not calling her Wilma, I'm playfully calling her 'that wicked woman', given she has doused me with sand several times already while dust-bathing only a metre or two away from the open roof of my 4x4.

Wilma has unquestionably become another firm favourite of mine. On this day Carol and I stumble upon her just hours after she has given birth. She is still dripping blood and the tiny baby—a girl—is struggling to stay upright on wobbly legs. Carol names the baby Worry as this tiny one is very swollen where part of the umbilical cord is still attached, and walking strangely with a bulky lump hanging very low between her legs. I am indeed a little worried about her. She's the first baby that I've seen on the actual day of its birth. But I hope for the best and look forward to monitoring her progress. I find myself hoping that I might be around to see her give birth to her own calf one day.

While new life is celebrated—and I, elated, start feeling like a proud grandmother to the newborns—human-inflicted injuries keep cropping up before my eyes, which then pull me into depths of despair. I so often feel like I'm on an endless roller-coaster ride of highs and lows, something that I've never had to deal with before.

Now, it's one of Lady's family who has been horrifically snared.

Louise is the mother of this latest snared elephant; a calf just two years old. Instead of cavorting like the others his age, he wanders around dejectedly, distressed and clearly in pain. His snared leg is a gruesome sight. It is the worst wound that I've seen to date, and it's even more heartbreaking for me given that he is part of a family that I've come to know well. Swollen and infected from an excruciatingly tight wire, his little leg has literally burst, with raw bloodied flesh dangling hideously. The wire has snapped and is thankfully now off, but the aftermath is sickening.

I agonise over whether to request for him to be darted, in order to administer antibiotics. Everyone is still learning about the best way to dart within family groups. Would Lady, the matriarch, have to be darted as well as Louise, the mother? Darting always carries some risks for the elephants, and it seems wrong to risk too many other lives unless it is absolutely necessary. I observe his snare injury over several weeks, and then finally manage to get Greg onsite. It isn't likely to make much difference, since the amounts are small, but Greg decides to take the opportunity to administer antibiotics in a series of non-barbed darts that will, by design, fall from the young elephant's hide once they automatically inject upon impact. Greg hopes these antibiotics might aid his recovery a little. It is evident from the calf's horrific injury that it will be a long, long road to recovery.

I revise the name I'd previously given to Louise's son, and now call him Limp—which is all that he can do.

One day soon afterwards, Louise is on her own in the bushes about 25 metres ahead of me. Limp is on my right, packing his little injured leg with sand in an attempt to get some relief. On my left I spot two lions, and I can taste the adrenalin. I hear in my mind the words often spoken by Parks staff: 'Do not interfere; let nature take its course.' I don't interfere, but with my 4x4 motor running, I am *ready* to interfere. How many countless times has man already interfered, with rifles and snares? Limp's injury is not nature's doing. He's surely been through enough, and to now get tackled by lions is simply too cruel. To my great relief, the lions show little interest and Limp eventually returns to the protection of his rumbling mother.

Days later I watch him take pleasure in a mud bath. He is having some fun. For the first time in a long time he's enjoying being a baby elephant. He's clearly feeling a little better but the moment is bittersweet.

I am so distressed by the sight of all of these snared, suffering elephants. Despite this heartache I can't give up, for by now my soul is wrapped up in the endeavour to help save them. It's a dream to be able to spend my days among elephants, but more and more often now this dream is fused with nightmares.

There's been an adult elephant with an oversized snare wrapped around his chest sighted only once. Two zebras, six buffaloes, and six sables were all found too late. All of them had been snared; all of them are dead. And another elephant has been found shot dead. Time and again I wonder where it will all end. I can't bring myself to think about how many years this has been going on, mostly unnoticed. It surely didn't start in earnest the moment that I arrived, yet the darters are only now run off their feet.

The loading of a rifle is a sound that I don't particularly like but there are dangerous animals out there, and dangerous people. It's a necessary precaution when searching for poachers. I walk into the bush with two armed men, after discovering human footprints that I can't identify.

We stop abruptly. Branches chopped off a tree signal that all is not right. A few metres away we see crossbeams, set high in a tree. It's a structure used for drying meat. The long horns of a sable, impressive no longer, are aloft in the branches. The sable's disembodied head is on the ground. We spot a yellow-billed kite in the sky above. Kites discover fresh meat before the vultures. We inch forwards, until it's clear that we are alone. Further on, a buffalo lies dead. Across the sandy road the poachers have boldly set up camp, leaving behind them a plastic *mealie* meal bag on the ground, ashes from a recent campfire, and more structures for drying meat. There is a zebra skin, and another buffalo skin.

Forewarned perhaps, the poachers have fled.

Fresh spoor around broken snare lines is disturbing proof that elephants have recently encountered these death traps. I fight an overwhelming urge to somehow be able to take the snare off the leg of the innocent giraffe that I sighted a few days ago, and wrap it tight—tighter—around the legs of these poachers, leaving it there to fester and debilitate, day after day. Would this be punishment enough, I wonder? My blood continues to boil.

Elsewhere, Jabulani and his anti-poaching team have been sitting quietly in ambush for days, waiting for someone to return to the snares that they've expertly uncovered. This time someone does return, and the team captures him. This poacher is old, short and extremely thin. He has no teeth, at least not in the front of his mouth. His grubby long trousers hang to his ankles, bare hardened feet poking out from beneath.

At first the old man professes his innocence and refuses to talk. But a few less than subtle intimations change his mind, and now he is ready, he says, to talk to the police. It is late by the time we escort him to the police station, and so it will be morning before he will be questioned.

After a night in jail though, he has once again changed his mind. Now he is innocent, he says. Nevertheless, under the escort of two policemen we tramp back into the bush. Warnings to him are becoming increasingly pointed, as patience wears thin. One of the policemen gives him a clip across the back of the head.

Eventually he cooperates, leading us to more of his snares set for guinea fowl and antelope, and under order, destroys every one. Fresh duiker spoor surrounds one of his traps, yet he seems undaunted that he very nearly had another fresh kill, right in front of the police. He admits to having snared larger antelope too—buffalo and sable—sometimes leaving their skins and horns behind in the bush. Sable meat, he finally tells us, is drying in his house right now.

We drive to a small mud shack not far off the tarred road. The tiniest, oddest looking wee dog runs around and wags its tail. A bigger dog is skeletal, with skin clinging tightly to clearly visible ribs. Inside the dark hut I'm overwhelmed by the stench of death. Fly-covered meat hangs from the roof, close to the poacher's ruffled bed. I quickly retreat outside, in need of fresh air.

The poacher hands over the lower legs of the recently poached sable. Then, while still being interrogated by the police, he casually bends down and brazenly gives the smallest dog some of the dried poached meat.

He had once been a lorry driver, he tells us. He's now divorced and unemployed. He has been poaching regularly for the past two years. The meat, he says, is sold and bartered in his village. His story changes often as he tells it. Clearly he has accomplices and knows of other teams of poachers but he will not rat on his mates.

'I can set snares up to pole 138,' he boasts. I shudder. The poachers have given the telegraph poles numbers; poles that I pass every day. Like lions, they have their own territories to hunt within.

While the police search other huts I sit and wait in the 4x4, looking at, and really seeing, the poverty that surrounds me. The gaunt-looking poacher walks, scruffy and barefoot, into his mud hut, reappearing with a handful of wild berries. He gums on them loudly as I watch him walk towards me. He holds out his hand, this desperately poor man with no teeth, and offers me some of his berries. Wearily, I close my eyes. And very slowly shake my head.

We drive back to the police station. The poacher is now wearing a dirty old pair of shoes with holes at the toes, and I find myself surprised that he actually owns any footwear at all. More than anything else, I am just taken aback. After leaving him in the hands of the police, I drive out into the field with my head spinning. I'm having difficulty reconciling the events of the morning.

There is little doubt, I remind myself, that this poacher has illegally killed and maimed probably hundreds of animals. Over thirty of his snares were destroyed just this morning. He's been stopped, at least for now. And there are many other poachers out there who are simply greedy, more so than poor.

I think of Limp, and I can see it all clearly once again. A snare set for a small antelope can rip off an elephant's trunk. A snare set for a larger antelope can horribly maim, and indeed kill, an elephant. It's an irrefutable fact that snares are despicably cruel, and deadly, to all who encounter them. I'm convinced that handing poachers—all types of poachers—over to the police is the right thing to do.

The animals have few friends, I remind myself. I know that we must continue to ensure that snares are destroyed, and that poachers are arrested. It's also glaringly obvious to me now that there are other fundamental problems that someone, somehow, somewhere, must strive to solve in this country where many of the Ruling Party elite, and indeed some of the safari operators in the area, are very wealthy. Such imbalances are disconcerting.

Of course it's not the only disconcerting thing going on in the world. In October I hear the news that 88 Australians and far too many other tourists have been killed in bombings in Bali. I am horrified and saddened, and struggle to comprehend the level of terrorism that has taken hold around the world since my move to Africa. Things in Zimbabwe are bad, but I'm not aware of a targeted attack on tourists here since 1982 (just two years after Independence), when six foreign visitors were kidnapped at gunpoint, seized as political hostages, as they travelled between Victoria Falls and Bulawayo, and later murdered. These days, they mostly target their own people.

Everywhere, it seems, innocent souls suffer at the hands of others.

# IN THE BUSH

# 2002

When I'm alone with the elephants, and there are no strange sounds and smells to distract them, I feel the ties between us growing. I don't force myself among them. I simply park in one spot, sit on my roof, and let them come to me. More and more often, as the months pass, they choose to congregate just a few metres away. And they now stay for longer periods of time, as I talk and sing to them, which they appear to find soothing and seem to genuinely enjoy. They stand quietly, opening and closing their eyes very slowly, in pure pachyderm pleasure. It is these times—when there's not a snare in sight—that refill my soul with joy and peace.

My connection with Lady in particular continues to intensify, as I doggedly search for her family, daily, in order to check on Limp. Despite the heartache of seeing his dreadful injury, there is relief in knowing that his leg is gradually healing. This L family in particular is teaching me so much about elephant bonds and relationships, about elephant joy and sadness. All four adult females happily suckle their youngest calves only a few metres away from me. Some days, when the world around me seems so screwed up, I find myself sitting with them for several hours. Some days I choose not to even open a notebook.

Sometimes I sleep out on the back seat of my 4x4 around a pan with my roof open wide. Brimming with contentment at these times, I might see a grey heron, silhouetted against a deep yellow sky, fly off into the night. The light evening breezes create ripples on the glassy surface of the water, which shimmers in the moonlight. As I lie on my back seat I frequently hear waterbucks enjoying their dinner of reeds, and the soothing rumbles of elephants. Fireflies dance with dreams and desires, extending an invitation to follow their light. If I was able to follow, I think to myself, I might arrive at some magical place. But I stay where I am. I'm already at a magical place.

Anything a little out of the ordinary, these days, is a welcome distraction from the poaching. A solar eclipse a few weeks before Christmas brings an opportunity for another break from it all, and a chance to rejuvenate my soul. But I choose to forgo driving one hundred kilometres deep into Hwange National Park with Julia, Greg and others. Instead I hope that my friends, leathered and feathered, will join me for a partial eclipse on the Hwange Estate. Sometimes now, just hanging out with the elephants, rather than with people, is all that I want to do.

By 8 a.m. daylight is fading. More than 50 elephants are unexpectedly around the pan where I'm parked. This is unusual for early in the morning, and I whisper a thank you. As the light diminishes and begins to resemble sunset, the elephants appear completely bewildered. I watch their confusion. There is an eerie silence. They bunch together and take on an almost purple glow. They move their heads from side to side, trying to make sense of this strange phenomenon, but make no audible sound. I realise that the loudest sound I can hear is the excited thumping of my own heart.

Through protective eye-wear I can see the almost total blackout of the sun; just a bright thin crescent remains visible. I wish that I had another two sets of eyes. I want to watch the elephants. I want to watch the sun. I want to watch the pair of saddlebill storks. I want to watch the zebras, waterbucks, kudus, sables and impalas; with their noiseless hooves I'd forgotten they were even here.

'Far out, this is absolutely incredible!' I say to myself, utterly mesmer-ised by it all. It all feels strangely dreamlike.

As incredible as I think this all is, many of my indigenous companions have made it clear to me that they believe a solar eclipse to be a sign of evil things in store; a dire warning that bad will now overtake the good for many years to come. I dismiss this notion without a second thought, rolling my eyes at the superstitions. But perhaps they know something that I do not. I have, since then, learnt not to be so insensitive towards the beliefs of others.

At the close of 2002, I choose to spend Christmas alone, searching for the seventeenth snared elephant I have sighted. I simply can't bring myself to join Julia and Carol in Harare for Christmas celebrations. I decide that I need to stay in the bush with the elephants.

I think about the joyous Christmas celebrations that must be going on elsewhere. I think about my family in Queensland. I think about my friends from my Ernst & Young days, who still get together—Anne, Sue and Susan—and our memorable parties, frequent bouts of laughter and scrumptious Mexican dinners. I think about my Air New Zealand friends in Auckland—Andrea, Bobby and Eileen—who watched, a little dumbfounded, as I fell in love with the African wilderness. In a box in a storeroom in Australia I have exquisite Christmas decorations, collected from all around the world, that I know Andrea would love for herself. And I wonder if Bobby is still pondering how I could possibly survive in the bush without a hairdryer. I think of Mandy in Melbourne, who I met on the seminar in the Dandenong Ranges. A talented singer–songwriter, she sends me tapes full of carefully selected music to enjoy. One song is 'Born to Try' by Delta Goodrem, which she says reminds her of me. Maybe this is so, but in truth it can all sometimes be intensely *trying*.

But do I want to be in Australia right now? No, I really don't. I want to be right here. With such clarity I can see that this is what matters most to me: being here, doing what I can to help the elephants. I now see, hear and feel everything so intensely. It's an electrifying, albeit heart-rending, way to live. As I pop open a bottle of bubbles, I am grateful. I wish my elephant friends peace and goodwill.

It is a sad end to the year. John is in the final stages of leaving Hwange forever and I wonder who will be next.

Perhaps he is better off away from it all. Earlier this year, images of the bloodied bedspread-covered body of white farmer, Terry Ford, had made headlines around the world. This 55-year-old had been bound to a tree on his farm by government-sanctioned land invaders, and shot in the head. For hours, his loyal Jack Russell terrier named Squeak remained curled up by his side, refusing to leave. These images are difficult to get out of my mind, even at Christmas. And they are increasingly impossible to ignore.

It hits home even harder when people you know are threatened. My friends Denzil and Shirley have been heckled, humiliated and mentally tortured this year. They are kind, animal-loving folk who are second-generation Zimbabwean. Their youngest family members are fourth generation.

'We were frog-marched to a place on our farm. There we were made to raise our right arm and clench our fist, mimicking the president, and ordered to chant slogans for hours,' Denzil tells me. 'Up with Mugabe, down with Tsvangirai.'

Morgan Tsvangirai is the leader of the only viable opposition, the Movement for Democratic Change (MDC). A raised clenched fist is the Ruling Party's official symbol of black empowerment. Conversely, a raised open palm is the symbol of the MDC. So you can't even wave in this place without being accused—and possibly arrested—for being an Opposition party supporter. You can also be arrested for criticising the president, even in private conversations if you happen to be overheard, since saying anything to insult or undermine the president or his office is a criminal offence.

'We were made to chant all sorts of other anti-Opposition slogans too, and phrases like "Down with the whites, Land for the people", Denzil recollects with a disturbing re-enactment. 'And when we didn't do it properly, we were made to do it again, and again. Then we were ordered to pack our suitcases and leave within the hour. "You are Opposition party supporters. You must leave immediately. This is our house now. This is our farm", the invaders bellowed at us, waving their axes around.'

There is nothing right or fair about how these land grabs are being handled, and by extension, they have a damaging impact on my attempts to positively promote Zimbabwe's flagship herd, which bears the president's identity. I'm alarmed by some of the realities, no matter how much I try to bury my head in the Kalahari sand.

When Denzil and Shirley purchased their land, well after Independence, it had been derelict, but with a lot of hard work and capital investment they'd turned the farm around. They built huge dams, and grew tobacco, maize, wheat, barley and roses, and bred cows, sheep and chickens. On their 4500 acres they employed close to 400 black workers. All in all, up to 700 people lived comfortably on this revived stretch of land. Housing was provided for the workers and their families in several well-maintained compounds across the farm, each house with its own toilet, water and electricity—luxuries that few of the rural folk living in this country's communal lands could ever hope for.

And Denzil and Shirley did much more. They paid the school fees so that all of the children who lived on the farm could be educated. They provided a free clinic, staffed by a nurse's aide, and supplied transportation to hospital whenever it was required. They built a crèche and a playground for the younger kids, and regularly handed out gifts of clothing. There was a trading store, which sold basic commodities like bread, *mealie* meal, dried fish, meat and milk. There was also a recreational beer hall with an entertainment area and a television and radio. They took pride in looking after their staff well.

Wandering around the farm, some of the unruly mob of youths and war veterans found a metal box, about six feet long—the outline and shape perfect for a coffin. It was in fact an old tobacco barn roof ventilator. In paint on each side of this makeshift coffin, they printed Denzil's name. He was forced to drive, excruciatingly slowly, behind his own coffin, as the pallbearers made their way up a road. Symbolic graves and coffins weren't unheard of, not that this made it any less terrifying for Denzil and Shirley.

This sort of thing was happening around the country with the blessing, and indeed the encouragement, of the president and his Ruling Party elite.

As 2003 approaches, I can only hope that the New Year turns out to be a better one for everybody. What is happening to this country is tragic. And I'm resigned to the fact that John will be better off elsewhere.

I think of the words of a poem by A. E. Housman I once learnt:

With rue my heart is laden,
for golden friends I had,
for many a rose-lipped maiden,
and many a light-foot lad.

Times change. Andy is dead. Other friends are gone. Friends and wildlife suffer. It is this increasingly troubled nation that I have chosen to call home. I escape into the past, and raise my glass in a melancholy toast, 'To rose-lipped maidens and light-foot lads.'

When I was a visitor, I used to favour Zimbabwe's April to October dry season, when animals in need of water are forced to congregate around the open pan areas and are therefore easier to spot. Now that I live here, and better understand how harsh the dry season can be for the wildlife, it's the wet season that I long for most. And it is finally here. Those who visit only in the dry often leave with the mistaken belief that the Hwange *veld* is perpetually grim, drab and hostile, looking unlikely to ever recover. But it always flourishes with the rains.

December heralds the beginning of summer, and the *veld* is instantly transformed. The terrible harshness of the long dry is forgotten. Soaking rain replaces the often-violent storms of late October and November. The longed-for changes are rapid and wondrous, the metamorphosis spectacular. Bare, sandy soil has been replaced by lush, green grass. The trees and shrubs are suddenly, once again, in full green leaf. Surface water sits where dust devils recently swirled and mushrooms push their way through elephant dung. Dusty mineral-lick excavations—created by the elephants—have been transformed into small pans, where lions love to lap and elephants love to play, despite them now being home to crocodiles. It's nothing short of miraculous to see the *veld* reborn.

It's such a rejuvenating time right now—for the elephants, for all of the animals, and for me.

# LOOPY

## 2003

With renewed inner strength, I decide to go alone to visit Andy's grave.

It's something that I do every now and again, when I find the courage to face it all, just to say hello. I went with Lol and Drew one time, and we lay together under the canopy of the huge ebony tree that protects Andy, staring up into its branches and marvelling at its magnificence. Now we call this place Andy's tree, rather than Andy's grave. Still struggling to come to terms with the fact that his body is a part of this tree, I lie flat on my back on the ground beneath it, and tell him my stories. I tell him about all sorts of things, including the bateleurs. I'm having frequent encounters with these large black eagles—adorned with stunning bright red on their face and legs—as they glide effortlessly through the sky with wing tips pointing upwards.

'I'm seeing bateleurs at my most vulnerable times,' I say to Andy, 'and when I do, it's really strange, but I think of you.'

It's not something that I have yet admitted to anyone else. It seems a wee bit weird, even to me. It's a little like the sign I asked Andy for the day after his funeral; just something to let me know that everything was okay. I was instantly, and mysteriously, rewarded with an extraordinary shaft of bright light that fell to earth in front of me. Enveloped in warmth, I had enough time to take a photograph, and then the light was gone. In the presence of others, I dismissed this as coincidence but I was never really convinced.

Later, I find out that the Shona people of Zimbabwe—from the eastern side of the country, where Andy's family live—believe the bateleur to be a spirit messenger. *Of course*, I think to myself. *A spirit messenger! What else could this bird be?* They're said to bring protection and good fortune. Now, they always bring a smile to my face. When I see one, I think of Andy with a hand on my shoulder, making sure that everything is okay.

When I first arrived to live in Hwange, I sprinkled some of my beloved dog's ashes close to Andy's grave. Chloe had been the only child in my life plan and, like Andy, was a profoundly important presence in my life. 'Please be careful not to step on her,' I said to Andy at the time. I'd spoken these words to him once before, when he was racing down the flight of stairs inside my Brisbane home, almost colliding with Chloe. She seemed to always be under his feet.

I sprinkled the rest of Chloe's ashes at Makwa pan, one of my favourite waterholes inside Hwange National Park. I pass Makwa on my way home from Andy's tree. It's a place where I've spent time with many a friend, and where I've always enjoyed especially memorable wildlife encounters. Today I'm by myself, just me and my memories. I cherish these alone times and hold them close to my heart.

The roller-coaster ride continues with more snared animals and more snare removals, interspersed with days of sheer ecstasy documenting the lives of my elephant friends.

I am particularly devastated when Lady's family is struck, yet again, by the horrific snaring. There's an aching numbness in my chest; my spirit once again stricken. This time it's Lady's nearly five-year-old son, Loopy, who has a deadly wire wrapped very tightly around his head and neck.

I've been waiting for this ghastly day, when poachers injure another member of my favourite family. Loopy was named for his cheeky, irrepressible nature. Now, unless we can remove the wire, it seems certain that he will die an agonising death.

I watch Loopy in disbelief. His spirit is clearly stricken also. I talk to him, willing him to somehow break the snare before it kills him. Three thin strands of wire are acting like a sharp knife, slicing into his innocent little face and neck. Lady is the only adult present. Except when mating, I've never encountered her without another adult female from her family close by. Is it so distressing for the family that she's chosen to bear this burden alone?

I close the door of my 4x4, trying to shut out this tragic sight, and hurry to arrange the approvals necessary to be able to remove the snare. The next day I sight the partial family group again, but I'm helpless and distraught when there is no one available to do the darting. I'm exhausted by the emotions of this awful discovery, but I continue to search for Lady's family every day, in the heartfelt hope that we will not be too late.

Three long weeks crawl by without any success. The anguish I've felt since first seeing Loopy's snare has been hard to endure. I have searched for him constantly, seen him occasionally, and each time his wound looks worse. There's never anyone available to dart. I've lost patience, and now I am losing heart.

But sweet reprieve eventually comes.

I last saw Lady's family two days ago, and for the second day running I've waited impatiently in the same place, on a calculated guess (despite no fresh elephant spoor heading my way), that Lady and her family will return to this pan. They arrive just before 1 p.m. With a knot in my stomach, I radio for assistance. Unfortunately Greg isn't available, but another darter is able to come immediately. It will take him twenty minutes to get to me. Meanwhile, someone else is hurrying to collect the required National Parks' scout.

Things don't start out too well. Lady's family drink from the cement trough where fresh water flows before running into the waterhole, and within five minutes they're starting to move off into thick bush, where it will be impossible to dart. Fortunately, I'd anticipated that this might happen. Help is still fifteen minutes away, with another fifteen minutes needed to prepare the required darts. I'd collected some *Acacia erioloba* pods that had fallen to the ground. They're a natural food treat elephants love. Reversing slowly for several hundred metres, I entice Lady and her family, metre by metre, up the sandy road by throwing velvety grey pods just in front of my bonnet. With Lady in the lead, all family members follow, picking up these pods as they lumber my way. I figure that if I can get them to the open mineral lick area they will feed there on the natural mineral salts, at least for a while. Thankfully, I am right. When the darter arrives, this is where he finds us.

There'd already been some debate over how this darting should best be done. We are all still feeling our way with darting within family groups. Right now some darters believe it's always necessary to dart the mother elephant as well as the snared calf. This assumes that someone can in fact instantly, and accurately, identify the mother of the calf, which in 'unknown' families is not always as simple as it may sound, since young elephants will often mingle with their cousins beside an aunt. An isolated observation of an adult female close to or even suckling a calf doesn't mean that this calf is necessarily hers. Over the years I've come to believe, especially with these well-known elephants, that every immobilisation scenario is different, and all of the known facts need to be taken into account before deciding on a plan of action.

I know Lady very well by now. I don't believe that she should be, or needs to be, darted—a recommendation that was earlier rejected by this particular darter and some of his companions. None of these men have spent any significant time with elephants. Even so, they think my input irrelevant. This is something that I am getting used to. To some, I'm just a lone, unqualified woman without the right letters after my name. But I understand well, as they do not, that Lady is suckling a younger calf and has recently been mated. She has three calves in fact, one younger than

Loopy and one older, and perhaps an unborn baby, dependent on her for their very survival. Lady is one of the best known and most habituated Presidential Elephants. I don't want to jeopardise Lady's life, and therefore the lives of her offspring, unnecessarily.

Of course it is the darter who has the final say. Despite my explanations he is still reluctant to dart only Loopy, however he finally agrees. A reversal can quickly be administered in the event that this turns dangerous, and I am prepared to be the only one out of the vehicle attending to Loopy if need be, putting only my own life in danger.

While the darts are being prepared, Lady, Loopy and the rest of the family enjoy the mineral lick. But time is running out. The family is again preparing to move off into thick bush. A few more acacia pods that I throw on the ground encourage Lady, with Loopy by her side, to stay for a few minutes longer while the darter finally takes aim. I can't hold them any longer. Just metres from the edge of thick bush, the dart—its contents determined weeks earlier based on Loopy's approximate age and weight— hits his rump with precision.

As I had hoped, Lady is preoccupied with looking after her youngest daughter, and the other family members simply follow her away into the bush. The most habituated family in the Presidential herd, they are not thrown into panic. When Loopy goes down, two family members come to help him, but as we approach in two vehicles they also move off without fuss towards Lady. Now we are alone with Loopy.

He has gone down face forward onto his chest (a potentially deadly position) and so, without a moment's hesitation, five hundred plus kilograms of elephant is quickly rolled over so that he is lying on his side. In this position he'll have no respiratory distress. I am thankful that he isn't a full-grown multi-tonne elephant. With armed support standing guard, the snare is quickly cut, the deep wound washed and antibiotics injected. It's a scene that has repeated itself endlessly in my mind for weeks, day and night. Now it is finally happening. Thankfully no elephants bother us, but the unpredictability of the environment we're working in never leaves my mind. It is not Lady who concerns me so much but rather her sister Leanne, who can sometimes be a little more aggressive than the others.

Standing now in my 4x4, I wait anxiously for the reversal drug to take effect. Still lying on his side, Loopy takes a trunkful of sand to dust his wound, and eventually gets to his feet. Loopy knows my voice well. In the months prior to him being snared, he had begun standing for long periods, and sometimes slept, right beside the door of my vehicle. I croon to him while he stands gently between our two vehicles, dusting himself. I suppose there is a comforting familiarity there.

He rumbles constantly, with family members answering him. I wonder, as I do so often, what the elephants are saying to each other in their secret conversations. 'It's okay, guys, I'm fine. Really, no big deal. I'm fine.'

He makes no attempt to move off, content to stay where he is. In the end, we leave before he does, to give him some space. Louise and son Limp are the relatives nearest to him. Loopy joins them in the shade of a tree. The other vehicles and helpers depart, and I sit alone with the elephants, talking to them. There is no sign of Lady. Within half an hour they've all taken off into the thick bush and I can no longer see or follow any of them.

The operation has gone extremely well, but I am never content until I know that the entire family has reunited. The next day at 10 a.m. I return to the same pan.

Unusually for this time of the morning there are already close to one hundred elephants around the pan. Searching nervously, I find Lady, but there is no Loopy close by. My heart sinks. Although not his normal behaviour, Loopy had rarely left his mother's side while the tight head-snare had been debilitating him. I switch off my vehicle and watch Lady and her family walk off in front of me, after first stopping by my door to say hello.

I can't see Loopy.

While begging whoever is listening to let Loopy be there, he suddenly appears from the mass of elephants, hurrying towards my vehicle. I am unspeakably relieved. And Loopy's own relief is obvious. Everything about him suggests that he is already feeling remarkably better. He clearly no longer feels a need to stay right beside his mother. He's holding his head higher than he has during the past three weeks when the tight wire was slicing his neck, and happily ventures his little trunk towards my outstretched hand before running playfully to catch up with his family.

This encounter delights and encourages me. Once again, my resolve to keep working with these elephants is strengthened. My heart fills with a peace that I have not felt in months. Distressed and preoccupied by all of the tragic snaring I'd been encountering, it is only now that I realise just how tired I am.

Loopy's snare wound is deep on the top of his head, and nasty on the side of his face and under his chin, but so long as no further infection sets in, I believe he will survive.

And survive he does.

While we were rescuing Loopy, Jabulani and the rest of the estate anti-poaching team were sitting out an ambush. Three days later the poachers—a man and his wife—are caught. They're clean, well dressed and obviously healthy. He is employed. I feel no sympathy. I look at their snares before he is ordered to destroy them. They are set at a height just right to snare an antelope—or the head of another young elephant. They're poachers, and they're breaking the law. They deserve whatever punishment the authorities deem appropriate. I know that the sentences are always much too light, but at least there's the added shame of being a convicted poacher.

With the sun setting on another day, I sit on the rooftop of my 4x4 and drink an Amarula. Indeed, I drink a few. I think about how I feel about all of this. What I decide is this: elephants are to me the essence of wild freedom. I am adamant that they do not deserve such agony and distur-bance at the hands of humans.

It is obvious, though, that not everyone agrees with me.

# HONORARY ELEPHANT

## 2003

All of those who've had the privilege of meeting Lady agree that she's an unforgettable elephant. She is huge and can be boisterous. She's unquestionably intelligent and powerful in more ways than one. She's wildly entertaining and affectionate to boot. Above all else, she is dignified and a great leader to her family.

Lady is the first wild elephant who has truly accepted me into her world, who has consented to my touch and responds with genuine excitement to my presence. This isn't something that I set out to achieve; it has happened by chance over the course of the two and a half years that I've been spending with her and her family.

One memorable day, when Lady was once again right next to my 4x4, I leaned out of the window and very tentatively placed my hand on her tusk. It was an instinctive moment; the same way that I might greet a human being. She didn't flinch or react in any obvious way, and I left my hand there for several minutes. This brief physical connection with my friend left my spirit soaring.

Since then, Lady has always gone out of her way to come and stand beside my vehicle, her trunk swinging like a pendulum as she hurries my way. Then she rumbles. Is she talking to me, I wonder? I always look up into her amber-coloured eyes, and place my hand on her tusk. She's an incredibly gentle giant, with an extra-special quality that always causes me to pause, and to breathe in the magic surrounding me.

Another day, through the window of my vehicle I placed my hand, so very gently, against her trunk. It felt as warm as the Kalahari sand, much rougher than I thought it would be, and deeply grooved. Lady tensed just a little at first, not knowing what this strange human appendage was against her skin, but she didn't try to evade my tender touch. In that moment, time stood still. A rush of adrenalin shot through me as we two creatures—such unlikely friends—were momentarily blended. I felt as if I was dreaming. Imagine! Such trust from a fully grown wild elephant! Holding her gaze, I talked and sang to her, as we placed our complete trust in one another. The reality slowly began to sink in and tears sprung to my eyes as I struggled to comprehend the enormity of the privilege.

Now—incredibly—I can rub my hand up and down Lady's trunk. I apply as much pressure as my own strength allows. She seems to revel in it, as do I. Sometimes when I rub her trunk hard, she concertinas it. It's like an accordion being played vertically, and I get the feeling she's about to sneeze.

I know that Lady is a wild, free-roaming jumbo who could kill me with one swipe of her mighty trunk. I continually remind myself that this is a truly wild elephant and, always attempting to read her mood while also keeping a close eye on her body language, I never push her level of tolerance, nor do I ever force myself upon her.

Sometimes when I croon to Lady and look up into her long-lashed eyes, her temporal glands erupt with liquid. It isn't a trickle, but more like a bubble of liquid that springs up from within, before streaming down both sides of her face. It is a sign of excitement. It's obvious to me that both Lady and I thoroughly enjoy our encounters with each other.

Friends who witness these encounters suspect that Lady, wild and free, has bestowed on me the status of 'honorary elephant'. I am moved beyond words.

Both Cynthia Moss and Joyce Poole have their own very close relationships with the elephants of Amboseli National Park in Kenya. They've
been studying the grey giants of Amboseli since the 1970s and are legendary in the world of elephants. I decide that it's worth spending time and
money to visit them and learn what I can from them. When I travelled
as a tourist, I loved the wide open spaces of East Africa and I'm keen to
return. I stay overnight in Joyce's spectacular home, full of huge panes of
undressed glass that afford panoramic views over Kenya's Great Rift Valley.
I've named a special J family elephant after Joyce. Even so, it's somewhat
surreal being in the home of this elephant legend.

I spend two weeks living among the elephants in Amboseli, practising sexing newborn elephants and estimating the age of older ones.
The Amboseli elephants have been monitored intimately for more than
30 years, many since they were newborns, so ages are precisely known.
From the Amboseli project I learn what a five-, ten-, fifteen-, twenty- and
thirty-year-old elephant *really* looks like. When I first see new babies on
the estate, I'm sometimes still confusing females and males, but I quickly
learn to tell them apart with ease.

Over the years the Amboseli project dispelled many myths about
elephants, and uncovered numerous fascinating facts. I admire Cynthia
and Joyce's supreme dedication and find myself craving their vast knowledge. During our days together in the field, devoted indigenous Kenyans
also share with me their intimate understanding and love of the elephants.

The splash of icing atop Mount Kilimanjaro provides a perfect backdrop to this study area. The purple sunsets are dramatic, the last rays
of sunlight illuminate the snow-cap with golden light. I awake in the
mornings, under canvas in a palm grove, to the call of fish eagles and to
buffaloes, hyenas and elephants wandering through camp.

The tusks of the charming Amboseli elephants bear little resemblance
to those of the Hwange ones. Some splendid tusks almost reach the

ground. Few sights are as awesome, and frightening, as a serious musth bull fight. One day, a clash of ivory, usually just a pleasing playful sound, signals the start of a battle between two dominant bulls. This conflict leaves one of them dead, having suffered a fatal tusk wound to his head. His own imposing tusks are over two metres long. It's a dreadful shock to Cynthia and others who'd known him for almost 30 years, ever since he was a cheeky teenager. I walk up to his body, lying still and noble on the ground, and place some grass in his mouth.

'For your journey,' I whisper sadly to him. At least it is a natural way to die.

Cynthia and Joyce ask after some of Zimbabwe's past elephant personalities, but I'm unable to shed much light. I am aware, though, that some of Zimbabwe's elephant management practices (like culling families and leaving babies alive, tied to their dead mothers, for later sale to the captive industry) haven't always been well regarded by others. I hope they won't tar me with the same tainted brush.

Zimbabwe's government press has also recently been declaring that there are some 75,000 elephants inside Hwange National Park, a figure widely believed to be inflated by around 300 per cent. 'Don't they know how to count in Zimbabwe?' is a rhetorical question that I'm often asked. On top of everything else going on, it's distressing to work with a species that is often the target of misinformation. The government loves to exaggerate things like birth rates, population growth and some vegetation impacts. Figures are blindly repeated until they become 'fact'.

I return to Hwange fortified with new information and techniques for identification and observation. I will also soon know first-hand exactly how frequently Hwange elephants are giving birth, and from what age, to then be able to dispel some of the myths.

There are certainly times when I feel a need to try and escape all of the misinformation and exaggerated talk. On these occasions, I sit on the roof of my 4x4 and watch the sun nudge the horizon, imagining what it would sound like if elephants could laugh.

Thankfully, things start to improve in the field. As the months pass it becomes clear that the snaring problem on the estate is under better control. Greg's Painted Dog project now has an additional anti-poaching unit, larger than the estate one, which also patrols the surrounds. Fewer snares are being uncovered these days, and I'm not finding as many snared animals. It feels like, at last, we are winning the battle.

And then, in July, another catastrophe strikes.

I'm getting ready to go to Bulawayo to buy supplies. I don't drive myself, since scarce fuel is better kept for field work, and besides, I don't like to risk my old 4x4 on long journeys. Instead I get a lift there and back in a truck that delivers supplies to various lodges in the area. The truck is due to collect me at any minute, when I overhear anxious chatter about Greg. He was flying the project's ultralight this morning, tracking rhinos rather than dogs. He didn't land where and when he should have.

Nobody knows if Greg is alive or dead. It's a bit like Andy's accident all over again. Andy had taken off from Sinamatella, the same National Parks base, and was also tracking rhino. He was in a helicopter, rather than a flimsy ultralight, and he didn't survive. So many of us had whispered to each other that we would never go up in that ultralight with Greg.

I first spent time with Greg back in the 1990s, when I was a tourist doing short-term voluntary stints. I opened his kitchen cupboard to see rows and rows of tins of beans. This is what he was living on. He had little funding at the time but he persevered with his conservation work regardless. At one stage his only way of getting around in the field had been a motorbike. With all those lions around. And when it comes to snakes, he is fearless. He once removed a deadly black mamba from the engine of a game-drive vehicle without thinking twice.

July days can be very warm, and the nights very cold. We don't know it yet but Greg is alive, and in excruciating pain. He has crashed far from his expected route and the search has been in the wrong area. Like his radio, both of his legs are broken in multiple places, as are his ankles and pelvis. He drags himself to shelter under the flammable remains of his plane. He makes what noises he can to fend off elephants, lions and hyenas during the 28 hours that he is alone and in agony, deep in the Hwange bush.

Late next morning he's finally found. Dehydrated and broken, he is airlifted out.

It will take years of rehabilitation for Greg to be able to walk again, and even then his legs will never be quite the same. He's exceptionally lucky not to lose them both—and not to have lost his life. If he had though, as dedicated as he is to the wildlife cause, I suspect he would not have regretted his fate.

# A MILLION MILES FROM MY CHILDHOOD

## 2003

By October Julia is making plans to leave Hwange, having decided that it is 'too heartbreaking' for her to remain in Zimbabwe. Her hyena colleague, Marion, is long gone. Val is living in Australia. John is living in South Africa. And now it's sounding like Dinks could be moving to greener pastures soon too.

And so I'm already feeling a little vulnerable, when there's an unexpected knock at the door of my *rondavel*. Standing in front of me is a manager from a nearby tourist lodge who delivers a message to me in the laid-back way of Africa. He tells me that a large portion of the Hwange Estate—the area called Kanondo and the adjoining area called Khatshana, where I spend much of my time—has been claimed by the governor of this province, a personal appointee of the president and the very government official responsible for handling land reform in this area. He has allocated this Presidential Elephant land to himself and to his relatives. No money or title deeds have changed hands. He has simply decided that it is now his own private property. Inconceivably, he has also managed to obtain licences from Parks and the Wildlife Ministry to hunt for sport. His approved hunting quota includes several elephants.

I am stunned. Feeling faint, I lean heavily against my door-frame, listening to this messenger in sheer disbelief.

White sport-hunters here and across the country are among those who have lost their land under the land reform program, to those calling themselves 'new farmers'. But this is an area that has not been hunted for more than 30 years. This is an area where wildlife has become habituated over these years to close proximity with humans. This is the key home range of the 'protected' Presidential Elephants of Zimbabwe and a key tourism area. This area is not white-owned. In fact Kanondo, according to old certified maps, has for decades been classified as 'State Land'; that is, protected land that at least some in government are clearly declaring can't be claimed.

How could anyone possibly now consider this claimable land? And how could the Wildlife Minister, Comrade Francis Nhema, have signed an approval to hunt for sport here?

Logic plays no part. This is Zimbabwe after all, and Mugabe's men do as they please. Equally concerning is the fact that Parks management, too afraid to do anything else, simply bow down to them.

From tomorrow, I'm told, I am no longer permitted in the Kanondo and Khatshana areas. From tomorrow tourists will no longer be allowed into these areas on game-drives, and the anti-poaching team will be banned too. From tomorrow, they will kill animals there.

Rich foreigners pay tens of thousands of US dollars to come to Africa and bag animal heads to hang on the walls of their homes. Since there are so many prime animal species on this land, this is easy money; nothing but a greedy get-rich-quick scam. It makes me shudder with fear and horror. So many joys that flourish only in the peace and quiet of the African bush will now be shattered by gunfire. As if the horrific snaring wasn't bad enough.

'What about the *protected* Presidential Elephants of Zimbabwe?' I challenge.

I get no response.

'What is being done to try to fix this?' I plead.

Still, there is no response. All I get is a shrug of the shoulders.

Is it really all over just like that? It is inconceivable. Of all the awful things that could happen, I never imagined it would be this: a high-level government official claiming Presidential Elephant land as his own. And worse, claiming it to hunt upon.

The whole situation holds the promise of deep pain, and I try—unsuccessfully—to shake the horror. Although I immediately set about informing the few people who I think may be able to assist, and draft my own pleas to government ministries, there is no stopping what is going to happen tomorrow.

I sink down on my sofa. I'd left Kanondo pan just a couple of hours ago, not knowing that it wouldn't be there again in the same way that it has always been, wild and free, a place with a light that is often indescribable. It's where I'd had my most memorable Presidential Elephant encounters, and where the best opportunities exist, in its open areas, to look closely for snare injuries. It is a place of life. Its wildness has called out to so many, who came with cameras and never with guns. It is simply impossible to come to terms with this new development.

My body will, I suppose, eventually recover from the shock, but my heart and mind won't heal nearly so quickly. Another very precious part of my Africa is gone forever. This though, is not the result of an accident. This is nothing but blatant, uncaring greed.

I find Lady in an adjoining area called Acacia Grove and I put my hand on her trunk. It is not a happy meeting. Her family is so often in the now-grabbed areas. Born wild. Living wild. Like all of the Presidential Elephants, they are extraordinarily trusting of human beings. I can only manage to say two words to her: 'I'm sorry.'

Ten days pass in a blur. Not unlike me, the gods are angry. Deafening cracks of thunder boom continuously in the night, and the rain finally comes. And it comes early.

'Let it rain. Let it rain. Let it rain,' I beg. 'Let the wildlife disperse, away from all of these new hunters.' I will it not to stop. It does stop, but not before depressions and waterholes, turned dry and cracked by the burning sun months earlier, once again hold life-giving water. It's good news for the wildlife, the animals no longer forced to congregate around just the few pumped pans that were the only sources of water before the downpour.

This first deluge doesn't penetrate very deeply into the baked ground. The fresh run-off water won't last for long without supplementary rain. But these first downpours are important: preparing the pans, enhancing their water retention capacity for when next the rain comes. Although this time I barely notice the smell of the first rain, it is in fact delightful, etched into the minds of all of us who live in the African bush. The lingering dust of the long dry months is washed away.

Out in the field, close to Acacia Grove, I'm near a pair of mating lions, now dozing only metres from my vehicle. Both male and female have been radiating a wild energy as they mate over and over again, muscles bulging around their necks. However, I'm not the only one taking an interest. A hunting vehicle pulls up beside these lions too, in this one small area that has escaped being re-designated for hunting.

I thought that my capacity for astonishment had been exhausted, but I was mistaken. This is a photographic area—one of the very few photographic safari areas left now—and the white hunters' brazen appearance here *does* astonish me. These men were seen a few days ago inspecting lion spoor. They want this lion—to hang on a wall. I can practically see them salivating.

They're hunting in an area full of habituated wildlife. There is no need here to track an animal for days, or weeks. There is no skill whatsoever involved in these hunts. So many of these animals walk right up to you— or at least they used to, before the gunfire started.

These hunters are, I decide, nothing but soulless, greedy men. When I look to memorise their number plate, I find there is no number plate at all. Why have they felt a need to remove it?

They move off, not soon enough for my liking, leaving my mind full of a thousand resentments. I try to enjoy the setting sun as it casts a stunning light on the lion lovers. They roll on their backs in lazy abandon, mouths wide with yawns of indifference. Thousands of white moths erupt from the damp earth, fluttering like snowflakes around them. It is beautiful, but my mind is elsewhere.

Suddenly I feel afraid, very afraid. By now it is painfully apparent to me that there are only a few people who truly seem to care about the wildlife tragedy that is unfolding here. Others just offer cursory acknowledgement. 'But this is Africa,' I am told repeatedly. And they know the risks of getting involved.

It is a response that exasperates me. I don't care that this is Africa, I don't care who owns land in this country, and I don't care who these land grabbers are. But I do care about the Presidential Elephants and about all of the wildlife that I've come to know so well over the past three years. Given that the head claimant is considered 'a big man' (politically connected), with an unsavoury reputation, most people are afraid of getting too involved. Thankfully, though, there are some who are genuinely concerned. There is some support from wildlife conservation organisations on this frightening road. The wildlife will not have to walk it entirely alone. And more importantly, there are two government officials who have indicated that they will try to help.

Back at my *rondavel* there is no power. Thousands of flying ants, making their regular appearance after the first rain, swarm around the few lights of a nearby lodge being powered by a generator. A toad jumps against my leg, giving me a slimy fright and a strange sense of connection to all wildlife. I am definitely on *their* side. My spirit hasn't quite failed me yet. By candlelight, a glass of Amarula—six times the price that it was twelve months ago, as inflation takes hold—warms what hope is left within me.

But the Presidential Elephant families are staying away, making close monitoring impossible. They do not like the sound of gunshots, and neither do I.

The next day in the field I'm reading *Flamingo Feather* by Laurens Van Der Post, waiting and hoping that some elephants will arrive. One sentence resonates with me: 'his life will achieve . . . something which is greater than happiness and unhappiness: and that is meaning'.

I read these words once, and then a second time, and a third. The familiar sound of the rainbird takes me back to times long gone, to my childhood home in Grantham and my parents who always linked its distinctive call with the rain that the farmers bank on. It was always just 'the rainbird' to me, calling unseen from the mulberry tree in our leafy, well-tended backyard. I listen to this same call now, in this different era and distant land far removed from my childhood, longing for the rain to return; longing for the hunters to leave.

The silence becomes intolerably loud inside my head. Fearing reprisal, so very few are speaking out. This is not a country of free and fair, and everybody knows it. I'm aware that my permit could be cancelled at a moment's notice, but I can't turn a blind eye. I continue to pass on whatever information I can to those who may be able to help.

My own thoughts and feelings are sometimes so intense they become unbearable, and my disillusionment grows daily. It's a heavy and unhappy burden, but I know that I must dig deep and find courage to continue on. Everything now though is soured with fear. And I am stricken with unease and deep sorrow: '. . . *his life will achieve . . . something which is greater than happiness and unhappiness: and that is meaning*'.

I am so pleased for John that he is gone. The house that he used to rent on the Khatshana side of the estate is now in the hands of the governor. The governor's brother-in-law walks around, threatening to bring out his AK-47 machine gun. It's a family affair and the governor's son is also on the scene. Already, nearby lodge staff have been forced to the ground, hands behind their heads, as gun-toting land claimants try to seize other wildlife land. One man, crudely calling himself 'Black Jesus', enjoys his own reign of terror.

My close friends email regularly to check on my wellbeing, but they're all hours, or oceans, away. While in the bush I've had to learn to get through things on my own and have become self-reliant. There are still wildlife researchers working in the area, but for the most part they're focused on their degrees and seem to care little about what's happening to the wildlife just down the road from them. To speak out would mean risking the permits that enable them to do their research work, and therefore their careers.

I keep looking for Lady and her family around Acacia Grove, the only part of the Hwange Estate not claimed. She has no hand for me to hold, but I want to hold her trunk; to tell her that everything will be okay; to beg her to stay safe. I look for all of the other families too, desperate to find out if they're still intact.

I realise there is no turning back. There's no running away, and no giving up. In the elephants' rumbles and in the feel of living ivory, I've found a life that has real meaning to me—and there can be no escape. Not now anyway. These elephants need somebody on their side.

My passionate desire to be out in the field all day every day is dwindling though. I now dread what I might see, and what I might not. Which of the elephant families are still around? Which are running terrified today from the sound of gunshots? Which are being forced to flee into snare-infested areas? Do I really want to know? My spirit beaten and bruised, I wonder if I'm strong enough to cope with the reality.

Few things are more distressing than watching a family of magnificent giants bunched tightly together, running terrified in complete silence with their tails high from the sound of gunshots, not game to stop to grab even a trunkful of water. Sometimes the shots aren't audible to my own ears, but the elephants hear them. Or perhaps they hear infrasonic warnings passed on by other elephants closer to the danger. Whatever the case, they flee at high speed.

With the hunting, and without access to Kanondo and Khatshana, my days with the elephants are not what they used to be. Their key home range is now inaccessible to me, and their behaviour has changed. For three years, I had always yearned to be out all day in the field with the elephants. Occasionally now, I don't even go out at all. Too often, the elephants are not around, and I know that it isn't only the rain that has chased them away.

It has been said that one can't live with animals without heartbreak. But heartbreak at the hands of greedy humans is so much worse to endure. I recognise that I've been happier with the elephants than I've ever been—although now, possibly sadder than ever as well. Perhaps it was inevitable, I console myself, that I would encounter this very bleak side of Africa. I wonder if I'll be forced to leave.

Yet I realise, with renewed clarity, that I no longer have any real place in a sophisticated Western society. It is a life that I've lost enthusiasm for, the wildness of Africa having called out to the deep wildness in my heart. I can't imagine going back. Zimbabwe, with all of its troubles, has still managed to keep hold of my soul. An adopted child of Africa, that's what I am now.

'You'll find the courage to stay,' Shaynie tells me in an email from Bulawayo. And I hope that she is right. The elephants have become an important part of me that I'm not ready to lose. By now I know over two hundred of them well, as individuals and family members. They have, in some ways, taken the place of people.

During these last months of 2003 I regularly watch the sun sink below the horizon, contemplating the unpredictable current of events in Zimbabwe. In the past, when chaos belonged to other people and not me, I'd had a boundless capacity for optimism. Now, I'm more world-weary, far less naïve. But though disenchanted, I still nourish hope that things will somehow come right for the elephants and other wildlife on the Hwange Estate.

For now, the hunting goes on and I wait impatiently for sanity to intervene. Sadly, I know only too well that things take time in Africa. They take even longer in Zimbabwe.

In an attempt to ease my troubled mind I search for diversions. I creep to Mpofu pan to watch the sunset. It's now also 'owned' by the governor.

The beauty of the fading day pierces me like an arrow. The sunken sun in the west has left the horizon orange, and the warm glow of the full moon is visible in the east. The dusk symphony begins. A saddlebill stork flies low from the pan, landing in a dead tree close by. Bare, contorted branches decorate the moon, the saddlebill exquisitely silhouetted in the middle of this distant yellow ball.

Everything is still. Their perfect reflections in the pan are the only evidence that four elephants are keeping me company. For a short time, I manage to disappear into my imagination. While watching the twilight die, I pretend that everything is right in my world.

My visit to Mpofu pan is so healing that I secretly return late the next afternoon. Just a few elephants are resting by the water's edge, now orange with the reflection of the sun just gone. Heavy grey clouds laced with deep blue hang in the sky, above bands of vivid orange and hot-pink. There are soft elephant rumbles. There is the familiar sound of dung balls hitting the ground and their sweet straw-like pungency. Sheet lightning is visible behind the heavy cloud cover, and the rainbird is calling. Eventually, the roosting commotion of the guinea fowls ends my quiet interlude.

On my way home in darkness, I stop at a lodge to find out how much further the local currency has devalued in the past few weeks. The numbers are now staggering and are expected to get much worse. The sky-rocketing inflation and exchange rates are indicative of a country in crisis. I've heard that the governor's family may be willing to sell their newly grabbed land for the princely sum of US$250,000, a huge amount of money in Zimbabwe at this time.

'How many Zimbabwe dollars is two hundred and fifty thousand US dollars?' I query. Numbers are punched into a program on a computer that's sitting on the reception desk. But it is too much, even for the computer. It displays no numbers, but instead responds with just two words.

'What does it say?' I ask, wondering why the receptionist is shaking his head.

'Numerical overload,' he laughs.

*Numerical overload?* Now I'm shaking my head as well. *What hope is there?*

I've been advised that I need to sit tight while correspondence about this land grab is being considered. It could take months, I'm told, which is terrifying to me. If nothing else, the hunting quota on this land surely has to be withdrawn as quickly as possible.

# GIVING SOMETHING BACK

## 2003

Something odd happens to the elephants around full moon. That invisible man sprinkles his moon dust, and his magic, and the elephants become a little crazy: more visible, more social, more vocal.

But the poachers have destroyed the beauty of even these nights. Nowadays, the full moon is referred to as the 'poacher's moon': the moon lighting their killing fields. And now the sound of the sport-hunters' gunfire combines with that of the poachers to ensure that there are far fewer elephants around than normal.

So I'm not in the best mood when I become stranded, alone one afternoon, in a remote location. It's the first time that I've had to admit defeat in the bush. While driving along a little-used road, essentially to show my presence to poachers, my back tyre hit a log hidden in long grass. Somehow in the process, my rubber fuel pipe dislodged and has been ripped in two.

The radio network is down so I know that I'm not going anywhere unless I can rejoin this rubber tube. I tell myself to get a grip and deal with it. Two clothes-pegs (used to fasten the mosquito net that I always carry in my 4x4 in case I'm forced to stay out overnight) keeps the rubber pipe ends bent and secured so that no more precious fuel is lost. Some all-purpose putty and tape from my toolbox doesn't help in rejoining it, although I try various imaginative fixes for over an hour. I feel surprisingly happy, pleased with my resourcefulness, all the while realising that I'm going to fail.

I know of only one vehicle that might pass my way, but it could be days before I see the dust of its approach. It is almost mid-afternoon. I've given up trying to repair the pipe, lying now on the sandy road looking up at it—as if that might help! I decide to lock my field equipment in my vehicle, leave a note on the windscreen and set off on the one-hour walk to the nearest lodge. I will take my water bottle, my little high-pitched air-horn, which will hopefully help to frighten off anything threatening, and my one-and-a-half metre hollow metal pipe that John gave me to help loosen tight wheel nuts. They seem like sensible protection devices to have on hand; a false sense of security perhaps, but better than nothing.

I think about John, who I know is struggling to adjust to his new life, and fondly recall the day he made me an expert in tyre changing. I wonder if he ever imagined that I'd be using his length of pipe for this purpose.

Then miraculously, I hear that vehicle. It is, just this once, an infinitely preferable sound to the silence that was surrounding me. A tow rope, never yet used but always in my 4x4, means that I'm quickly rescued. Previously, I'd always managed to limp back to base, but not this time. Resident mechanics, exercising their superb bush skills, have me mobile again quickly and I'm soon back off into the bush, smelling distinctly of petrol.

Although it sometimes feels like my 4x4 is held together mostly by wire and optimism, it has, for the most part, proven to be an extremely reliable bush vehicle despite its unenviably high fuel consumption. It does, though, have a few little foibles. During one of my trips to Bulawayo for supplies I ask Ernie, a father figure and friend, to help me source some brake fluid, which is often in short supply as so many things are now. Soon afterwards, he returns with a small pot.

'What's that?' I ask.

'It's brake fluid,' Ernie replies.

'That will last me for *two weeks*,' I grumble.

Ernie turns to his companion and shakes his head. 'She's got the only vehicle in the world,' he sniggers, 'that runs on brake fluid.'

We all still manage to laugh a little. But laughter—and sleep—no longer come easily for me. I think constantly about the snaring, the land grabs and the sport-hunting. I think about the past few years, which have passed more quickly than I could ever have imagined. And I realise there is something missing of the person that I'd been three years ago, since seeing and going through so much. I'm so grateful for my friends in Bulawayo and Harare, who understand this country well and who have helped me keep things in perspective. I continue to cherish my Down Under friends too, who encourage me on and enjoy living my life vicariously. Together, they're my backbone, my team.

What my family have been going through in Australia also helps me to keep things in perspective. My eldest niece, Rebecca, was diagnosed with Hodgkin's lymphoma last year, only a few months after I sold my Brisbane home. Cancer at age seventeen. It was a shock to us all, especially since there's no family history of this dreaded disease.

After four months of weekly chemotherapy, Rebecca was deemed to be in remission. But six months later, after starting a law degree, her cancer was back. She wasn't keen to commit to more treatment, but she wasn't ready to succumb to this disease either. Mater Children's Hospital in Brisbane became her home for two months. This was, on top of everything else, a logistical battle for my sister Deborah, since there were two younger siblings in their family home, 130 kilometres away in Toowoomba, who also needed their mother.

Rebecca required higher doses of chemo, and also a stem cell transplant. A month of daily radiation treatments to her neck and chest would be necessary following the transplant, which raised concerns about breast cancer and infertility, which also had to be addressed. Her own stem cells were harvested and then transplanted. Her weight plummeted to 42 kilograms.

'Once you get through this, Bec, you'll have to come over and visit the elephants,' I tempt, trying to give her something else to focus on and look forward to. I realise, though, that she can well do without Africa and its array of diseases and disasters.

For me, this is another poignant reminder of just how fragile life is and how important it is to make the most of every day, doing what you really want to do with your life. In a strange way, Rebecca has given me the courage to stay in Hwange and battle on.

'God doesn't give you anything you can't handle and get through,' she tells me.

'How are you feeling, really?' I ask her.

'My body feels like it's been stampeded by elephants,' she admits. 'I'm dying for a Hungry Jack's double decker cheese combo,' she tells me, after not being allowed any take-away food for months.

'I'm craving a McDonald's cheeseburger, with fries inside the bun,' I say (knowing there's no McDonald's anywhere in Zimbabwe).

At least we're both smiling.

Rebecca's sixteen-month ordeal is finally over, although it will likely take as long again to properly regain her strength, and there's no getting these years back. Her cancer, we all hope, won't return. She's due to begin university again next year, where she'll leave law behind, and study to become a schoolteacher instead.

'Life's too short to be arguing for a living,' Rebecca decides. 'It's time to give something back.'

She's come through her own battle much wiser, which gives me hope that I will get through mine.

# CHRISTMAS IN THE MIST

# 2003

Dinks and Shaynie are determined to ensure that, this year, I enjoy a peaceful Christmas. We decide that the spectacular Bvumba Mountains, in Zimbabwe's east, is where we'll go together.

We sit three abreast in a borrowed vehicle, taking turns to drive and singing songs (not often in tune) out our windows to the great African outdoors as if we haven't a care in the world.

We pass boulder-topped *koppies* and gnarled, bulbous baobab trees. When we arrive, we drive cautiously up winding roads. I'm amazed by the seemingly endless vistas of rolling green hills cloaked in patches of forest, with glimpses into neighbouring Mozambique. It's an entirely different world from the one I've come to know so well in Hwange, and I'm grateful for the change of pace and scenery. And for some sanity.

Our cabin is nestled high in the Vumba, in 'the mountains of the mist'. Mist rolls in tangibly over the hills and soon rain begins to fall. We sit in front of a crackling log fire, allowing our bodies to relax, listening to the peaceful tinkling of frogs.

We awake on the morning of Christmas Eve to the sparkle of count-less raindrops suspended from the tips of pine needles, the soaring pine trees dwarfing our cabin. A Livingstone's lourie—green with red under the wing—flits gracefully among the trees. It seems fitting to see these Christmas colours in the sky. Flame lilies (Zimbabwe's national flower) are abundant, including the yellow variety, as are the stunning large blue flower-clusters of the hydrangeas.

It is enchanting, and we find it impossible to leave. Literally. Having driven our vehicle down a steep slippery incline to get to our cabin, we now find that we can't get back up. The overnight rain has made it 4x4 terrain and we're not in a 4x4. Our first rescuer has to be rescued himself, and we wait for a second knight in shining armour. A visit from a beautiful Emperor Swallowtail butterfly, with sizeable wings and distinctive clubbed tail found only on this eastern border of Zimbabwe, lifts our spirits.

After our rescue, we stand quietly on the roadside as a troop of elusive canopy-dwelling Samango monkeys—with chubby silver faces and dark grey bodies—swing swiftly through rain-sodden branches. In Zimbabwe they only exist in these misty mountains.

The African new moon is lying on her back in a crystal clear night sky. Around the log fire we toast marshmallows, while enjoying good South African wine, a treat for our often deprived palates. A firefly appears, flashing its bright light just above my head, willing me to make a festive season wish.

'Here's to lots of everything good,' toasts Dinks, forever the optimist. And we clink our glasses together in genuine hope.

We take a trip northwards to Nyanga the next morning, where the mountains are more rugged. Pine forests dominate the landscape and there are sparkling waterways and waterfalls.

Some days the mist and the rain lingers all day, which is a welcome respite from the Hwange heat. We wander around in it, collecting pine cones to put on the fire and admiring the oversized toadstools, snails, slugs and frogs. The evenings are spent playing Scrabble, laughing and inventing new words, while enjoying endless cups of hot Milo.

'Look what I've got!' I grin, holding a bottle of Amarula high above my head, to claps and cheers from Dinks and Shaynie.

We eat freshly picked mushrooms from the Vumba forest floor, and survive. We eat berries growing by the roadside, and survive. We visit the renowned Tony's Coffee Shop, and barely survive the shock of the prices. In Zim dollars, a slice of cake costs what you'd have paid for a roadworthy vehicle here just a few short years ago. It isn't Tony's fault; Zimbabwe's economy is in free fall. None of us are prepared to pay *that* much for a piece of cake, but Dinks and Shaynie, unable to resist, order a very expensive hot drink while I sit and watch them savour every mouthful.

I find that I can't avoid talking about the Hwange land claim altogether. The last two months have passed in a blur of disbelief, outrage and grief, and even here in this distant location, it's always at the back of my mind.

'Do you think the land will ever be returned?' I ask, searching for some thread of hope. Dinks and Shaynie want to hand me that hope. They know what I long to hear, but false hope is not their specialty. They urge caution. They urge me not to try to take on powerful people. One of the hunting companies now operating on the estate is a South African one that has been officially banned from Zimbabwe, although it's still managing to operate underhandedly.

'You must know how corrupt a hunter has to be to be banned from Zimbabwe,' Shaynie states, 'and what sort of connections they must have to still be able to operate.'

I cringe inside just thinking about it.

'But this is the land of the Presidential Elephants,' I say, for what feels like the hundredth time.

My mum once told me a story about a highway in Australia that was being diverted 'because a frog lives there'. I'd grinned at her, rolling my eyes. It was clearly not just one frog; not just any old frog. A unique family of frogs. Frogs, and their habitat, deemed worthy of preservation.

'Well, it worked for frogs in Australia,' I say meekly. 'Maybe it will work for the Presidential Elephants?'

'We certainly hope that it will,' Dinks says gently. But I can tell she's not convinced.

'Here's to staying alive in 2004,' Shaynie toasts with a half-smile.

I smile too, knowing that if Dinks leaves Zimbabwe to live elsewhere next year, it will be Shaynie needing the comfort that is now being lavished on me.

The next morning we forget all of this depressing talk, and head south-west to Great Zimbabwe, a World Heritage site close to the township of Masvingo where Shaynie once lived, said to have been the royal capital of a Shona community. The town ruins exhibit extraordinary workmanship: a maze of well-finished stone block walls, astonishingly wide and tall, built without mortar. They're considered the most spectacular ruins south of the Sahara.

Back in Bulawayo, we welcome in the New Year watching videos, while struggling to adjust to the high temperatures. Separated by just seven hours' drive, but seemingly another world, log fires are definitely not needed here. Dinks expertly makes *sadza*, the maize meal staple of Zimbabwe; white and bland and somewhat of an acquired taste. With the smell of the accompanying relish tantalising our taste buds we tuck in, eating it in the traditional way with our fingers.

We celebrate New Year's Day among the spectacular rocky outcrops of yet another World Heritage site—the Matobo Hills—a twenty-minute drive south of Bulawayo. This is 3000 square kilometres of some of the most spectacular granite scenery on earth, superbly sculptured by nature over hundreds of thousands of years, resulting in extraordinary castles of balancing rocks. It's a place of bushmen rock art, where in bygone days, these hunter-gatherers used caves and crevices as canvases.

There's an overwhelming sense of power and grandeur here that leaves us feeling awed and humbled. The lime-green, grey and rust-coloured lichen on the huge granite boulders resembles splashes of paint—an unex-pected smattering of colour among the leafy trees and the breathtaking towers of stone.

The unmistakeable call of the African fish eagle echoes hauntingly, but it is the larger black eagle that is the master of the skies here. On terra firma, rhinos roam, leopards have their lairs, and rock dassies (also known as the rock hyraxes) scamper over the boulders. Small and guinea-pig-like, the dassie has—astonishingly—been genetically proven to be the closest living relative of the elephant.

With a glass of wine in hand, while watching the sun sink behind the boulders of smooth rock, we take in the overpowering spirituality and mystery of these timeless rocky hills.

'This is my favourite place on earth,' Dinks declares, and we raise our glasses in a toast to that.

It's been an extraordinary ten days with special friends, in some of Zimbabwe's most beautiful places. Now it's time for me to return to Hwange and the heartache of my own reality. It would be easy to pretend that the destructive and often violent land take-overs, now in prime tourism areas, are not even happening. After all, everywhere we visited on our trip seemed so normal.

It feels a bit like I'm about to be catapulted back into someone else's life.

# INTO ANOTHER WORLD

## 2004

After time away, even if it's been only a week or so, it always takes a few hours to get myself organised. There are inevitably spiders, rodents, bats, ants and termites to deal with, and a mess in my fridge from the constant power cuts. Sometimes there's a snake. There's likely to be thatch everywhere too, the baboons and vervet monkeys having partied in my absence, feasting on the insects living in my roof. Still, I quickly adjust back to my life in the bush, where an ancient 4x4, a pair of binoculars, a camera, a tyre compressor pump, jumper leads and a can opener are my most treasured possessions. In this country, which continues to crumble around me, my small fridge remains all but bare with basic commodities like bread and dairy products constantly in short supply.

I slip into a stretchy knee-length black skirt, in preference to shorts or long pants, and a black spaghetti-strap top underneath a loose open shirt. Even as a tourist I never fancied trying to look like Tarzan's girlfriend, fitted out in designer khaki, although some people seem to think that I should look like Jane of the jungle. I wear only thongs, which Aussies know that you wear on your feet, unlike Shaynie, whom I horrified one day as I walked around her flat looking for them. She was imagining that my knickers were hiding somewhere in her house! I might have been looking out for my bare feet but Shaynie was looking out for my bare butt.

I haven't worn closed shoes since I arrived in Africa and I'm certain that I'll never feel comfortable in them again. I now cringe at the mere thought of an underwire bra. In fact I no longer even own a bra.

I sit down and wonder if perhaps this really is someone else's life.

'Your boobs will be hanging down around your waist when you're 60,' Shaynie once declared, admitting though, that she had never actually noticed my lack of underwear. 'You'll be wishing, then, that you *were* in someone else's life.'

I have, at least, returned to the bush to some extremely good news. The Wildlife Ministry has conceded that a mistake was made, and has now officially withdrawn the sport-hunting quota so rashly issued to the governor and his family. They're still on the land however—and it looks like they might be here to stay—but at least, for now, they can't legally hunt. It is encouraging news indeed.

The governor's family are unaware that I've had anything to do with this decision, and I'm not about to enlighten them. Instead, I decide to befriend them. Now that they have no approval to hunt, I suppose I'm going to have to try to work with them if they're really here to stay, which I'm prepared to do so long as they allow game drives and snare patrols to continue.

'Be very careful,' I'm warned time and again, by those who know first-hand just how ruthless some of these ZANU-PF politicians can be.

Soon I'm back in Bulawayo for a meeting with the head land claimant, the governor himself. In an office building in the centre of town, a small rickety lift lands me in a nondescript reception area. Before long, I'm sitting at a large wooden table with him and a couple of members of his family. I can't help but notice that they all look extremely well fed, in this country where so many go without.

The meeting goes well. In fact it lasts for several hours. We talk and even laugh together. They're exceedingly polite and charming. Perhaps,

I think hopefully, they mightn't be as ruthless as so many are claiming, after all.

'Appearances in Zimbabwe can be very deceptive,' I'm cautioned time and again. Even so, I'm ready to give them a chance. There is, however, one statement that keeps racing around and around in my mind, setting off alarm bells; one sentence that makes me doubt their integrity. 'We do not want to hunt,' the governor says to me.

Although I sit quietly listening, I know this to be a lie. I know that the Parks Authority is no longer allowing them to hunt in the Kanondo and Khatshana areas, despite their application to continue to do so. I know, too, that this man has already allocated himself and his extended family at least two other farms, on which they are hunting. But in Africa so many things are all about not 'losing face'. So I say nothing. Without me having to go to higher levels, the governor agrees that I can return to my elephant work in the areas he has claimed as his own.

For a few months after this meeting my life returns to a degree of normality, as long as I ignore the sideways glances and the criticisms from those who believe I'm doing the wrong thing by giving them a go.

'Have you lost your mind?' (white) people ask me. 'You will never be able to work with these men,' they declare.

But surely not every ZANU-PF politician is deceitful and immoral.

I keep searching for Limp, who is still suffering from his snare injury. The last time I saw him, his leg was hideously swollen once again and I'd feared for his life. When I finally catch up with the Ls, I'm grateful to find that he's looking better, although still limping badly. Thankfully, the rest of his family are fine. Lady is as gorgeous as ever. As I tick off each member, I'm relieved to know that the family is intact.

'You stay safe, Lady,' I tell her, as I always do, while giving her trunk a friendly rub.

While I've been granted permission to return to these Kanondo and Khatshana areas, it's awfully worrying to me that tourist game-drives have not recommenced, and the anti-poaching team still hasn't been allowed back to patrol. Frustratingly, the Parks Authority doesn't try to intervene and make this happen, despite this being the land of the Presidential Elephants.

I'm trying to find as many elephant families as I can—a survey of all members of each family—to check on their welfare since the bout of hunting; to check if anyone is missing. I run into various families in addition to Lady's—the Ws included. Matriarch Whole never fails to melt my heart with her placid, caring nature and gentle rumbles, right beside the door of my 4x4. But I see relatively few elephants during my daily rounds. I'm not too concerned yet, as sightings always decrease during these rainy months. As always, I wonder where they disappear to. Are they following centuries-old migratory instincts? Is there perhaps a favoured plant—a tree, a flower, a pod, a particular type of grass—that they go off in search of? Or are they just hidden in thick bush?

By the time the dry season arrives, the elephants should have returned in bigger numbers. But they have not. Kanondo and Khatshana are often devoid of elephants—of any animals in fact—day after day, week after week, and month after month. And I become increasingly suspicious. Something is just not right.

I return to Australia for a month's break from Zimbabwe, arriving on my birthday in early May. A visit, especially to see my family, is long overdue; I haven't been back for over two years. Airfares and associated time away are expensive, and I choose to keep my dollars for field work as much as possible.

Only two of my three sisters, Deborah and Catherine, know that I'm coming since we thought it'd be fun to keep it a secret. Catherine is my youngest sister, who I tormented when she was young. Apart from (accidentally) dropping her head-first on the linoleum floor of our bathroom, I was suspiciously close when a droplet of water from the hot tap soaked her cardigan, scalding and scarring her little arm. And later I was close by when she thrust a digging fork straight through her foot, so that it poked out on the underside. How the plastic bottom plug of a biro got so far up her nose that it had to be removed by a doctor is another of our family's unsolved mysteries. Needless to say, as we grew up, it felt safer to spend time apart.

Deborah fetches me from Brisbane airport, and drives me the hour and a half inland to Grantham. She has the good grace not to tell me how tired I look. She's bought me an extra large packet of cheese Twisties and a McDonald's cheeseburger, with fries to put inside the bun. She knows that I've been craving this comfort food. I rip open a little squeeze packet of ketchup, spread it liberally on the bun, and tuck in.

When we pull up at my childhood home in darkness, Deborah walks up the stairs and goes inside, where my parents are clearing up after dinner. I remain quietly downstairs, listening to her reminding them that it's my birthday.

Then I appear without warning. I learn this is something that should never be done to parents in their seventies! My eldest sister Genevieve, and my nieces and nephews, are equally bowled over by my unexpected appearance.

I find it difficult to talk about all that has been happening in Zimbabwe in a way that my family and friends can relate to. It's an effort to find ordinary words to explain so many extraordinary and incomprehensible events, especially to those living in a stable country where life is fair, where shops supply your every need and where everything functions as it should. In Australia, you can say whatever you like, to whomever you like, without fear of repercussions. Sitting in my parents' living room, my words suddenly seem unbelievable, even to me. It's easier to avoid speaking too much about it, and besides, for these few weeks, I just want to forget.

Everything seems so alien to me. I can't bear to sit in front of the television, not even to watch the news. I marvel at how clean and tidy everything is. I struggle to readjust to the fact that there's always electricity and running water. I adore how soft and thick the bathroom towels are. I snuggle into a real bed, that isn't a thin piece of foam on a concrete floor. There's nobody snatching land, nobody making hateful proclamations, nobody walking around with rifles. But, of course, there are no free-roaming elephants either and this for me, now, is hard to bear.

It's a rejuvenating month of fine food, rest and relaxation. Nonetheless, as it draws to a close I'm looking forward to my return to Zimbabwe, despite my fears that the worst is still to come.

It's incredible how quickly we can be transported into different worlds. Back on the Hwange Estate, the logic and luxuries of the First World disappear, and it doesn't take long for my worst fears to be realised.

'Why are there hunting vehicles on the land?' I ask the governor's men, trying hard not to raise their ire with any visible hint of alarm or concern.

'Arrhhh, they're just sight-seeing,' I'm told.

*Sight-seeing! What a load of rubbish. Why am I seemingly the only person who can see through this?*

'Oh, that's nice for them,' I say, my blood already beginning to boil.

When I catch one hunting party at Kanondo, on foot with their guns, I'm told that they're 'after a wounded elephant bull'. Never in all of my years on the estate have I ever known an animal wounded elsewhere by a hunting client to be followed into Kanondo. When this happens a second time I become more than a little suspicious.

Another day I find one of the governor's vehicles driving around Kanondo pan. The gun-toting occupants in the back are very clearly looking for an animal to shoot.

I am incredulous.

I would give the devil my soul, I declare, rather than close my eyes to what I am now seeing. If I cause trouble, I will immediately become the governor's target—but it is another risk that I will have to take. I tell only those who need to know, and ask once again that they handle my information with discretion. This is a country where some simply 'dispose' of those who are in their way. I try not to worry unduly about the possible consequences.

I am constantly distraught about how little wildlife I'm now seeing, day after day after day. Usually during July, Kanondo hosts what I've termed 'reunion month'. For some unknown reason, this is the time when the largest number of family groups regularly mingle in the middle of the day, creating an unforgettable spectacle. Several hundred Presidential Elephants revel in the mud-bathing area, and feast on the mineral licks and surrounding vegetation, regularly returning to the pan to drink and playfully splash around in the refreshing water. These memorable displays are made even more special for me because I know who the elephants are, and am able to interpret their interactions with one another. I don't know for sure why they meet up like this, but I like to think they're simply having a party, by infrasonic invitation only; celebrating their close bonds, and catching up on gossip after long periods apart.

But this July there is no sign of a reunion at Kanondo pan. For the first time in four years most elephant families stay away. With so little wildlife activity, the once pristine Kanondo pan is becoming choked with reeds and, more concerningly, with an inedible weed.

One afternoon, however, Lady and her family appear here. They seem as happy to see me as I am to see them, and they surround my vehicle to sleep. I've just finished singing 'Amazing Grace', which has them all nice and relaxed, when all of a sudden the entire family race off in complete silence, their tails up, into the bush, alarmed by a sound or smell that is beyond my human senses. I sit bewildered and saddened, presuming that they've heard a distant gunshot. But it is one of the governor's vehicles that appears in the open just 30 seconds later. It is further evidence of what is going on unseen: the elephants clearly associate the sound and smell of this vehicle with danger. I remain calm enough to greet the occupants, but beneath the surface I am incensed.

I can't imagine it getting any worse than this, but what if it does? I did not come to this country to play policewoman. This is not something that I want to get involved in. But what choice do I have?

# CARRYING ON

## 2004

Dinks has moved to South Africa. It's heartbreaking to watch friends leave, especially when you know how much they love their country despite everything. Zimbabweans are searching for a better way of life and families are split as millions are forced to make their way over the borders, or overseas, in order to try to survive.

Now that Shaynie has lost her flatmate, she's decided to take on work away from Bulawayo. She would leave Zimbabwe too, if she could—but where would she go? She has no ancestral rights to claim citizenship in another country and so has no choice but to stay, unless she manages to get herself sponsored in elsewhere. At one point, she makes enquiries about a job in Mozambique.

'Shaynie, come on, that's just stupid. Why on earth would you even consider Mozambique as a place to live, even if they could in fact get you a work permit?' I ask bewildered. 'A country suffering from decades of civil war, that's where you now want to be? It's one of the poorest countries in the world forgodsake. You'd be jumping from the frying pan straight into the fire.'

I quickly realise that I'm definitely not the right person to be preaching to anyone about jumping into a fire! But I'm starting to believe that

Shaynie would consider a move to Afghanistan if it was offered to her. What she eventually decides she really needs is a kibbutz in Israel to ease her troubled mind.

'I'll come with you,' I announce in support, despite the idea being way too communal for me—and secretly confident that she's not likely to walk this path. Shaynie is a survivor; she grew up during a war after all. She's going to be okay.

Shaynie remains in Zimbabwe and we stay in touch by email. I miss her presence (and also her couch) in Bulawayo. She's been to Hwange National Park just once—and that was last year. I think of my own circumstances in Australia and realise that I was always so tied up with my work that I, too, visited relatively few of the wild places in my own home country. Too often we take for granted what's right in front of our noses. So I don't criticise Shaynie for not making more of an effort to escape to Hwange on weekends; she knows all about the awful goings-on after all. Now, at least, she's determined to one day meet Lady and some of my other special elephant friends. That will have to wait a while however, as she spreads her wings, searching for relief elsewhere.

And then there is more tragedy on the estate.

At Kanondo, Whole comes to me when I call to her. She seems more eager than ever to say hello. I'm crooning to her as she stands beside the door of my 4x4, looking forlorn, when I'm distracted by an awful gasping sound. I look around and spot her three-year-old son, Wholesome, nearby. He has a snare wrapped tightly around his little head and neck.

'Oh please. I just can't bear this anymore,' I blurt aloud to no one.

Wholesome is gasping for breath and I realise that his windpipe must be partially severed by the strangling wire. I know that I'm too late, but I fumble with my radio and try to organise urgent assistance regardless. Wholesome dies in front of my eyes some 30 minutes later, before help can reach us.

I've known Wholesome since he was just days old.

Whole races to him when he falls, as does his sister Whosit. They both use their trunk and tusks in a frantic effort to lift him and hold him upright. It is the most heartbreaking scene I have ever witnessed in my life. Other family members race to assist as well, and with so many elephants now trying to help, Wholesome's little lifeless body ends up being pushed into the waterhole.

I shake myself out of my own grief, and realise that I should be video-taping this event. But how does one do that at a time like this? It seems heartless, but I force myself to pick up my video camera.

Mother Whole, sister Whosit and grandmother Wendy remain close by the little elephant who has been such an important part of their lives. They wander right into the water and stand by his side, constantly touching his lifeless body. Occasionally, they try again to lift him. Later, after Wendy moves off, Whole and Whosit return to his carcass again—and again and again. They move off, sometimes as far as 25 metres away, and then race back to his lifeless body. Even though several hours have passed by now, they continue to do this over and over again.

Eventually, Whole comes and stands by the door of my 4x4. The way she holds her head, her mouth, her eyes; everything about her spells intense grief. Whosit resolutely refuses to leave her dead brother, even when all other family members have wandered a short distance off into the bush. My heart aches for them all.

Tuskless Debbie and Delight and others from the D family later pass by, spending eerily quiet time beside Wholesome's body, paying their respects. By now it is dark, and I drive home dejectedly.

Spoor around Wholesome's body the next morning confirms that many elephants have visited him during the night. The governor's family then butcher Wholesome's little body, taking his hide, his ears, his tail and the meat—for sale. Humans had killed him, and humans then greedily took all that they could, for profit.

Elephants have a sense of death like few other animals. They will walk straight past the remains of another animal, but they'll always stop at the new remains of one of their own kind. Family, extended family and clan members stop frequently at Wholesome's butchered carcass, touching it gently with their trunks. It is Anne and Andrea, and others from the A family, now spending extended time beside his remains. They silently back into their dead companion, and slowly move a hind foot in a circling motion over the carcass in a chilling gesture of awareness.

As I watch them, moved and saddened, I vow that Wholesome's death will not be in vain. He will help to highlight the plight of the remaining Presidential Elephants.

This time, I choose to ignore the orders of Wildlife Minister, Francis Nhema, to not speak publicly of snaring. How can we possibly fix the snaring problem if the officials refuse to acknowledge it exists? How can we get assistance with expensive immobilisation drugs, antibiotics, dart guns, anti-poaching unit supplies and the like if we can't show people what is happening here?

I send around graphic photographs and the story of Wholesome's death. I mention the land grabs, although I don't name the governor or his family. I don't send these to the press, but somehow they end up there. Without my knowledge or approval, one of the tightly controlled government newspapers publishes the story. Obviously it hasn't done its homework, and doesn't actually know who these land grabbers are, since stories are never published that are disparaging to those in power.

Needless to say, the governor is not pleased. In fact, the governor is furious. I am immediately banned from the land again. He targets me as the person he needs to get rid of if he and his family are to keep this land.

Suddenly I have the police, from the nearby township of Dete, searching for me, asking endless questions and demanding to see my passport and my permits. The governor is using his considerable political weight to try to have me expelled from the country. Clearly I am now *persona non grata*. If I had been a local, I would likely have been thrown in jail by now or have simply disappeared. Being a foreigner affords me some small measure of safety.

I think about the white Zimbabwean journalist and esteemed author, Peter Godwin, who dared to investigate and report internationally on something much worse, the Matabeleland Massacres, including first-hand accounts of bodies being dumped down abandoned mine shafts under cover of darkness. He was forced to flee his own country, hurriedly boarding a flight out from Harare after a tip-off that he was about to be arrested for doing so and thrown into the notoriously awful Chikurubi maximum security prison, where overcrowding and disease is rife. He was warned he would languish there for years. Shortly afterwards, Peter was declared an enemy of the state by the ZANU-PF government. '*Persona non grata* in my own home,' he later wrote of himself.

'Sharon, get out of there,' Shaynie emails to me, knowing exactly what her government is capable of. 'And if you don't, I'll come and kidnap you myself,' she threatens.

'Shaynie,' I say, 'you know that I have to stay.'

Out in the field I battle with thornbush roadblocks erected to deter me, and regular shouts of abuse. One unidentified man runs after my 4x4, waving an axe. This is the most frightening time that I have faced in Zimbabwe to date. I know all about threats and intimidation in Africa. I never expected, though, to be on the receiving end of them.

Yet the more they want me gone, the more I become determined to stay. I carry on as best I can.

I come upon Andrea the elephant, with her immediate family in tow, and email a photo of them to my friend Andrea in New Zealand. A reply drifts back across the ocean. After deciding firstly that 'she' is a good-looking elephant, Andrea declares 'if you look between my legs I've got great breasts!' And then, making a comparison to her own, she adds: 'Not that they should really be between my legs but it's a major size improvement on what I have now!'

I'm grateful for friends who make me smile.

Carol, her friend Lynn, and a group of their friends arrive from Harare out of the blue one morning, and this brings another smile to my face. They're heading to a lodge inside the national park for a few nights of rest and relaxation.

'You're coming with us,' Carol declares, immediately sensing the anxiety behind my smile.

'But . . .'

'There are no buts,' Carol says, in a voice that invites no discussion. 'You're coming with us,' she repeats. 'Grab some clothes. You need to be away from here.'

Soon we are all heading to an upmarket safari camp called The Hide, close to where Andy is buried. It is far enough away to be peaceful. It's Carol's great pleasure to spoil her friends, and I am exceedingly grateful for this thoughtful gesture.

It is certainly enjoyable to play tourist, when you can very easily pretend that nothing horrible is going on behind the scenes. Tourists rarely see evidence of any of it. A third bed is placed in Carol and Lynn's large luxury tent, and I hope that I won't disturb them with another restless night's sleep. My dreams have turned dark and disturbing.

My dream on this particular night is peculiar and unusually vivid: I am a passenger in an open game-drive vehicle. We hit a bump and I go sailing up into the air, higher and higher, while the vehicle continues on its way. Carol quickly realises that I am no longer in the vehicle and looks around frantically trying to find me. There I am, floating high in the sky, strangely suspended in the cool air above. The guide reverses at speed to try and catch me before I plummet to earth. I don't plunge to the ground however. Instead, I sail gently back down through the clear air and land, unharmed, precisely where I'd been seated beforehand.

I awake in a fit of uncontrollable laughter. Fearing that I'll wake my room-mates, I bury my head beneath my pillow. For some reason though, I can't stop the laughter that's so intense it leaves me gasping for breath.

Early the next morning I tell my friends about my dream.

'I heard you,' says Carol.

'Me too,' says Lynn.

'I thought you were sobbing, needing to rid yourself of all of the tragedy that's been going on,' Carol says softly. 'So I left you alone. I'm so pleased to hear that you were actually laughing!'

We laze on our beds, analysing my dream and speculating about its meaning. We finally conclude that I'm on a bumpy journey, experiencing things totally alien to a normal way of life, but everything will be okay in the end.

I love how my friends tell me what I need to hear.

# SKIDDING SIDEWAYS

## 2004

The police are waiting for me on my return.

The governor and his family have nothing on me. My permits are in order. It is intimidation, pure and simple.

At one stage I'm advised by a concerned colleague to leave the country, if only temporarily. I think this surely isn't necessary, but after listening to what he's heard from others in the know, I decide that perhaps I should. I start throwing clothes and toiletries into a bag.

Soon afterwards I receive more frantic advice: 'You may not make it to the airport. Stay where you are.' He's worried that I might meet with an 'accident'; that I might get run off the road. It's something that used to happen in the post-war period. 'Death by puma,' it was called back then, after the heavy army trucks called pumas.

I think people's imaginations are getting the better of them, but I can't be certain. They've lived in this country far longer than I have, and know better than me what some are capable of. Suspicious 'accidents' are still very much the norm. Blowouts are all too common. When a marked car goes in for service, a bullet from a heavy calibre rifle is placed in one of the tyres. When the vehicle travels at high speed the bullet generally gets hot enough to go off, causing the vehicle to spin out of control.

'Never be at your *rondavel* on a Friday afternoon,' I'm warned by another person with first-hand knowledge of what can happen. 'If they lock you up then, you will spend the entire weekend in jail. And you don't want to spend that long in a Zimbabwean jail.'

All of this is not just bewildering to me. It is shocking. I haven't done anything wrong. In fact I'm the one—and one of the very few right now, it seems to me—trying to do the *right* thing by the wildlife. But this is Zimbabwe. It does not matter.

I've somehow found myself embroiled in games that I have no stomach for, struggling against powerful adversaries. It is something that I never bargained on or sought out. I imagine my body floating in a pan, chewed on by crocodiles, my death somehow having been made to look like a careless accident on my part. I warn my friends, rather than worry my family: 'If something like this ever happens, don't you believe it'.

I alert the Australian Embassy in Harare to my situation, feeling better just knowing that more people are at least aware. The embassy makes it clear to me, however, that other than providing a list of lawyers and making sure I have food, they can do little to help if I'm thrown in jail.

All of this is draining away my spirit and my zest for the elephants. I long for things to be as they were when I first arrived. There are awful days now when I can no longer see beauty in anything.

'Did you really think that it would stay as it was?' a friend asks me one evening.

'I thought it might . . .' I whisper sadly.

The Kanondo and Khatshana of sanity and peace. They have disappeared before my very eyes.

My days of innocent enchantment are long gone too but the nights are the worst, increasingly filled with torrid dreams. It is at night that I hear most of the spine-chilling shots. And I feel an unspeakable despair. I close my eyes and weep in grief and frustration at what is going on around me.

I no longer like to get to know any of the big-tusked elephant bulls well. Sooner or later they disappear, leaving only those with small or broken tusks to roam the estate. These days I'm always relieved to see broken tusks, making these elephants less attractive to the sport-hunters and the poachers.

I remain disheartened that so few people in the area are speaking out. Sometimes it's as if there's an echoless void out there. Australia seems so far away. I know that I could be there. But my elephants in Australia are only statues made of stone. I am dogged in my determination to stay, for the sake of the animals that I've grown to love. The most dangerous predator in Africa, I've come to realise, is not the lion. Nor can the hippo, the buffalo or the elephant hope to compete. The most dangerous animal by far is man.

Hwange once seemed so seductive, so serene and largely untouched. Now I'm constantly alert. I've ceased to harbour even the slightest romantic notion of the Zimbabwean bush. I muster my resolve, and continue on. But the harassment continues.

Gunfire is now out of control. The elephants are moving in large aggregations, probably for safety's sake. One minute there are no elephants in sight and the next scores of them are racing, terrified, out from the tree line. Today there are several families fleeing in tight formation, with ears flat and tails out. One of them is Whole's.

It takes me hours to find the W family again after this distressing episode, and another two hours to regain just a little of their confidence. It is Willa who comes close to my vehicle before the others. She approaches hesitantly, while I alternate between singing 'Amazing Grace' and talking gently to her (something that I do frequently now, especially after distressing episodes), reassuring her that everything is alright. Just as most family members are beginning to settle, a game-drive vehicle approaches and the elephants take off into the bush yet again at speed, and in complete silence. Now they're frightened of a game-drive vehicle—specifically this particular vehicle.

When I find the W family again the next day, I spend the entire morning with them—attempting to rebuild what has been broken.

Soon after, six officials arrive at a nearby lodge and demand to see me. Some are from the Immigration Department and others are believed to be from the dreaded CIO—the Ruling Party's Central Intelligence Organisation, or secret police, feared for its brutality. They have travelled all of the way from Harare, on the other side of the country, to talk to me. They're no doubt acting on instruction from the governor. Although the CIO has a reputation for harassment and provoking fear, all six people leave quietly after a short and trouble-free meeting. I am feeling rattled however. I can only hope that I've convinced them that I have nothing to hide.

Still, I now feel that I have no choice but to escalate all of this to a higher level. I travel to Harare, to the offices of three different Cabinet ministers. This is a little daunting, since these men are practically worshipped by the masses. They get around like mini-gods, with their own state security details.

I meet first with the Wildlife Minister, Francis Nhema. Having previously signed the governor's sport-hunting quota, he does little to boost my confidence. He won't look me in the eyes. During our meeting he speaks vaguely, and so softly that I have to strain to hear him. His eyes burn into my chest. I have no idea what to make of him. All I know is that he has done little to save the wildlife under his watch. If nothing else, I suppose, at least I have met him. I'm left with the impression that he's unlikely to follow through on anything, unless specifically instructed to by the President's Office. His distant and dry style unsettles me.

I next meet one of President Mugabe's closest advisers, one of the most powerful and feared men in the country; the minister responsible for state security (which includes the CIO), and for the land reform program.

'Don't be afraid,' Minister Didymus Mutasa says to me, holding my hand within both of his and looking me in the eyes.

'I'm not afraid,' I lie. I'm aware that Minister Mutasa, like Minister Nhema, must know the governor very well. They're all colleagues after all. Clearly he believes that there is good reason for me to be afraid.

'Your work is crucial. It must be allowed to continue,' Minister Mutasa says to me.

I am fully aware of this man's reputation. I know that he could have me taken out just as quickly as he could arrange for my protection. But having been involved in the original Presidential Decree years earlier, he appears to have retained some interest in these elephants and my gut tells me that he'll be a useful ally.

Then I meet with the Immigration Minister to try to find out what's holding up my work permit renewal. His face registers something close to shock that I'm asking to be allowed to *stay* in this troubled country. He spends most of our meeting lamenting the fact that he's struggling to pay for the education of his children.

I leave Harare with increased confidence that my permit will be renewed and that the governor and his family will be evicted. I also believe that I have the support of at least one very powerful man. I'll need this if I am to survive here. I've been assured that I have the support of the Wildlife Minister too, although I'm still not convinced about this. I find it difficult to trust somebody who doesn't look me in the eyes.

Back on the Hwange Estate I continue to battle with thornbush road-blocks, and another order from the governor's family that I am banned from 'their' land. Sightings of the Presidential Elephant families have reduced from an average of eight families in one day, to eight families in one month—if I'm lucky. For the past twelve months, the *veld* has been disturbingly quiet.

These quiet spells have allowed me time to write my very first book, which I've named *In An Elephant's Rumble*. It's just a self-published,

Zimbabwe-only edition, to try to raise some in-country awareness, and hopefully a few dollars that will go towards my fuel and vehicle expenses. With access to foreign currency, it's cheap to produce and print a book in Zimbabwe right now, and so my profit margin is high. There is much fanfare over its launch in Bulawayo; a distraction that I'm grateful for. My Camera Centre friends and Shaynie (who is dressed as a zebra, while another friend is dressed as an elephant) help to make it a particularly memorable occasion, and I manage to put on a happy face. For safety's sake, I'm forced to hold back on many facts in this book. Some things I leave out entirely. I end it with a variation of Hunter S. Thompson's words:

Life's journey is not about arriving safely at the grave in a well preserved body—but rather let us skid in sideways, totally worn out, shouting triumphantly: 'Damn, what a ride . . .'

What a ride indeed.

The battle with the governor's family drags on for more long weeks, the days blurred with uncertainties. Finally, though still banned from the land, I climb determinedly into my 4x4 and drive to Kanondo. On the way I bat away unsettling images of possible ambushes and tyre spikes. A sixth sense has told me that something is very wrong and I need to find out what it is. And there, at Kanondo, I'm met with a huge tract of felled trees. With shaking hands, I quickly photograph this alarming scene of deforestation and get out of there. This is the final straw. I'm assured 2005 will commence with the governor's family finally gone.

*Why do I still find this so difficult to believe?*

During this madness, what keeps me sane is Misty's adorable new baby boy, who I've named Merlin. Misty lost her previous baby, also a boy, two years ago, when he was just a few weeks old. I'll never know if he was caught in a snare, or if it was a natural death. She's revelling in suckling a little one once again, and I love the slurping noises that go on right beside the door of my 4x4. If only I could spend time with

them every day, but I'm still not seeing the elephant families as much
as I once did.

I find solace in keeping in touch with wildlife people who I trust. I email
my British friend Karen, who lives for the hippos of the Turgwe River in
the Savé Valley Conservancy in the south-east of the country, to see how
she's getting on with land grabs that are also going on around her, and to
offload about my own problems. Karen and I first met in the late 1990s
when I spent time with her at Hippo Haven doing a short-term voluntary
stint. We've remained in touch ever since.

I still can't think of Karen without thinking of scorpions. While
staying with her, I slept in a quaint little wooden cottage, quite open to the
elements. Drying myself off after a steaming shower, I reached for my long
black trousers and a sweater, and pulled them on. Then I started making
my way towards her house.

'Hollllllllyy crap!'

My hand instantly shot inside the back of my trousers and I flung
whatever was in there onto the lawn. Karen came racing out at the sound
of my bellows and took on the task of examining the burning cheek of my
buttock. What I'd briefly held in my hand felt like a scorpion, although we
couldn't find the little bugger anywhere. I quickly pulled my underwear
back up, hoping that scorpion venom wasn't something that someone had
to suck out of you!

'What colour was it? Was it big or small?' Karen probed.

I had no idea what colour it was, nor its relative size, but judging by
the degree of pain, it surely had to have been big. I was taking no chances.

'It was big,' I declared.

'It's the smaller ones with thin pincers and thick tail that are the most
venomous,' Karen explained (which taught me that there's really no need
to exaggerate), and thrust a generous helping of antihistamine tablets into

the palm of my hand. She kept a close eye on my temperature. I couldn't sit down properly for days and a hard red lump remained for months. Being bitten on the butt by a scorpion is definitely not something that I recommend.

I went on to do my own wildlife work in Zimbabwe knowing that I could always count on Karen for kind and timely words of support, particularly now during the land invasions. Neither of us are interested in Africa's animals as subjects for academic advancement or financial gain. She understands better than most why I stay on, and I'm grateful for her presence in my African life.

# NOTHING BAD LASTS FOREVER

## 2004

There is a saying: 'The Earth is made round, so that we cannot see too far down the road'. If I'd been able to see further down my already bumpy path, perhaps I might have followed Val, John, Marion, Julia and Dinks, and left Zimbabwe at once. I am, though, still hopeful about what 2005 might bring, and I'm heartened by a visit from a stranger, who arrives on the doorstep of my *rondavel* wanting to talk. He tells me his name is Trymore Ndlovu.

'I am trying harder to see an elephant,' he jokes, making light of his name.

He hasn't seen an elephant for eight years, he says, and longs to see one during this visit to the Hwange Estate. We both know the chances of this happening have, since the land claims, been significantly reduced. We talk about the Presidential Elephants and the ongoing restricted access to their land. His dark, intelligent eyes express confusion and sadness.

'*Okungapheliyo kuyahlola*,' he says in isiNdebele. He translates as he leaves, his hand patting his heart in a gesture of respect, 'Remember, *Mandlovu*, nothing bad lasts forever.'

Soon afterwards my friend Eileen in Auckland emails me with just a few words: 'Shaz, come home.'

I am torn, but I can't yet bring myself to abandon my elephant friends. I can't yet give up.

I haven't ventured into neighbouring Hwange National Park for months, and the prospect of staying overnight there is invigorating. This trip is with another friend called Marion: a young French researcher who works inside the park. Her love of Africa is very real. She always manages to provide cheerful company and compassion. She's also kind to the core; she once left pizza on my doorstep, which was somehow still intact when I arrived home, despite monkeys everywhere. Her handwriting on the box read, 'A surprise for you'. Inside the national park—away from the troubled Hwange Estate— I'm hoping that things might be clearer. I need to rest the bones of the old year.

Stunning two-tone red and yellow flame lilies, which flower for just a few weeks, are in bloom along the roadsides, as are the sickle bushes with their tiny Christmas lanterns in mauve-pink and yellow. They always radiate my hopes for the coming year. The sight of newborn impala and wildebeest babies, fragile and long limbed, also reminds us that Christmas is close. This is the wet season, a particularly beautiful time of year.

What strikes me most about this excursion is how much I love it all, still. We make our way past Makwa pan, past the area where Andy is buried, towards Ngweshla pan. We stumble upon a white rhino bull along the way and stay with him for a while, admiring his ancient splendour. Had we known that poachers would soon wipe out all of his kind in this part of Hwange, perhaps we would have stayed longer.

I recall an American visitor's response to my question, posed earlier in the year, as to whether we were looking at the backside of a black or a white rhino. 'This rhino is *grey!*' she had exclaimed. Indeed, she had a good point: both the black and the white rhinos are certainly grey. It's a wide mouth rather than a pointy one that distinguishes the white (grey) rhino from the black (grey) one.

The many tortoises on the sandy road are a prelude to the spectacle awaiting us at Ngweshla pan at sunset: there are waterbucks, impalas, kudus, elephants, zebras, giraffes and ostriches. And most spectacularly of all, a huge herd of more than eight hundred buffaloes, known to frequent this area. No sooner have we settled ourselves—G&T in hand and with other small luxuries of olives, smoked mussels and cheese to be savoured—than we are completely surrounded by the buffalo herd.

It is as though no other humans exist in the world, and we respect this notion with our silence. Watchful and wise, the buffaloes seem to have intentionally made this wide, grand circle around us, before breaking off and moving further away.

'Wow! Do you think they had a message for us?' I ask Marion over the sound of their grunts.

'Nothing bad lasts forever?' she offers, with a smile.

Carefully avoiding the many nightjars and the occasional springhares (Africa's miniature equivalent of kangaroos) bouncing along the road, we find a place inside the national park to sleep for the night, to share our wine and our stories. Our incessant talking, now quite foreign to my increasingly solitary existence, doesn't diminish the tranquillity. It is wonderful that, though we've both spent thousands of days and nights in the African *veld*, we both still truly treasure the sublime beauty that surrounds us, even under cover of darkness.

But even so, I find myself envying her Hwange existence, safe and warm within the confines of the national park and with several months of each year spent in her homeland. I choose not to burden her with the latest land grab sagas.

Back on the estate, it's difficult to get excited about Christmas Day, but it turns out to be a special one in the field. I unexpectedly come across Lady and her family in an area where I've never seen them before. I haven't encountered them for more than eight long weeks, so I'm thrilled to see them all again. Toddling among those so familiar to me are two new wee packages of pure pleasure: a dashing little boy for Leanne (later named Litchis, which is the Zimbabwean version of lychees) and another for Louise (later named Laurie).

I can barely contain my excitement. Both youngsters are probably already six weeks old, and play together around a rainwater pan. Limp is there too, showing little interest in his new baby brother, his snare injury no longer bothering him too badly although there's still a noticeable limp. The great matriarch, Lady, herself heavily pregnant, comes to share her mud with me. I'd seen her in oestrus twice during 2003, and assume that she conceived during her second session. So, I'm expecting her to give birth in early April of the new year, an event that I'm already looking forward to. She looks huge—but even when not pregnant, Lady always looks huge.

'Thank you, my girl, for visiting me for Christmas,' I tell her, as she rumbles contentedly beside me.

Back at my *rondavel*, I think about my family celebrating Christmas in Australia. Christmas is a big deal for them; a time of too many presents, too much food and far too much noise. While enviously imagining their platters of succulent prawns, I watch the African children who live around me racing behind old car tyres, which they're pushing along the sandy tracks. They play hopscotch, the outline for their game etched with a stick in the damp ground. I watch them throw balls that are nothing more than a plastic shopping bag, stuffed with more plastic bags, shaped round. And I know that with no material gifts, but endowed with a natural ability to create their own fun, they're really not missing out on all that much this Christmas. As little banded mongoose friends follow me inside—to lie for a while on their bellies on my grass mat with their legs outstretched—I'm content in the knowledge that neither am I. This is still exactly where I want to be.

Two days later I'm sitting on the rooftop of my 4x4, admiring a sizeable zebra herd, dramatic against a backdrop of green-topped acacias and bulbous grey storm clouds. The quiet beauty is abruptly broken when I spot yet another gruesome snare injury. The young zebra, the stripes on her rump not yet jet-black, wears the death trap around her neck. The ring of wire is digging in deeply, the wound so horrific that I fight the need to turn away. But having watched young Wholesome die, I know that I can now bear anything. Harder to stomach is the knowledge that the anti-poaching team is still not allowed to properly patrol this estate.

Thankfully the zebra herd is still around when a darter comes the next morning. The wound is even more horrific than I first thought; it's something you'd expect to see only on a dead animal. Her neck is very deeply sliced. The maggots are nauseating and the snare is particularly difficult to remove. The loop of wire is wrapped hideously around her windpipe, and I fear she will not survive the ordeal. Antiseptic washes, ointments and antibiotics are used liberally.

Somewhat remarkably, after the reversal drug is administered she gets to her feet and rejoins her mother and the four others who had put their heads to hers, concerned, when she first fell to the ground under the effect of the immobilisation drug. Back together again, they all begin to feed.

I always experience a great sense of relief, knowing that we've done what we can to treat these human-inflicted injuries. Nothing will ever make it right, but we can continue to try to make it better.

When New Year's Eve arrives, I have grand plans to toast the new year at three different times. Firstly at 1 p.m. when friends in New Zealand will be popping champagne corks; again at 4 p.m. when family and friends in Australia will be celebrating; and again at midnight Zimbabwe time. But yet another snared elephant sighting—another gruesome neck wound, this time on a youngster in Misty's extended family—means that 1 p.m. and 4 p.m. pass without me even noticing.

There is, disappointingly, no one available to provide immediate darting assistance, and I ask myself again why I don't just go and do the dangerous drugs course myself and become a qualified darter. In Zimbabwe you don't have to be a vet in order to complete this course. I am, though, too closely connected to these elephants to take on the responsibility of darting them. I could never successfully load the deadly immobilisation drug while I'm feeling so distraught about the injuries. And besides, the courses (and required follow-ups), and a dart gun, are expensive and I don't have that kind of extra money to spare. It's also not possible to dart an elephant alone, so I'd still be reliant on others. I'm better placed being a key spotter and coordinator.

I know that police are now based around the clock on the Hwange Estate, at both Kanondo and Khatshana. I can't yet be certain this is a good thing, although my fervent New Year's wish is that they're on the right side. Here you can never tell. But their presence does seem to be a sign that the governor's family has finally been displaced, at least for now. I'm once again driving in all estate areas.

While there's still some light, I grab the opportunity to take three of the policemen to see the snared elephant. Frustratingly, I can't work out who he is. He is wandering alone, and there are so many elephants from the extended M family in the vicinity that I need more time to determine who he belongs to. For now it's more important to give these policemen a first-hand glimpse at what's happening here.

'We don't need to get too close,' one of them says to me anxiously, clearly afraid of these imposing creatures. 'They are too big.'

The sun is setting and so there's no time for me to help them feel more at ease. Instead, I pass my binoculars around so that they can properly see the snare injury for themselves.

'But this is terrible,' one of the men declares—and I hope this is genuinely how he feels. We can hear my little grey friend struggling to breathe. It's a horrifying sound that I've heard before, too often.

When I arrive home from the field, feeling weary and despondent, I check my emails and receive more upsetting news: the Boxing Day tsunami has claimed several hundred thousand lives, among them a Zimbabwean who was in Thailand and was a close friend of folk I've stayed with in Bulawayo. It's another reminder of the fragility of life. 'This is just getting too much now,' I say to no one, feeling like somebody has cast a hex on the entire world.

I decide that it's time to rest my weary head—well before midnight—so I'm going to miss the last of my three New Year toasts as well. Before climbing into my bed on the floor of my *rondavel* I light a candle, and take a moment for a quiet chat with the man upstairs. I admit that I find this a little ridiculous, since I haven't had very much to say to him for a couple of decades.

I think about Australian billionaire Kerry Packer and the heart attack he suffered in 1990, which left him clinically dead for six long minutes. Later, he famously declared, 'There's nothing there.' No tunnel of bright light, no one waiting for you, no one to judge you, so you might as well 'do what you bloody well like!' I've often wondered if he might be right.

While President Mugabe and his henchmen make public declarations about their devotion to God, I'm more and more convinced that if there are angels out there, some of these men would be among the first to rip their wings off. With the increasing levels of violence, corruption, revenge and insatiable greed going on around the country, surely the Ruling Party elite must actually believe, too, that there's nothing actually out there.

I light my candle anyway, not really knowing what I believe anymore. Singing 'Amazing Grace' to the elephants still gives me goosebumps regardless.

I never see the little M family elephant again. Later, I manage to work out that the snare victim was the five-year-old son of the elephant named Monty. His name was Manu.

(Left) I grew up on a vegetable farm in Grantham, Queensland. I'm grateful for the 'toughness' I acquired from this small community. (Right) With Chloe, who lived until she was nearly eighteen, during my high-flying years Down Under.

It was a very different life in Africa. (Photo courtesy of Brent Stapelkamp)

(Left) Andy and his son Drew eighteen months before he was killed in a helicopter accident. (Photo courtesy of Laurette Searle). (Right) The local people believe the bateleur eagle to be a spirit messenger.

In 2000 Lol, Drew and I went together to visit Andy's grave inside Hwange National Park.

The grand Lady was the first wild elephant who truly accepted me into her world.

(Left) The collared rhino that chased me up an acacia tree. (Right) John, my old-timer Zimbabwean friend, with a sample of his hand-tooled leather. (Photo courtesy of Laura Walker)

The tiny one-room rondavel that was my home for more than a decade.

Once I got to know her well, Lady came when I called her, with her offspring in tow.

How could anyone possibly want to harm this?

(Left) Gladys, who named me *Thandeka*. Later, I became known as *Thandeka Mandlovu*. (Right) Carol and Miriam both lived in Harare.

My friends Shaynie and Dinks in the Matobo Hills.

Whole has a distinctive hole in her left ear.

Hanging out with Misty. (Photo courtesy of Mark Stratton)

Members of the Presidential families often followed my 4×4 as if I were their matriarch. (Photo courtesy of Brent Stapelkamp)

In the early years wildlife, such as this sable bull, relaxed right beside my 4×4, but with increased gunfire they became less trusting over time.

Elephants have a sense of death like few other animals. Sometimes they move their feet over the remains of one of their own in a chilling gesture of awareness.

Elephant youngsters are always entertaining. They helped keep me smiling.

Barbara and her daughter Dee during a visit to Victoria Falls.

Jabulani (left) and members of his anti-poaching team spent their days destroying wire snares.

Eyelashes to die for! In the right light, an elephant's lower eyelid takes on the colour of the ocean.

Makwa pan, inside Hwange National Park, holds many special memories for me.

Lady and her family.

Cheeky vervet monkeys frequently kept me company in my garden.

With the beautiful Whole as she catches forty winks.

I didn't often see other vehicles when I looked out the window of my 4×4, but I did see this.

You know you're among friends when they fall asleep right beside you.

No matter where I parked, the elephants would always want to be there too.
(Photo courtesy of NHU Africa)

Joyce, like all the other elephants, liked to share her dust with me.

When they weren't showering me with dust, they were splashing me with mud.

A live leopard in the field is infinitely better than a dead one at my rondavel.

Sometimes when my elephant friends greeted me, their temporal glands erupted with liquid, a sure sign of excitement in the ladies.

All shapes and sizes, desperate for some pumped water in the dry season.

I will always
remember the
young elephant
I named Future.

# THE ELEPHANTS WILL
# SPEAK TO YOU

## 2005

Unless it's raining, I always have the roof of my 4x4 wide open to the great expanse of African sky. Seeking shade in the middle of the day, I decide to park under the sprawling branches of a tall *Acacia erioloba*, laden with the scruffy nests of sparrow weavers and the large communal nests of red-billed buffalo weavers. I'm whiling away the heat of the day, working on my laptop, waiting to see if any elephant families arrive. Sightings of them are as important as ever, especially since I'm still working out various family trees.

The loud thud of something hitting my bonnet startles me and I look up in alarm.

'What the—?' I gasp in sheer terror.

There, covering more than the length of the bonnet, its body in a curl, is a horribly long, mottled, greenish snake. With its head held aloft, very close to my wipers now, it's about to slither up and over my windscreen.

I shout and swear and bang on the glass of the windscreen to try to scare it away. My other hand is already opening my door, preparing an escape route. I frantically bang some more. The snake turns and slides off the bonnet.

I jump out, terrified that it might now be coiled somewhere underneath my 4x4, but I can't find any sign of it. I stand there for a few minutes, hugging myself and looking around anxiously, hoping to catch a glimpse of where it has gone.

*What sort of snake was that?* My heart is still pounding. *Boomslangs are that colour, and are known to prey on birds' eggs and fledglings. And they are deadly!*

I am totally freaked out.

I eventually climb back into the driver's seat, look high above my head and shudder. If that snake had fallen just one metre further back, it would have landed right on top of me, through my open roof!

*How long had that slithering reptile been up there, hovering above me in those branches?*

I determine never to park under that tree, or perhaps any tree, ever again. Death by sunstroke is preferable to death by snake, I decide.

'Death by the governor would be worse,' Shaynie says to me, after I tell her this story.

We do not laugh.

The reappearance of some of the governor's men makes me extremely uneasy. It's very clear that they believe themselves to be above the law. I'm so tired of their ongoing harassment and verbal abuse. I report them again, directly to Harare.

One week later, official notification is received at last. The governor's family have been ordered to vacate. Tourist game-drives and anti-poaching patrols will soon be able to recommence.

'Do you believe it?' Shaynie asks.

'It's been almost sixteen months since they claimed this land. If it doesn't happen this time,' I say, 'it never will.'

During this period, I'd discovered powers of resilience that I didn't know I had. However, the situation is now unendurable. Either they're really gone this time—or I need to be. I'm assured by the policemen, still based on the estate, that they're really gone for good this time.

'So why then are you still here?' I ask them, searching for reassurance.

'We are just waiting for orders to leave,' they tell me.

And then, suddenly, one of them who has only recently arrived is jumping around, pointing with excitement, a huge smile on his face.

'Arrhhh, arrhhh. He is *too* big. It is my first time to see one,' he says with astonishment, staring at an approaching elephant. 'Arrhhh. He is *too* big,' he repeats, again and again.

To the Shona people he is *Mhukahuru*, the hugest animal of them all.

Another of the policemen looks deep into my eyes and says: 'One day, *Mandlo*, the elephants will speak to you, but only to *you*. It will be a miracle.'

'But they do already speak to me, in their own unique way,' I say with a smile.

'Arrhhh but no. They will speak to you with *our* words, *Mandlo*. A real miracle it will be, just for you.'

He is trying to give me hope, I think; trying to give me something to look forward to. 'I will be sure to listen closely,' I say. There are, after all, plenty of little miracles happening all of the time in the Hwange bush.

There are indeed heart-warming miracles like this one, which I witness a little while later.

There's one male bushbuck that I see regularly when in the field, always at the same pan. His ears are a little tattered, his horns worn, and the hair on the back of his neck is balding, but he is a handsome gentleman nonetheless.

I'm sitting in my 4x4, door open, watching this buck while he nibbles on tasty leaves about twenty metres away. He seems so peaceful; I can't bring myself to start my noisy engine and move off. I have no wish to frighten him. Instead, I watch some more. He drinks and browses and then stands quietly in the shade of a bush, having covered his horns with mud.

Then, he walks straight towards my vehicle and puts his nose to the petrol tank. He moves slowly towards me, my legs dangling out of my open door. He comes closer and closer and I wonder, bewildered, if he is perhaps blind or deaf. Now no more than an astonishing twenty centimetres away from my knee, he puts his head down and sniffs the elephant identification folders that are on the floor behind my seat. Then retracting his head just a little, he gazes up into my eyes. His own trusting eyes are huge liquid pools.

I hold my breath and dare not move even my eyelids. He is definitely not blind. He looks particularly old and wise. Slowly, I move a finger towards him, unbelievably close to his handsome face. He twitches his moist nose, but still does not move. I sit awestruck.

I remember the camera on my lap, already knowing that he's too close to photograph even his eye. It's a terrible habit, this overwhelming urge to photograph everything. He stays next to my leg as I very slowly put the camera to my face. I know that it won't focus, but the photographer in me has to try. He jumps back, startled by the noise of this strange machine. Yet still he stays close by.

Eventually, he moves off slowly into the bush while I sit mesmerised by what has just happened, my heart pounding.

And for a moment I believe it. Nothing bad lasts forever.

# WILL THE EAGLES
# LOOK OUT FOR ME?

## 2005

There is always life and death on the African plains. New births bring great joy. Elephants give birth roughly every three and a half to four years on average, and so most adult females have by now given birth in the years that I've been in Hwange. Some births, though, are infinitely more exciting than others.

When I see my elephant friends wandering with just their youngest calf in tow, as they do when they're in oestrus, or when I occasionally see them actually being mated, I note the dates with excited anticipation, knowing that 22 months later there will likely be a new little bundle of joy. Sightings of all of the families reduced significantly during the land take-overs however, with months sometimes passing before I would see a particular family again, putting a big hole in my data collection. I do know, though, that Lady is due to give birth.

It is late March when I finally come upon the L family again, at Kanondo. I'm so relieved to see them all happily together now that the governor's family is gone, and I look expectantly for the tiny baby that I think might be among them. But the baby is still in Lady's belly, I can see that for certain. She is huge, her breasts—which are very human-like and visible between her front legs—are enormous.

I pull up just a metre from her while she continues, on her knees, to use her tusks to break away large chunks of minerals. In her heavily pregnant state she can't get enough of them. Clearly, pregnancy cravings are not limited to humankind. Lady has not seen me for three long months, and she is completely ignoring me.

I am indignant!

'Lady, you don't even want to say hello to me?' I ask her, shaking my head. 'I am hurt. You need to rethink your priorities,' I tease her.

Actually, I am secretly honoured that a wild elephant can ignore my close presence so totally. After several long minutes, having had her fill of natural minerals, Lady snakes her trunk inside the window of my 4x4 and gives me a friendly throaty rumble. I'm tempted to ignore her! Of course, there's no chance of me being able to do that.

'Finally!' I exclaim, my hand rubbing her trunk. 'You wicked woman. You've got a baby in your belly,' I tell her.

She shakes her huge head in response, ears flapping like sails in the wind, as if to say, 'I've been carrying this 120 kilogram burden for 22 long months. Don't you think I know that?'

She must surely give birth any day.

Two weeks later I'm cursing a flat tyre that has delayed me while following a mating pair. With other elephants only a few metres away, I crawl around in deep sand—keeping as close an eye on them as they keep on me—and manage to change the tyre, but not before the oestrous female has wandered off. Covered in sand and grease, I drive on, filthy and frustrated.

Then, I come upon something so much better, and immediately feel extremely grateful for the delay. It is Lady—and she has a tiny baby girl in tow.

I'm as thrilled as any surrogate mother would be! Lady brings her newborn right up to my 4x4, the little one oblivious to this metal monster before her, and suddenly there is a tiny trunk pressed up against my door.

'Look at your baby! You've got a baby,' I croon to Lady, over and over again.

This is the most adorable elephant calf I've ever seen—although for sure I am more than a little biased. She is still bright pink behind the ears, with bright blue eyes. Led astray by her two five-month-old cousins, Litchis and Laurie, and ten days old at most, she leaves her mother's side to fool around with them. She's unusually adventurous for such a young elephant and Lady makes no attempt to curtail her wanderings. Beside her mother's huge form, she looks like a tiny doll, no bigger than Lady's ears. The whites of her eyes are, unusually, very prominent, giving her a permanently 'surprised' look. The soles of her feet are a very pale pink.

She is wonderful.

To repay my friend Carol for her thoughtfulness and generosity towards me and my work, I give her the privilege of naming this gorgeous little baby. She agonises over this task for many days, umming and ahhing and deliberating, and further tossing and turning in her bed. She imagines me, out in the field, crooning to this young elephant, and wants her name to be special.

Carol eventually names her Liberté; Libby for short. It is an undisguised plea for freedom, equality and sanity in this troubled country. For now, there is indeed more trouble.

The Ruling Party has initiated what has been dubbed 'Operation Murambatsvina', which means 'Drive the rubbish out'. Hundreds of thousands of people across the country have had the only city homes they've ever known, and their vending stalls, demolished by bulldozers. These have suddenly been deemed illegal slums. Throngs of desperately poor unemployed people, trying to find a way to feed themselves, are homeless and distraught, left with nothing but a couple of items salvaged from the rubble. The Opposition describes it as a heartless and ruthless campaign to drive out a large chunk of those city-dwellers who voted overwhelmingly against President Mugabe's regime in the March parliamentary election. This election was widely reported to have been marred by intimidation, threats and electoral fraud. Amnesty International declared it not free and fair. There is outrage around the world over this latest violation of human rights and the government's indifference to the suffering of its own people. Once again, I'm pleased to be in the bush with the wildlife, trying to concentrate on other things.

But revenge now permeates the bush too. In Zimbabwe, if you dare to stand up to the unethical and unscrupulous, you will pay the consequences. And so what happens to me next is no real surprise.

The governor's family are gone from Kanondo and Khatshana, but they're still in the area of the Presidential Elephants. During his time as governor, this man allocated yet another prime piece of land to his family: a small strip on the *vlei*, sandwiched between two photographic safari lodges, that he placed in the hands of his son and brother-in-law. Despite this land being right in the middle of two tourist lodges, they'd managed to secure a quota to hunt for sport here as well. So, these men are still in the vicinity and causing ongoing problems. Together with other concerned people, I've been urging for this third hunting quota of theirs to be withdrawn.

In the meantime, they have continued to hunt, driving their private vehicles (and hunting vehicles with international clients) up and down the *vlei* among tourists who've come to see live animals, not dead ones. The very last thing that any photographic tourist wants to see is hunters, guns and slaughtered animals.

When I see the governor's son once again driving towards the gate to the tourist *vlei*, I approach him on foot. I force myself to greet him, and then remind him, as politely as I can, that these are private roads, which he has no approval to use. I suggest that he park his vehicle and go and speak to the general manager of the lodge, who has overall control of them, and whom I know would like to speak to him.

Already angry that his family lost Kanondo and Khatshana (land that was, clearly, never theirs to lose), and holding me primarily responsible for it, he responds by thrusting his arm through his open window, and punching me forcefully under my chin.

I am lucky that he is sitting lower than I am standing. If we'd been at the same level, I would have borne the full brunt of his punch in the middle of my face. The incident leaves me shaken, but not seriously hurt. By now I expect no less of this family.

When I report this incident to the police and then to my Harare contacts, I receive a phone call from a high-level police commander in Harare encouraging me to prosecute.

'Do not get involved with these people,' Shaynie cautions me. 'Which of them can you trust?'

'You want me to sit back and let these thugs physically attack me?' I ask, knowing that Shaynie would never agree to that.

'Just be very careful,' she urges, determined now to stay in daily contact in case I disappear. It's a phrase you hear regularly here: that someone has 'been disappeared', in a similar way as you would say someone has 'been murdered'. Those who have 'been disappeared' occasionally turn up again, the worse for wear, but not often. Their bodies are usually never found.

I agree to prosecute, in the belief that somebody has to start standing up to these politically connected men. Then I get cold feet, and withdraw my case. But the police and some members of the (usually dreaded) CIO convince me once more to proceed, so that there's a public record of what is happening in these wildlife areas. These organisations, which once sent emissaries to intimidate me, now appear to be my allies. This is the way of Zimbabwe. You simply never really know whose side anyone is on, which makes things even more scary.

I've never been to court before, let alone in Zimbabwe. I arrive under police escort to ensure that I make it safely. There are people everywhere.

Both the waiting area and the courtrooms are spartan and chilly. Perhaps for my benefit, the proceedings are in English. I'm asked to give my version of events. To my surprise the magistrate is writing everything down, in longhand, on a sheet of white paper. I slow my words, and finish my account. I am not cross-examined. My witnesses give their accounts next. Then it's the turn of the accused. He does himself no favours, initially denying that he assaulted me, and then constantly contradicting himself, his story making little sense.

Unusually perhaps—in a country where political intimidation is not uncommon—the magistrate takes no account of the accused's family connections and justice prevails. The court system in Zimbabwe works strangely, however. The convicted get to *choose* their own punishment. My assailant is asked to choose between community service, a fine, or jail. Naturally, with plenty of money at his disposal, he chooses to pay a fine. But, once again, he's in front of the wrong magistrate.

'You are too rich,' says the magistrate. 'A fine will not hurt you. You will learn nothing from a fine.'

So, the son of a cabinet minister (no longer a mere governor following the recent election) is sentenced to 40 hours of community service, cleaning in a clinic. I imagine that he's never cleaned anything in his life. The black African spectators in the courtroom are perhaps thinking a similar thing, since murmurs and chuckles fill the air. I sit quietly.

'Now there's really going to be trouble,' is all that Shaynie can say to me when I later relate these proceedings to her.

Words from Karen Blixen's book, *Out of Africa*, subsequently play over and over in my mind: 'If I know a song of Africa . . . does Africa know a song of me? . . . would the eagles of Ngong look out for me?'

*Will Hwange's bateleur eagles keep looking out for me?*

It doesn't end there of course. When the family's sport-hunting quota for the piece of land between the two photographic lodges on the *vlei* looks likely to be withdrawn by Minister Francis Nhema, a so-called 'professional hunter' (that is, a Zimbabwe-based hunter who accompanies foreign paying clients) arrives to confront me, practising his art of intimidation. He's a man with a dubious reputation.

'You are causing us too much trouble. Do you understand?' Headman Sibanda spits at me, his face mere centimetres from mine. Too angry to care, Sibanda has cornered me at one of the big photographic lodges so there are many witnesses to his threats.

Mustering all of my self-control, I tell him calmly that he is speaking to the wrong person; that I will go and find the general manager of the lodge for him. But he isn't interested in speaking to anybody else.

'You're just a fucking white. Fucking white trash,' he lashes out.

I look him in the eye and slowly raise an eyebrow. *Is that the best you can come up with?* I think to myself.

I've had enough. I move to walk away but he herds me, just like I'd recently been herding a snared buffalo, and uses his shoulder to impede my free movement. He's obviously aware of the recent court case, since he is one of the ex-governor's hunters, and knows not to actually touch me. I shake my head, and eventually manage to get my body away from his. He climbs back into his vehicle, while I immediately report the incident to people I trust.

'Is this worth risking your life for?' Shaynie asks.

'What will be, will be,' I say, in resignation.

Things will never change unless we properly expose these bullies. I'm no use to the elephants as a martyr but I can't lie low out of fear. Bobby, worried about my wellbeing, asks me from New Zealand, 'When and how do you make the decision to stay or leave?'

'I think somebody else will probably make that decision for me,' I tell her.

# ENOUGH TO PEE YOUR PANTS

# 2005

The rains all but failed in the January to March wet season months this year and won't come again until November. We're heading into an extremely harsh period of drought. To make matters worse, the ex-governor's family rarely pumped water and left the pans in a terrible state. Some were dry as a bone and others were covered with weeds from lack of use. The photographic safari operators now need to resurrect these pans.

In the meantime, I decide to spend time introducing the L family to some of the estate's photographic safari guides. Tourism is so important to Zimbabwe, and I'm in a position to assist. Lady's sheer magnificence isn't something that I can keep to myself any longer. I want the guides to be able to share her splendour with guests, but I'm very aware that the delicate balance between familiarity and strife could be fractured in a flash. I've spent countless hours with the Ls and have earnt their trust. I know and understand the family hierarchies, the family relationships and the elephants themselves, not just as individuals but as members of a close-knit group. I've become expert at reading their moods. I choose guides who I believe will be responsible, who understand and appreciate their own limits, and won't be tempted to break rules and push boundaries in pursuit of a bigger tip.

When I find the Ls on the *vlei*, I race to fetch Bheki, the resident safari guide of the largest lodge in the area, keen for him to at least be able to identify Lady. By the time we return to the *vlei*, Lady has wandered some distance away and is hidden behind bushes.

'Lady, Lady, come on, girl,' I call.

'She'll come right here?' Bheki questions, in disbelief.

'Come on, Lady. Come here, my girl,' I call again.

Before Bheki realises it, Lady is right beside his door, flaunting her unique charm, with Libby in tow.

'She knows her name,' Bheki declares, shaking his head in bewilderment.

I'd never really thought about it like that, believing that she probably reacted more to the tone of a friendly voice, and the sound and smell of a friendly vehicle. But why not, I muse? If a dog can know its name, why not an elephant?

So, during the next few weeks I test Bheki's theory. Lady comes to me only when I call *her* name. She always responds to the sound of my voice by lifting her head, but if I substitute her name for any other, she stays where she is. Her daughter, Lesley, does exactly the same thing, as does Whole and others from the Ws, and Misty and others from the Ms. Members of the B and C families however don't seem to care what name I call. 'Come on, girls,' is all it takes for them to all hurry my way.

One day, with the Ms surrounding my vehicle, I take the opportunity to play a game of catch. Not yet two years old and still without tusks, Mertle's son is standing a few metres away, using his trunk to investigate a small log on the ground. He knows I'm watching him, and he picks up the log and hurls it towards me. It hits hard against my door. He looks quite pleased with himself and, although stunned by his cheekiness, I admire his fiery spirit. I open my door with a smile and throw the log back to him. He smells it and after deciding that it is okay, promptly picks it up and hurls it back to me. This time it lands on my bonnet with a loud thud. By now I'm having no end of fun, but everyone seems to want to join in. There is quite an excited commotion, with elephants appearing from all directions, rumbles filling the air. I decide that it's best for me to move off. I name this little guy Mettle, in celebration of his daring.

It's a fun time among my elephant friends. I wish these periods of light relief would last forever.

During my early days in Zimbabwe I used to truly loathe leaving the elephants to spend a necessary few days in town, but as the years pass and the problems grow more and more frightening, I now look forward to a few days away to catch up with mates in either Bulawayo or Harare, and enjoy videos, pizza, ice cream, and other necessities of life! I don't take weekends off, and so having some days away every few months gives my mind and soul a rest from it all and helps ensure I don't go 'bush crazy'.

I get on a bus to Harare and wander around Carol's garden. I listen to bird song and stop, literally, to smell the roses. And I read.

'Why on earth are you reading *that*?' Carol asks in dismay, as she walks into the room she has made up for me to sleep in. I'm reading a second-hand copy of Harold Hayes' *The Dark Romance of Dian Fossey*, written after Dian's 1985 murder. 'You don't need to be reading that!' Carol says, shaking her head.

I'm intrigued by the life and work of Dian Fossey, of *Gorillas in the Mist* fame. How isolated she must have felt living primarily alone in the remote Virunga Mountains in Rwanda for thirteen years, without even the luxury of email. She battled with poachers and corrupt officials. It is her murder, never properly solved, that has me absorbed. Although the Rwandan government eventually charged an American researcher—one of Dian's colleagues, *in absentia*—few people believe that he is guilty. Many think it was the work of poachers. I've always felt that she was most likely killed by a hired hand, on orders from a powerful Rwandan government official.

She was bludgeoned to death inside her cottage, her face sliced by a fatal blow from a machete. This image of Dian Fossey feels awfully close to home these days.

Carol drags me out for ice-cream, to get me away from this book. We reminisce about a memorable shared encounter with a glossy black-coated sable bull, with massive sweeping horns, at Kanondo before the land claims. He'd walked so very close to my 4x4 and then sat down on the ground just a few metres away, totally at ease in our presence. We recall, too, the warthog families that grazed right beside us. It's these sorts of encounters, now lost, that we long to experience once again. But with all of the disturbances going on, animals like these are no longer so trusting.

Before returning to Hwange (the book still with me), I briefly stop in Bulawayo to buy supplies. So many things are 'short' these days. Bread is short; cooking oil is short; sugar is short; flour is short; butter and margarine are short; soft drinks are short; crisps are short; long-life milk is short; tinned goods are short; soap is short; toothpaste is short; engine oil is short; brake fluid is still short . . . and fuel is shortest of all.

A little billboard, advertising the small piles of newspapers for sale on the pavements, catches my eye. 'Shortage of shovels delays burials,' it reads.

'You surely can't be serious,' I mumble to myself. Even shovels are short.

I arrive home to no water, and to the usual mess that needs to be cleaned up. But I'm pleased to be back in the bush.

Just after midnight, I'm rudely awoken by extraordinarily loud munching. Elephants are around my *rondavel*. They've walked over wire fences and are, I assess, in my neighbour's big backyard, very close to the circular wall of my little home. Wrapped in a blanket on my piece of foam on the floor, I calculate that the one munching the loudest, no doubt an adult bull, must be less than two metres from my head. His great weight against the wall of my *rondavel* would be enough to bring it crashing down with me inside.

I climb out of bed and rather futilely put my laptop under layers of soft pillows in case the worst happens. Then I walk outside. As I open my door I hear a loud, determined voice and forceful banging on a windowpane. It seems my neighbour, Morgan, doesn't particularly want the elephants in his backyard either. The six-tonne jumbos turn and run, thankfully away from me.

It is an odd feeling standing there in silky pyjamas in the moonlight, my arms folded against the cold, listening to our nocturnal visitors hurrying away, vegetation scraping against their leather hides. Morgan notices my silhouette, though I can't see him.

'Hello, Sharon,' he says calmly, in the darkness, as if this is the most natural thing in the world.

'They were too close,' I reply, without pleasantries.

'Arrhhh yes, very, very close,' he agrees.

We moan and joke about those responsible for keeping the perimeter fence electrified, and eventually go back to our beds. I think about my parents' nocturnal visitors: possums that scurry across the roof of their home, which they complain about endlessly.

'I win,' I think to myself, as I drift back to sleep.

Shaynie is now living and working back in Bulawayo, but feeling disillusioned. I convince her to finally drive to Hwange and meet my elephant friends. She sponsors me with town accommodation and countless other kindnesses, all of which ultimately benefit the elephants. So, as I've done for Carol and a few others who have done their utmost to assist me, she'll come out with me in my vehicle, despite the trouble some people have begun trying to make for me whenever I do this. Some seem to think that I should never have anyone beside me, despite it happening so infrequently, and only with those who've supported me in some tangible way. It's clear there are still people in the area, friendly with the ex-governor's family, trying to frustrate me.

It's only Shaynie's second ever visit to Hwange. For someone who loves the bush she is, for the most part, terrified of her country's wildlife. Like any good friend, I choose to completely ignore this fact.

The Presidential Elephants dazzle us with one of their uniquely sociable performances. The beautiful, gentle Misty is the first to acquaint herself with Shaynie, perhaps a little too closely. Shaynie just about pees her pants! But terror gradually changes to awe, and there's no doubt that she'll always remember this first remarkable encounter. Later Whole, Willa and Whosit practically sit on her lap.

I admit that I keep positioning my 4x4 so that the elephants walk straight up to Shaynie's window. Whenever she starts winding it up, I reach over and wind it back down! Unfortunately Lady, Libby and company remain out of sight.

'It's a good excuse to have to come back soon,' says a transformed Shaynie, desperate now to meet up with Lady and the Ls.

# HOW LONG IS
# THE FUEL QUEUE?

## 2005

Although a child of farmers, I had no true appreciation for the rain when I was small, except that it meant I could play in the mud. I often noticed my parents on the veranda of our Queensland farmhouse, leaning against the wooden railing watching a still distant storm, hungry for rain. But I didn't really understand. Years later, while working in the cities, the rain or lack thereof didn't trouble me either. There were water restrictions occasionally but I didn't fret over them unduly.

Now though, after years in Africa, drought pulls at my heart-strings so intensely that I feel a physical ache in my chest. Over the next few months, I'll watch the wildlife suffer shortages of both water and vegetation.

To top this off, we again have a serious problem with snaring. Some days we appear to be losing the battle as we catch up from when patrols were prohibited by the ex-governor and his family. Jabulani and his team once again search tirelessly, destroying all of the snares they come across. The bush is thick and vast however. They can't possibly uncover every death trap.

Calls for assistance to remove snares start to overlap, tragically. Over one three-day period, seven snared animals are seen, some with truly horrific injuries. Five are animals that I have spotted. Working frantically, the snares are successfully removed from most of these animals, and I long for a period of respite.

'We're finding hardly any snares, and we haven't seen a snared animal for a very long time,' declares the spokesman for a nearby anti-poaching unit at the same time, intent on keeping their reputation intact.

'Well, you'd better open your eyes,' is all that I can say. I could have said a whole lot more, but I've learnt there's no point arguing with some people. The circumstances speak for themselves. Ultimately, no one is able to deny the snaring problem around Hwange National Park. It is there. And it is, once again, getting increasingly worse. Already, more young Presidential Elephants have died from snare wounds.

I come upon a group of 80 elephants together, from three different Presidential families. Of these, seven have shortened or sliced trunks. There is Brandy and Bubble and Bobby's six-year-old son, Bailey. There is Grace, and Tarnie's four-year-old daughter, Tabitha, and there are two adult bulls. Some are old injuries, with which the elephants manage remarkably well. Other injuries are newer, and it will be a waiting game to see whether these elephants manage to survive. It's a distressing fact that no Hwange Estate elephant who has lost half or more of its trunk in a snare has ever survived for long.

It's a real comfort to arrive home to an email from John. He's finally found someone to send one on his behalf. It's signed 'Spiderman'. I'm thrilled to hear from him.

'U our hero', he writes, speaking on behalf of his wife, Del, too. These words bring a lump to my throat. I have frequently wondered about them, and wished they were still around so that John could teach me more about the bush. I've recalled *braais* in dry riverbeds, campfires in new places and long talks of philosophy. I've often wondered if John was still sharing his bed with snakes, as he unwittingly did on more than one occasion, and whether he'd continued to befriend spiders and climb naked onto the rooftop of his home. I'm happy to hear that he still has his Akubra.

'I miss everything so much I could scream,' he laments.

I understand, but during the twenty-fifth anniversary of Independence, a few months ago, President Mugabe had chanted, 'Africa for Africans!' What he meant of course was, Africa for black Africans. John, with his short fuse, is better off away from it all.

What's interesting at huge annual ceremonies like this one is that black Zimbabweans, from the poorest to the very rich, and from all the ethnic groups, dress in Western-style clothing. Zimbabwe appears to have no traditional dress as is found in most other African nations. The only tradition there seems to be on these occasions is to wear a garment with the face of the only president they've ever known painted all over it. President Mugabe is still a hero to many. He attracts standing ovations here, and in other African countries. But then, so does Libya's dictator, Colonel Gaddafi. And so too did Uganda's Idi Amin.

When I ask a black Zimbabwean about Zimbabwe's cultures and traditions he says simply, 'We have kept few of them. Our culture now is to loot from others. All our chiefs do this.'

Despite everything, there is plenty for John to miss. The Hwange bush is still a sanctuary of great enchantment and I try harder now to find the beauty, especially in the ever-changing detail of the smaller life forms. They're often overlooked, yet they are, in their own way, as dramatic as the elephants walking proudly across the plains.

But even looking closely at the trees these days can break my heart. A huge mature teak tree—a familiar sight on my regular route through the *veld*—is severely wounded. Its sturdy trunk has been hacked out by poachers looking for honey, lured there, perhaps, by the greater honeyguide—a dull-looking but clever bird, renowned for deliberately leading people to beehives. I can only hope that they did not leave a portion of their find for the honeyguide, because then, as legend has it, evil will befall them on their next trip into the bush.

It's gruelling coming to terms with just how much has changed around me for the worse, in the four short years since I arrived in the Hwange bush. People now get away with doing as they please. There are so few controls in place nowadays and nobody seems to care.

I awake to a raging bushfire, much earlier in the season than normal.

Some men are out whacking at the flames, trying to contain it. They set a back-burn, which nearly goes catastrophically wrong. They manage to limit the damage. Smoke chokes the air, hiding the sun. Birds soar, feasting on insects flushed out by the flames. The vegetation crackles and burns all day. There'll be more fires than usual in this drought year, some deliberately lit as uncaring poachers strike a match, making it easier to find game to kill.

'I'm taking the old Dete Road,' one of the helpers calls out to me, over the drone of our 4x4 engines. 'Watch out for me on your way home. I'm running on air.'

I look down at my own fuel gauge. Frequently now the only way to obtain fuel is to buy it on the black market. The cost of it is crippling me, talk of assistance rarely materialising, and I wonder how much longer I can keep this up. I drive home with the setting sun behind me, a ball of hazy fire cloaked with glowing pink, and the almost full moon ahead, round and smoky pink. Even now, there is beauty to behold.

The fuel situation, though, is desperate. When I'm unable to source a delivery, I have no choice but to queue in the township of Dete, a 40-kilometre round trip, on the rare occasions when this filling station actually gets fuel.

'How long is the queue?' I always enquire, before using more of this precious commodity to get there.

Every time, the response is the same: 'Arrhhh, but it is not very long.'

I'm not sure why I bother to ask, since I always sit in a winding queue for at least five long hours. And the queue ahead keeps lengthening, vehicles constantly barging in.

'It is our culture,' they say. 'You put a stone. You come back later.'

A policeman, smartly dressed with hat, belt and other finery, stops by my vehicle to chat. By now I've come to know the police force quite well. 'Arrhhh, Pincott', he says to me, extending his hand. 'How are you?'

Given the circumstances I don't give a full account, simply replying that I don't like fuel queues.

'Arrhhh, but you are close now,' he assures me.

Yes, I can see the pump now—but I am still two hours away.

I gaze at the old bakery on my left. Gone are the days when you could buy greasy cream buns and sweet rolls. Now it doesn't even sell bread, the doors tightly closed. Across the road, shabby square shops of brick and tin are brightly painted, attempting to disguise, perhaps, all that is not available within.

By the time I reach the pump they're no longer selling a full tank of fuel. It is being rationed to 40 litres. Five hours for a mere 40 litres. What can I do but sigh and try to smile? This is Zimbabwe after all.

# ON FRIENDLY LAND

## 2005

Zimbabwe is a country of extremes. There is poverty and abundance. There is beauty and cruelty. And although at times it makes me just want to sit down and weep, there are still occasions when all I can do is laugh out loud.

A big daddy baboon occasionally appears from nowhere at the open door of my *rondavel*, to sit for a while on my doorstep. He's friendly enough, but he flashes his dental weaponry to make it clear who's the boss and always shows up so unexpectedly. I fear that one day he'll give me a heart attack. I learnt long ago not to leave any food items in sight, but a kind friend has just gifted me a packet of potatoes, and I haven't yet put them away.

In just two lightning-fast steps Mr Baboon has the packet in his hand and is racing out of my *rondavel* with them. I take off after him, determined to recover some of my meagre fresh produce. I lose ground. He sails over my thatched fence, potatoes under his arm, while I have to run around it. We must look ridiculous. I hope there's no one recording this bizarre scene. In a rather undignified manner I run and shout and throw stones. In his scramble to get away from me, the plastic packaging breaks. As I'm closing in on him, he picks up as many scattered potatoes as he can, lining the length of one hairy arm. Thank goodness he has no kangaroo's pouch! In the end, I have more potatoes than he does, but I resent this big bugger's thievery, and tell him so in no uncertain terms. I hobble back to my *rondavel* with a victorious grin, carrying what's left of my potatoes in the fabric of my shirt.

When I email this story to my friends in Australia and New Zealand, bragging that tonight I won't have to eat three-minute noodles after all, I receive bewildered replies. They're not about the baboon or the potatoes: 'Why are they three-minute noodles?' I'm asked. 'They're two-minute noodles Down Under!'

'Well,' I say, 'things always take time in Zimbabwe.'

While I continue to wait, impatiently, for an official announcement concerning the third hunting quota issued to the ex-governor's family, more tragedies unfold.

Now an F family youngster's trunk has been ripped off by a wire snare. My records show that he was born to the Presidential Elephants in early February 2003, making him not yet three years old. Due to all that has been consuming my time in the years since his birth, I haven't yet named him. When I last saw him with his shortened trunk, he was still suckling from his mother, Freida, and was fat and seemingly doing okay. But he has only a very short section of trunk now. I know that ultimately, unless he can somehow adjust and become a browser once his mother's milk is no longer on offer, he has no chance of long-term survival. I am still deliberating as to whether or not we can intervene in a constructive way.

I'm driving along the *vlei*, thinking about the latest bushfire, smoke choking the distant air, and there he is. Alone. Abandoned? Or has something happened to his mother? I simply can't believe he's been abandoned since Freida has always been particularly protective of him, both before and after he was cruelly stripped of his trunk. The last time I'd seen them, less than two weeks earlier, Freida had been unconditionally tolerant of his suckling.

Something seemed very wrong. I would look for Freida later. Right now, all I can think of is trying to save this little Presidential Elephant. He is much too young to be wandering alone, and he has no trunk to speak of with which to feed himself. He is already agonisingly thin and lethargic. Clearly, he's been wandering alone—traumatised and unseen—for some time.

I step out of my 4x4 and walk towards him, calling to him, remembering a previous newborn elephant found alone by a roadside who had walked straight up to me and frantically tried to suckle from my arm. This little fellow, though, is older and much less trusting. He attempts a mock charge, forcing me to sidestep behind a bush. Even in his weakened state he could inflict harm. It would have been comical I suppose, if it hadn't been so tragic. I race to the other side of the *vlei* and pick up some *Acacia erioloba* pods from the ground, imagining that he might be able to get down on his knees and feed with his mouth if I throw them in his direction—but he just doesn't know what to do with them.

It is late in the day. I have no choice but to leave him, praying to invisible forces that he will, in his vulnerable and fragile state, survive the night. I need to make the necessary arrangements. He deserves a chance. We have to try to save him.

Plans are in place quickly. A facility in Victoria Falls named Elephant Camp has a good reputation, and although it's a captive facility that offers elephant-back rides—a practice increasingly frowned upon by animal lovers—it is known to treat its elephants well. A Zimbabwean named Gavin immediately agrees to take him in, and further agrees to never ride him. There, at least, he will be given a chance to live in a caring environment—and to become an ambassador for the Presidential Elephants, and for snare victims everywhere. I then ring for the necessary approvals from the Parks Authority who, surprisingly, quickly give permission without fuss. These officials know by now I won't back down easily, nor will I be quiet if reasonable requests are denied.

To be able to capture him though, we have to find him again. When I left him, he was heading slowly down the *vlei*, towards the land grabbed by the ex-governor's family. How could this little elephant know that this small slice of the *vlei* is currently off-limits to us all? No one is even permitted to drive across this land, which these family members angrily reaffirmed just a few days ago. There always seems to be *something*.

'If you have a problem, speak to the president!' I find myself preparing these words in advance under my breath, in anticipation of yet another hostile encounter. I'm determined to be ready to stand up to them, should they try to interfere with this operation.

After a few hours sleep, I drive along the *vlei* searching for this little elephant, but I can't see him anywhere. I quickly ask Jabulani and his anti-poaching team to track his spoor, and I drop them off in the area where I'd last seen him.

It's after midday when Jabulani's radio call finally comes in. '*Mandlovu, Mandlovu*, this is Jabulani. Do you copy?'

'Go, Jabulani', I say.

'We have the *ndlovu*', Jabulani states.

'Is he alive?' I ask with my heart in my throat.

'Positive', Jabulani confirms.

'Is he on problem land?' I ask, my heart still in my throat.

The response is what I want to hear: 'Negative *Mandlo*. He is on friendly land.'

'I need to organise the others, Jabulani. It'll take time. Stay with him. Let me know if he's moving too far. I'll bring you and your men food and water as soon as I can', I say.

'Copy that. Out', says Jabulani, and he is gone.

The men from Elephant Camp have been ready to depart, and are immediately on their way. They will dart and transport this little elephant back to Victoria Falls. I've decided to call him Future—for the future of the Presidential Elephants, and the future of anti-poaching and snare-destruction efforts everywhere.

It becomes necessary for me to make last-minute phone calls to high-level authorities, and to give further explanations, but no one tries to impede the process. Permits such as these take time—usually a very long time—but cooperation is at its best. Future is weak and any delays will certainly cost him his life.

The Elephant Camp team arrives after a two-hour drive. The Parks Authority scouts arrive with the transportation crate that will supposedly take a three-year-old elephant.

'Will he fit in there? I don't think he's going to fit in there,' I say, shaking my head.

We can't delay now. We need to get down the *vlei*. Time is running out. With a convoy of helpers in tow, we finally arrive at the place where Jabulani and his team are watching over Future. No one can tell for certain, but we all agree that the crate appears not to be tall enough. There's a frantic dash back to the maintenance section of the nearest lodge to find a way to cut the top off this sturdy crate.

I stay on the *vlei*, concerned that the day is fading fast. 'What time is it?' I ask, again and again.

Finally, the radio call comes in. They are on their way back down the *vlei* with the modified crate. It is 5.35 p.m. Soon the sun will set. There is no time to lose.

The darter looks to me for the go-ahead and I nod. He immediately takes aim, with a reduced amount of immobilisation drug. In his weakened state, there's always a chance that Future will not survive the drug. Soon he is down. He's even thinner than I'd realised. His skin lacks lustre and his trunk is so tragically short. His breathing and heartbeat are being closely monitored.

I kneel down beside him, and while gently touching him with my hand, I whisper a quiet prayer to the god of wild things.

The helpers now move in. A path has to be frantically cleared to where Future is lying in the bush, the truck carrying the crate has to be reversed in, and Future has to be lifted by scores of able-bodied hands onto the back of the truck. And then he has to be pushed into the crate.

The loading work is successfully completed, but the moon is already shedding light. I look up at little Future, his head well above the top of the crate, thankful for the foresight and assistance of others. I step up onto the back of the truck, place my hand against his shortened nose, and once again I wish him well.

We head back up the *vlei* in darkness. Future is to be immediately transported to Victoria Falls. I watch him standing in the crate on the back of the truck, heading out to the main tar road towards his new life.

My chest is tight with quiet hope.

When there are no messages I assume that all is okay. I telephone early the next morning from the nearby lodge (as there is still no mobile phone network here) to confirm that Future did indeed survive the night-time journey. Everyone is asking about his welfare. There is jubilation and excitement at the prospect that he will now survive.

But Future is just too weak. Despite gallant efforts, and a drip to help him regain his strength, Future dies, peacefully and with company, the next evening at 6.30 p.m. A little piece of me dies with him. His mother, Freida, is never seen again.

We are all desperately sad, but I try to focus on the positives in all of this. Two years ago, I would likely have never been given permission, at least not in such a short timeframe, to do anything to assist. And I may not have found anyone willing to take on the dedicated care of an elephant with such a major injury. Cooperation has improved ten-fold. I will always remember little Future for his part in helping this along.

# WAITING FOR THE RAINS

## 2005

'Don't we lead such different lives!' I exclaim in an email to my Kiwi friend, Andrea.

It's strange that less than ten years ago we led such similar lives. We jetted around the world together making recommendations for major system installations. We travelled first-class, in the air and on the ground, never doing without. Now Andrea is the doting mother of two, living in a sprawling home surrounded by green rolling hills dotted with the inevitable flocks of sheep. She successfully juggles family life and a thriving career, and talks about extraordinary parties and First World fun and adventure.

An email from Bobby ignites a momentary ache in my chest. She tells me that she and her husband jumped in a plane and flew from the North Island of New Zealand to the South Island—for dinner. Oh, how I dream of enjoying that sort of extravagance again. Once in the 1990s I did a similar thing, and flew from Auckland all the way to New York for dinner. It's a little different for me these days. For my birthday earlier this year Bobby emailed me and asked, 'Did you manage a cake? ... candle? ... *cupcake?*', which made me laugh at her own plummeting expectations of what I might have available to enjoy.

Mandy has been ending her emails with celebrity and world snippets of news, so that I'm not completely out of touch. Even so I am frequently having to admit that I have no clue who she's talking about! (Our own Princess Mary of Denmark? Who on earth is Princess Mary?) Feeling well over participating in the bar and club scene, Mandy tells me she's taken to internet dating to try to find a perfect man. Is that what people do now? I am definitely out of touch, and can't help but wonder if someone will find her body before they find mine!

I crawl into my sofa bed on the floor of my *rondavel*, in a space not much bigger than my walk-in wardrobe used to be, my thoughts with the elephants. I feel a deep contentment—despite the many struggles—that I've experienced in no other place. From this landlocked country, though, I do find myself yearning for seashells and children's sandcastles and flying kites on a beach by a rolling ocean.

The next morning I untangle myself from my mosquito net, and crawl off my foam mattress onto the cement floor. Although it's standard practice to hire help here, I do my own washing, gardening, cooking and cleaning so my early morning hours are filled with these chores. By 10 a.m. I'm loading my 4x4, preparing for another day in the field.

In this year of drought there's barely any grass, and right now not an animal in sight. I'm driving slowly towards Kanondo pan and am struck by a feeling that I'm driving towards a beach. The ground is an expanse of white, a cooling morning breeze is blowing gently, a few clouds are dulling the sky. There are babblers, but I pretend that they're seagulls. I fight an overwhelming urge to get out of my vehicle and run, pretending to fly that kite.

'What the hell,' I say to no one. 'Why am I fighting it?' Impulsively, I'm out of my 4x4, doing just that. And it feels good to chase those dreams!

It's such a relief to really laugh again. I feel young and carefree. I feel free. I run and run and run, looking over my shoulder and up at my colourful bright kite, floating high in the sky. But I'm much too unfit for this, the possibility of lions a good excuse, I tell myself, for not running too far. My breathing laboured, I laugh some more as I run back to my

4x4, still flying that imaginary kite, hoping there's nobody in the bushes watching me.

It was a crazy flight of fancy. But it relieved some of the pent-up frustrations that have been growing inside me since the land invasions began, which have had me feeling more trapped than free, even in these wide open spaces. And if my beach was fantasy, I think to myself, my need to escape the seemingly endless problems is not.

'You really need to get out of the bush more often,' Shaynie says to me afterwards, trying to visualise me flying that imaginary kite. 'That can't have been a pretty sight!'

At long last the official announcement comes, banning the ex-governor's family from sport-hunting between the two photographic lodges on the *vlei*. Minister Francis Nhema is quoted in the press saying, 'We have banned hunting activities in those areas where we find the Presidential herd of elephants for sanity and order to prevail.'

Given that he is the very person who carelessly signed off these hunting quotas in the first place, I find his talk of sanity and order a little pitiful. I do, however, allow myself to feel relief, and a little hope that at last we might be able to return to life as it was in the days before the land invasions. It's doubtful that it will ever again be exactly as it once was though. And I know that the ex-governor's family will be out to get further revenge, so I'm not exactly filled with joy.

I do dance around with joy however, whenever I'm able to source a jerry can of fuel.

'Only in Zimbabwe,' one of my indigenous neighbours named Busi says to me, 'can you get *that* excited about twenty litres of petrol!'

Busi, intelligent and level-headed, once had me reeling in excitement at her staggering kindness. She unexpectedly gave me a gift that I knew she could not really afford. It was a bracelet of silver: eight exquisite elephants all chained together.

'The perfect gift for *Mandlovu*,' she declared.

With so many people struggling to feed, clothe and school their families, it was an exceptionally generous gesture. So many have relatively little, but what they have, they share.

I also try to share in different ways, particularly with the children of Main Camp primary school. Photographs are a real novelty for these kids, and some have never even seen a live elephant despite living inside the national park boundary. I want them to learn the importance of protecting their elephants. Every now and then I've been spending a couple of hours sharing stories and surplus photos, watching students create their own drawings and tell their own stories. I long for them to have something more—a better quality life, with more positive influences—but I have little spare time and even fewer resources.

Sometimes, the innocence of childhood speaks volumes. 'This is my father,' one little girl says to me, pointing to a bright red stick man that she has drawn, with big blobs of grey elephants all around.

'What is he doing?' I ask.

'He is poaching,' she says. And before I have a chance to say anything she adds, 'I can teach him it is bad.'

It's a tragic fact that some national park and safari lodge employees— whose jobs depend on the wildlife—are among those who add to our poaching problems. Indeed, it's becoming increasingly clear to me that poachers are often related to, or in cohoots with, Parks employees, police or government officials. And sometimes, alas, even with anti-poaching scouts from a privately run team. Of course there are very ethical and dedicated people as well. It's a tragic fact though, that some of those in trusted, paid positions are the ones I'm now most wary of.

Out in the field, I attempt to get my records up to date with births, deaths and disappearances, which is a task that is ongoing. All families by now hold a special place in my heart, but some remain firm favourites. Lady's family always react immediately when I call to them, trunks swinging rhythmically as they hurry my way.

Little Libby is growing up fast. Ever the playful clown, she uses her mother's thick legs as poles to scratch her backside on. The sight of Loopy always brings a sense of pride, in the knowledge that we saved him from certain death. Limp's snared leg is finally starting to properly heal, three long years after his injury. It's exciting to watch Lady's adult daughter, Lesley, become increasingly mellow; she's soon to give birth for the very first time. She leans her trunk against my side window, standing just centimetres away with her eyes closed. Soon, all five adult females will be nurturing babies under twelve months old, making it a particularly beautiful period to spend time with them. Louise places her trunk on the back of Lazareth, son of Lucky, who leans against Libby, who is suckling from Lady. Lee swirls his trunk around and around and around. Litchis and Laurie lie down on their sides in the sand. Lady's sister, Leanne, welcomes my hand on her tusk. Lucy, Levi, Lindsay, Lol, and Leroy are around me too. I feel like the most privileged person in the world; an honorary member of this family. It's sad that I spend time wondering who their third snare victim will be.

There's never time, these days, to hang out with a family for too long. The list of daily demands is staggering. There are snares set right beside lodges; animals falling into lodge sewerage pits; rubbish pits not properly maintained attracting wildlife to what certainly should not be eaten; fallen electricity cables that could easily electrocute giraffes and elephants; cement drinking troughs carelessly dug out too deeply so that they trap baby elephants; more snares; more elephant carcasses. As the exodus from the country continues, the capabilities and energy levels of some of those who remain, here in the bush at least, is deeply concerning. So much is not properly done or not done at all without prompting.

Now in October temperatures soar above 40 degrees Celsius, day after day, the heavy, thick air making it difficult to take a deep breath. Feeling dejected by it all, I find myself sitting on the parched ground, head on my knees. Flat tyres in the sweltering heat don't help.

'No wonder they call this suicide month,' I groan.

I look once again at Kanondo pan and feel a sense of desperation over the neglect. There have been changes in lodge management during the land grab madness, and those now in charge don't seem able to grasp what needs to be done. The neglect during the land grab period worsened everything. This key pan is not only dry, it's full of weed-covered silt. It must surely rain soon, and then it'll be too late to clean out and deepen this important pan, using a mechanical scoop, to improve its water-holding capacity. Tired of waiting for those responsible to act, I jump into action. It simply needs to be done, and done now. I speak to my neighbour, Morgan, who works for the Painted Dog project, about borrowing a tractor and scoop that might do the job, and negotiate a deal to secure a skilled operator. With a few phone calls, I manage to get diesel donated. Within just a couple of hours, we are set to go.

The scorching heat of the day is relieved somewhat by puffy white clouds intermittently hiding the sun. Sables, waterbucks and kudus look on hopefully as the scooping begins. It is a long and noisy process. Much of the pan is deceptively still damp beneath the layers of crumbly dry soil, threatening to bog down the 4x4 tractor—which unfortunately has the scoop attached behind it, forcing the tractor to go in head-first. The men, working through the blazing heat, do what they can, carting load after load of silt out of the pan, dumping it far enough away so that it won't wash back in. Soon though, the tractor is hopelessly bogged.

'Can't you get your friends to assist, *Mandlo*?' Morgan asks.

It takes me a moment to understand his meaning. I follow his gaze, focused a few hundred metres away on my big grey friends.

'They could pull us out easily,' Morgan declares. 'Can't you get them to help?'

Unfortunately, it isn't quite that easy.

On Day 2, as I stand overseeing this scooping, I realise that the job is much too big for the equipment being used, and I realise, too, that at this rate we will never finish before the rains arrive. I'm also aware that the tractor and scoop will soon need to be returned to the Painted Dog project. I need to prioritise. I select just the outer rim of the pan for the men to concentrate on, so that at least this smaller section will be complete and ready to capture decent rainwater.

When thunder rumbles three days later and more powerful equipment has still not been secured to finish the scooping, I finally admit defeat. We've done our best. The pan is in better shape than it had been, but plenty more could have been done if those responsible had tried to secure more powerful front-end equipment.

This pan will no longer hold the quantity of water that it did in past years. There is little more that I can do though. I have nagged enough. Now, the rain can fall.

As the year wanes I eagerly await the full moon, for it's said that with it comes a change in the weather. The night of the October full moon turns out to be practically cloudless. I search the night sky for a hint of rain, but there is none. Most of the Presidential Elephants are forced to move elsewhere since the estate pans now hold more mud than water. The adults in Lady's family have learnt to use their trunks to skim the surface of shallow water, in order to get a clean mouthful. Their youngsters are learning this skilled behaviour too, but they're struggling. It's heartbreaking to watch such despair.

At long last, on an early November evening, while an unknown elephant bull attempts to demolish the coral creeper in my garden, cracks of thunder split the silence. For a short while, rain pelts my thatched roof. I lie on my sofa bed on the floor of my *rondavel*, with lines from *Bambi* from my childhood racing through my mind. Rather than Bambi asking,

'What's all this white stuff?' I imagine little Libby out there in the darkness asking her mother in a wee voice, 'What's all this wet stuff?'

'Why, it's rain!' I hear Lady saying.

'Rain?' little Libby questions innocently, never having felt anything like it before on her young body.

'Yes,' says Lady, 'the rains have finally come.'

And so, mercifully, I can stop willing it to happen: the drought is broken at last.

As Christmas approaches, I gaze out from my *rondavel* at all the mistletoe in the rain trees. These large clumps of greenery drooping from high boughs appear to favour this type of tree, so named because of the clear liquid secreted by a spittle bug that falls from it like rain.

'Mistletoe is a symbol of love and peace,' my friend Miriam tells me from Harare. 'Long ago it was decreed that those who pass beneath it should kiss, to proclaim the strength of love; to seal a friendship.'

Perhaps that's why I find myself so drawn to it, not just at Christmas time, but throughout the year. Only now do I understand that it signifies my relentless longing for peace and tranquillity in this, the animals' world.

It's a longing that never seems to be fulfilled.

# THE LETTER

# 2006

The Swahili-speaking people in Kenya have a saying: '*Wapiganapo tembo nyasi huumia*' ('When elephants tussle, the grass gets hurt'). For me the meaning is already very real: 'When officials wield their power, innocent people get hurt.'

I've been living in Hwange among elephants for almost five years now, the most tumultuous five years of my life.

The ex-governor's family have realised that the Parks Authority really won't be issuing them a sport-hunting quota for this year, for the *vlei* land that they claimed as their own, and they are seething. A story in the Bulawayo government-controlled newspaper, *The Chronicle*, quotes the brother-in-law as saying, 'That Sharon Pincott is bad news and until we deal with that woman once and for all, we will always have problems. She is destroying the whole conservation.'

The words 'once and for all' have only one meaning in Zimbabwe.

These never-ending threats and attempts at intimidation are so draining, although I'm actually pleased that this is at least now in print for the world to see. When I complain to authorities in Harare about this threat on my life, the story quickly disappears from the newspaper's website.

Taking advantage of his new ministerial position, the ex-governor writes me a three-page letter. The letterhead reads 'Khanondo [*sic*] Safaris & Tours'. He's misspelled the name Kanondo and clearly hasn't bothered to change the company name after their eviction. He formally accuses me of being a spy, writing that I am 'an agent of the Australian Government assigned with the task of frustrating [Zimbabwe's] land reform programme'.

They hang spies in countries like this! It's a desperate, laughable allegation and yet another attempt to scare me into leaving the country—or to get me expelled.

Why is this little Aussie girl from Grantham in country Queensland considered such a threat to this man, who calls himself Mugabe's 'obedient servant' and is fast becoming one of the richest men in the country? I suppose I should be terrified, but I am simply dumbfounded at the crudeness of it all. There's not one person in the Australian government— apart from the Australian ambassador in Harare, with whom I've made contact for my own peace of mind—who would have any reason to know that I even exist.

The ex-governor refers to me as 'an Australian reject', calls me 'illiterate', and states that my 'provocation deserves to be stopped one way or the other'. 'It is common knowledge,' he writes, 'to all patriotic Zimbabweans that you were sent to this country to frustrate the land reform programme especially in Matabelaland [*sic*] North Province where you were to work with the opposition in this diabolic act. Your mission totally failed as I frustrated it during my term as governor hence your anger.'

These are the desperate words of a very desperate man.

My activities in Zimbabwe are 'nefarious', the ex-governor writes. It's a word I've never heard before. 'Evil, despicable', my thesaurus clarifies. Well, at least that might explain how *he* knows it, I think to myself.

He further claims that he 'voluntarily moved out from [the Hwange] estate after realizing the area was infested with anti-land reform agents like you . . . Never was there a request or order from anybody for me to leave the area serve [sic] for your lunatic and imaginary eviction, which only exists in your mind and that of your informers ... I am clear in my mind that you are nothing but an Agent of the Australian Government assigned with the task of frustrating the land reform programme when most racist white Rhodesians started running away from this country to Australia ... The truth will soon be told about you and your local corrupt accomplices.'

He accuses me of having 'sent reports to your country Australia demonizing this country and its leadership' and goes on to say 'your country is totally Anti-Our President and its leadership and continues this demonization of him on a daily basis using false information from its spies and agents like you.'

Demonise. Demonisation. Demonic. Satanic. These words are often used in Zimbabwe's government press, particularly to describe the Opposition party.

The letter concludes: 'I think its [sic] high time you cautioned your handlers that soon and very soon you will be working for the Australian Kangaroo Conservation Project', and is signed and dated 23 January 2006.

The President's Office has been copied into this letter, as well as the three Cabinet ministers I had previously visited in Harare.

What this man hasn't banked on, is that unlike the vast majority of people in Zimbabwe right now, I won't allow myself to be bullied. I immediately fax this letter to all of the people listed as copied in. I'm hardly surprised when I learn that none of them have in fact received a copy of it.

I can't decide if I'm frightened or pissed off. The locals are scared for my life. They know what would happen to them, if they were in my position: 'accidents', beatings, rape, disappearances, murder, and not only of them but of their families too. Being a foreigner affords me just a little extra protection and these thugs are forced to be a little more restrained than usual.

'But are any of us really that stupid?' a friend declares after reading the letter. 'Does he think we fell off a paw paw tree? They are just trying not to lose face.'

'This is the quality of the men running our country,' says another. 'It is an embarrassment to our race.'

Shaynie simply says: 'Sharon, get the hell out of there.'

Shortly after receiving 'the spy letter', as it becomes known, I spend a pre-arranged month in Australia and New Zealand visiting family and friends. It's almost two years again since I've been Down Under. I'm one of the lucky ones, able to leave Zimbabwe whenever I wish. Many of my friends, restricted by no spare money and tough visa requirements when travelling on a Zimbabwean passport, are not so fortunate.

On my departure, a customs officer asks me if I'm carrying any Zimbabwean dollars, as it has become illegal to take more than the equivalent of a few US dollars out of the country.

'Why would I *want* to take Zimbabwean dollars out of the country?' I retort, bewildered. 'I couldn't even give them away if I wanted to. They're worth almost nothing in this country, and they're worth absolutely nothing in every other country.'

I can tell that he's heard it all before, no doubt millions of times. I know that he is only doing what he's been instructed to do, regardless of whether he agrees with it or not.

Onboard my Qantas flight out of South Africa, 'I Still Call Australia Home' streams into my earphones, and I feel tears sting my eyes. This song manages to pull at my heart-strings every time I hear it. The truth is that I'm more confused than ever about where home is. But I still feel that it's the wild spaces of Zimbabwe, and the elephants, that hold my heart—even though it sometimes feels and sounds like hell on earth. I am relieved, though, to be about to spend time in a safe, sane, functional country, at least for a while.

With my family, I feast on a much longed-for seafood smorgasbord in Toowoomba, and I eat chocolate and more chocolate, and share excellent red wine and cheese with my dad. I allow myself to enjoy the comforts of First World life. I also visit Eileen, Andrea and Bobby in Auckland and delight in the sight of the sea; endless vistas of crystal clear water. Eileen and I sit on a bench in an open-air restaurant built over the sparkling ocean, devouring delicious, melt-in-your-mouth calamari, and chips, the best that they can be. It is this normality, I realise, this cherished mateship and the lightness and laughter of it all, that I miss most.

Meanwhile, back in Zimbabwe, the ramifications of 'the spy letter' are still being dealt with. One afternoon, while relaxing in my childhood home, I receive a phone call from the Australian Embassy in Harare. 'We recommend that you consider not returning to Zimbabwe,' says the voice on the end of the line. It is what they have to say. I appreciate their concern and promise to think about it.

I also receive other advice. My contacts in Harare assure me that 'the abuses of the past will cease'. But I've had many such assurances over the past 28 months since the ex-governor first laid claim to Kanondo and Khatshana.

It would certainly be easier, safer, not to go back. Yet the more the land claimants and the hunters push, the more I'm determined to stay on and continue my work with the elephants.

My parents, approaching their mid seventies, say to me, 'If you feel good where you are, then so do we.'

I'm actually unsure how good I feel about it all. In fact I feel more exhausted than I ever have. But the pull of Africa, the yearning for this other less-routine life, is still ridiculously strong. The enormous Australian sky, the great Aussie outdoors, the reassuring pulse of a safe, secure life, is not enough to hold me here. I return to Zimbabwe, hurled back to this frightfully different existence, with armfuls of goodies in my suitcase—as if that might help me to cope. It doesn't, of course.

With new personnel in the local Parks Authority office, the ex-governor's family decide to try their luck, and reapply to hunt on the land sandwiched between the two photographic lodges on the *vlei*. The fact that the Parks Authority actually investigates the feasibility of reissuing a quota, in total disregard for Minister Francis Nhema's previous directive banning them from ever hunting there again, is further evidence of corruption and collusion.

Nothing has changed. It never does.

# AN EAGLE IN THE WIND
# 2006

'You need to get your smile back,' observes an anti-poaching colleague as we stand together in my garden, amid beds of succulents and colourful bougainvillea that I've planted and tended lovingly. He is right.

Although the ex-governor and his family appear to have disappeared from my day-to-day life, it frequently seems like there's little left to laugh about. I once read that the average four year old laughs 300 times a day. The average 40 year old, having battled through a few decades of life, laughs only four times a day. How sad is that? The average 40-something year old living in Zimbabwe has even less to laugh about.

I resolve to get my smile, and my laughter, back.

One thing that does frequently make me smile is the *ten* sausage trees growing in my little garden. It took a few years for them to appear but the phallic sausage shapes I brought back from the roadside during my Mana Pools trip have propagated alarmingly well, without any help from me. I gaze at them now, wondering if I'll be here to see them produce stunning flowers and fruit.

Something else that does make me smile is that I've managed to write and release a second book. (I think everyone should live without television, radio, newspapers and internet for a while and rediscover squandered time!) It's another self-published, Zimbabwe-only edition; my diary of 2005 together with a record of the changing months and seasons, which I've named *A Year Less Ordinary*.

Another book of elephant and bush tales never goes astray here, and it's a source of satisfaction to me that it is complete. I learnt so much about the trees, the wildflowers, the insects, the birdlife and all of the animals, large and small, during 2005, simply by forcing myself to be more observant each week and writing it all down.

It's not easy to even find a bookshop in Zimbabwe these days, although I still manage to buy second-hand books occasionally. My friends and I often present each other with little gifts for no particular reason, and I once placed some pre-loved paperbacks on Shaynie's bookshelf, knowing that she enjoys reading when she can. At exactly the same time she happened to surprise me with a little gift of her own; something that she knew I'd never seen. Actually, it wasn't all that little. I'd bought Shaynie some books. She'd brought me a one-kilogram bullfrog!

And then there are the elephants to keep me smiling. They're never idle, always effortlessly entertaining. There is the best of human behaviour in all that they do.

The strain on my pocket has been somewhat eased with the release of this second book. What's more, SAVE Foundation in Australia is now contributing towards my 4x4 and fuel expenses. I'm really grateful for this show of support from my home country. Financial assistance allows me to be able to patrol more intensely each day without worrying unduly about the costs—that is, when I manage to source fuel. Yet entertaining donor groups in the field complicates my life even further. All sorts of jealousies and accusations overshadow any donation made to me, and having folk in my vehicle, no matter who they are, always causes more allegations to fly. There are people around who just like to try to make trouble for me at every turn, and this makes it difficult to even be able to reciprocate the kindness of donors.

Right now I need to take it just one day at a time. I must stay especially mindful of the ex-governor and his family, and the influence they wield.

Given all that I know, it's increasingly difficult to find the beauty that holds me here. But I try to keep alive inside me my deep feeling for wild Africa, the yearning and the ache in my bones for the extraordinary beauty of the Hwange *veld*.

Mandy emails me with news of Steve Irwin's death, killed by a stingray barb at the tender age of 44. I admit to sometimes having felt a little embarrassed by his broad Aussie accent and over-the-top style, but one of my nephews grew up with the Crocodile Hunter and adored him. There's no doubt that Steve was loved and admired by people all over the world, and was an inspiration to millions.

'What happens for you after the elephants?' I'm asked.

The best that I can usually answer is 'I don't know'. It's not something that I think about. I have no retirement policies or plans for my old age. Indeed it's difficult for me to see myself even making it to an old age.

I can't help but grin when a colleague writes to me saying, 'My god Sharon, it often sounds like you're auditioning for a *Die Hard* movie!'

The truth is that I'd be content with a short life—and perhaps that's what gives me fortitude in difficult times. I haven't worked full-time in a paid job since I was 31. I retired altogether from the salaried world at age 38. How could anyone wish to change that? I would much rather be happy in my 40s doing what I truly want to do, than be rich in my 60s.

And immediately I think of my dad, who once scolded me with a half-smile. 'I hope someone asks you if you still think that when you're 60 . . . What about planning for your old age? You might think you're not going to live all that long but God will punish you. He will make you live until you're 105!'

Forget 105. Shaynie has frequently thought that I won't reach 45.

'*Now* you're thinking about leaving?' she asks me perplexed. 'I know it's been a tumultuous time, but maybe the worst is over?'

'Maybe,' I say.

'Always remember,' Shaynie urges me, 'an eagle flies further when in a turbulent wind.'

Carol and Miriam decide that I must join them for a couple of re-energising days at Wilderness Safaris' Makalolo camp inside Hwange National Park. This responsible photographic safari company knows how to run a concession, and I'm forever wishing it had a presence on the Hwange Estate. It's incredibly cheap for locals with foreign currency to visit these luxury lodges right now. For the Zim dollar equivalent of around US$45 each per night we get accommodation, meals and two game drives each day.

It's so unusual, and such a pleasure, for me to see bush roads so well maintained, and so much dry season water in pans. The poisonous ordeal trees, abundant in this Kalahari sand region, are producing young foliage in stunning shades of purple, making our drives through the *veld* especially beautiful. I'm glad that I've come. We manage to laugh a lot.

'What on earth is *that*?' Miriam shrieks loudly, crouched in the grass, glaring at a scary-looking tarantula-like creature.

'It's a Parktown prawn,' our guide tells us.

'It's a *what*?' we screech in unison.

'Sounds like something you'd eat at a fancy restaurant in Cape Town,' Miriam chuckles.

'Or on Queensland's coast,' I say, with longing. 'My goodness, they're running around everywhere!'

They're actually exceptionally ugly oversized crickets that look like miniature mechanical monsters. 'If that's a cricket, I'll eat my hat,' I mutter, still amazed at how many African critters leave me aghast.

An oversized eight-legged solifuge also manages to give me the heebee-jeebies every time I see one. Known as the 'rain spider' or 'Kalahari Ferrari', it's an extremely fast-moving, hairy and downright scary spider-like creature with beady eyes (and definitely not your speedy game-drive vehicle)! Everything seems to grow so big here.

One of the first thunderstorms of the season brings a deluge of rain and the smell of the earth reborn. Standing in the glow of sunset, we watch flying ants of a pint-sized variety emerge from slits in the now damp ground, floating up to the stars like tiny fairies. At my feet are miniature frogs having a feast. The local people feast too, on the larger variety of flying ant. They place buckets of water under lights, attracting millions of these insect delicacies to their deaths, and into frying pans.

With the rain, tortoises return out of nowhere from their hibernation, and a ballet of butterflies gathers around puddles on the ground, proudly displaying exquisite markings. The booming thunder and rain urges throngs of frogs into a deafening, full-throated chorus. Everywhere, there are *toktokkies*, an adorable wingless black beetle that attracts a mate by tapping its abdomen on the ground. And *shongololos*, giant black milli-pedes that move in graceful waves on countless little legs.

Even without elephants in sight, it is beautiful. It is what helps to hold me here.

One morning I walk towards the base of an *umtshibi* tree, easily recog-nisable by its blackened bark. This tree holds particularly fond memories for me because it's also the name of the national parks base where Andy, Lol and Drew had lived. Miriam and our guide inquisitively amble on towards a large hole in its trunk.

'Watch out,' I say playfully. 'There might be a black mamba in there.'

The very next instant they jump back from the tree, their eyes wide. *Oh no! Don't tell me there really is a black mamba in there!*

'Ssshhhhh, sssshhh,' they urge, gesturing at me to come and look. 'There's a genet asleep in there,' Miriam whispers.

I see the beautiful black-spotted coat and long thick tail of this nocturnal cat-like creature, slumbering now inside the tree trunk.

I smile at the wonder of it all.

Rain has not yet reached the Hwange Estate, where Kanondo pan and most of the other pans are once again bone dry. Waterhole maintenance has not improved at all over the past twelve months, and Presidential Elephant sightings remain few. Where once I could taste hope, now I can taste only neglect and it is bitter.

My concerns intensify over land degradation, unethical sport-hunters, far too much snaring (so many fences destroyed for wire) and never-ending gunfire. I'm also alarmed by speeding vehicles that hit animals, including elephants. And by lenient or no penalties for just about everything. I'm as tired of people's indifference as I am of the neglect, the lack of care, the threats and the intimidation. Some people do have plenty to say in the safety of their own private gatherings, but so very few do more than talk among themselves. I throw caution to the wind and publicly relay facts. Some think that I'm being too forthright, too fiery, too honest. Many do not like to hear or believe what is happening on the estate. Hwange's wildlife—Hwange's elephants—deserve better. I soon decline to attend time-wasting group meetings where people aren't prepared to say aloud what needs to be said.

Every day now, to relieve the strain, I play a little game with myself. As I drive along the road to Kanondo I stretch my open hand out of my window, trying to catch my dreams. But they just whizz past. I used to like to imagine that 'Hope' occupied the passenger seat beside me, but now I see nothing but an empty space. I am bone tired of dancing with despair all of the time. And I'm tired of being tired.

There is one saving grace. For the past two years, following Whole-some's traumatic death from his neck-snare, Whole has appeared terribly forlorn, but now she has a new baby girl in tow. There's a lot of joyous slurping going on just centimetres from the door of my 4x4. I ask Miriam to name this little one. She calls her Winnie and I desperately hope that she will survive.

It's only the sight of Whole, Lady, Misty and my other elephant friends that reaffirms that it hasn't been for nothing. What is happening to Zimbabwe is heartbreaking and devastating. It's now time to make some decisions.

'You've done more than your share,' I'm assured by friends time and again.

This doesn't help to lessen my grief.

'I must leave here,' I whisper one evening with a tight knot in my stomach, finally surrendering after close to six arduous years.

'Leave here? I think you'll leave here on the twelfth of never!' says my friend, Reason, who works nearby.

I know in my heart that my friend is wrong. He's trying hard to be cheerful, but he can sense my fatigue.

I think about Karen Blixen, who died the year that I was born. In 1937 she wrote *Out of Africa*, which was later turned into an epic movie of the same name. For seventeen years she lived in Kenya's eastern highlands, and loved it dearly, yet after her enforced departure, she never returned—not once during the remaining 31 years of her life. Only now do I understand how someone might never go back to a place so well loved but where so much heartache was endured.

At least I'm not alone in my sadness. Emails flow in from thought-ful strangers once they hear of my plan to leave. One in particular I will always remember: 'You passed this way and touched the history of the Presidential Elephants. They would thank you if they could.'

I don't quite know how I will leave. The words of Beryl Markham weigh heavily on my heart: 'I have learned that if you must leave a place that you have lived in and loved and where all your yesterdays are buried deep, leave it any way except a slow way, leave it the fastest way you can,' she wrote in *West with the Night*.

But it seems easier, better, for me to leave in a slow way. I spend time at Kanondo—the Kanondo that I once loved so much; the Kanondo that I now barely recognise given the neglect. I sit alone and let the tides of uncertainty and disillusionment wash over me.

# JUST CAN'T DO IT

## 2007

With the new year, I try to sharpen my hopes but find little reason to celebrate. It feels like it really is time for me to take a different path.

Carol drives me south more than 2000 kilometres to Port Elizabeth in South Africa's Eastern Cape. After six years working full-time in the field with elephants at such an intimate level, I've gained specialty experience and skills that relatively few people hold. These would hardly get me a job in Australia, but I'm not ready to give up working with elephants just yet. I've offered my time to Addo Elephant National Park and am travelling there to meet with Graham Kerley, who is in charge of its elephant program.

We travel via Botswana to try and escape the worst of the notoriously inefficient border-crossings. I'm astounded to see Tim Tams in a supermarket! My mouth waters. One packet is the crazy equivalent of US$7. I fondle it longingly, and reluctantly place it back on the shelf. Down the next aisle I pass a woman who has six packets in her trolley—and she doesn't even sound Australian! I think about mugging her as she walks to her car.

Our first stop in South Africa is at a McDonald's for a cheeseburger—which I wolf down, with fries inside the bun. And soon it's down to business.

Addo is such a completely different ecosystem to Hwange.

'There are no trees!' I lament.

The vegetation is dense and low growing. At least this means no snakes falling on my head from towering trees.

The park is soon to be expanded considerably in size and then the elephants will range in a stunning, wider habitat. The females in this population are tuskless so at least they won't be the target of ivory poachers. I know that once I get to know the Addo elephants personally, I'll love them in a similar way to those in Hwange. And there won't be sport-hunters and land grabbers to contend with.

Graham offers me a position, one that will help to link science with tourism. He is flexible and leaves the start date up to me, understanding that there are things in Zimbabwe I need to finalise, and things in South Africa that he will need to finalise for me.

'And you talk about me jumping from the frying pan into the fire,' Shaynie retorts when I tell her about the job. 'Not only is South Africa one of the most dangerous countries in the world, it's fast going the same way as Zimbabwe, and that's downhill.'

South Africa's crime rate is indeed sobering. The murder rate is five times higher than the global average. The killing of white farmers happens so frequently that it doesn't even make the news. But at least South Africa hasn't tried to rid itself of the white population.

'Not yet . . . ' Shaynie shivers.

While I feel the need to leave Zimbabwe, I'm not at all keen to leave elephants altogether. South Africa's tourism areas are typically very safe. I decide it will be okay.

I take my time and say heartbreaking goodbyes to Lady and Libby, to Misty and Merlin, to Whole and Winnie, to Willa, Wilma, Cathy, Courtney, Belda, Brandy, Joyce, Grace and to hundreds of my other special elephant friends. I wonder if they'll eventually realise that I've left them. I wonder if they will forgive me. I beg them to stay safe; to stay away from the hunters and the snares. My goodbyes, especially to Lady and her family, are excruciatingly painful. I watch them wander away down a sandy road, not knowing if I'll ever see them again.

I feel deep sorrow over this parting of ways. And I feel aching grief. It's not possible for me to hand over to anybody else. I've worked with no salary, while also funding the bulk of the project equipment and costs myself. I've had to make my own way. Contemplating setting someone else up out of my own pocket is out of the question. I haven't found anybody who can continue on in the way that I have, on the long-term basis that is needed.

I know my giant grey Hwange friends will always be part of my future hopes and dreams. As heart-rending as it all is, I hope to still be able to return, every now and again.

And after going through all of that, I don't leave. I just can't do it.

'I understand,' says Graham when I tell him at the very last moment.

'Do you?' I say, surprised. 'I'm pleased one of us does.'

I feel dreadful that I've mucked Graham around like this. He knows, though, what the Presidential Elephants mean to me. He knows too about my endless troubles and that I won't have made the decision easily.

'They're lucky to have you,' he says.

Four disturbing incidents occurred while I was preparing to leave, all within just a few weeks, and these combined to change my mind about leaving Hwange. I reached this decision in spite of Australia's Prime Minister John Howard inadvertently putting all Australians in Zimbabwe in an even worse position than we already were.

'Did you hear what your prime minister publicly called Mugabe?' Carol rang to ask me. I can barely remember the name of the Australian prime minister, let alone know what he said.

'He called him a grubby dictator,' Carol laughed.

'Really? He said that? Aloud? Oh god,' was all that I could say.

While I quietly applauded John Howard for speaking his mind, I knew that this sort of statement would affect me, merely by association. And indeed, President Mugabe already takes every opportunity to lump Australia in with the United States and the United Kingdom as his top three most loathed nations. He prefers, these days, to deal with the likes of Russia and North Korea. Australia has imposed targeted sanctions and travel restrictions on members of Mugabe's regime following ongoing human rights abuses and reported election rigging, and these are now reinforced. I'm already an Australian government spy in the eyes of some, so what might I become now? Despite this, a sequence of concerning events persuaded me to stay on in Zimbabwe.

Lancelot, born to Lesley six months earlier (grandson to Lady), became the third snare victim in the L family. Thankfully his wire came off his right front leg without our intervention, leaving a slight injury that remained for just a few weeks. But I knew in my heart that this wasn't the end of it for Lady and her family.

Then the T family was hard hit, with three snares in this much larger family within just a few weeks. By the time I spotted Trish's tiny six-week-old daughter with a very tight snare around her neck, I was already beside myself with concern. A skilled darter named Roger responded to my radio call. As he took aim to dart both the baby elephant and her mother out of the window of my 4x4 (this was an exceptionally young elephant so the mother did need to be darted as well), I took an audible deep breath and involuntarily clasped my hands to my face. I just hated these dartings so much.

'It'll be alright,' Roger assured me.

And all I could do was think, *No, it's not alright. This is not alright. This can't be allowed to keep happening.*

When the young calf—who I subsequently named Tuesday (the day of the snare removal)—awoke from the immobilisation drug, she gave a deep, open-mouthed roar as she attempted to get to her feet. She wasn't old enough to know what to do, or where to go. And she was alone, with only me by her side. Roger was in another vehicle, attending to her mother elsewhere. All of a sudden, her eight-year-old cousin, Twilight, appeared at the treeline, running at breakneck speed, her ears waving as she ran, her body barely able to keep up with her racing feet. Squealing and roaring, she headed straight towards my vehicle, and stopped a metre away. Gently caressing Tuesday with her trunk, Twilight ushered this de-snared baby off into the bush, safe and sound. It was an extraordinary display of how elephants look after one another, even at such a tender age.

Then, a few days later, vultures led me to the remains of an illegal elephant hunt. This was photographic land, but the surrounding areas had been grabbed for sanctioned sport-hunting. Some hunting guides could not care less where they kill, so long as their overseas clients get to pull the trigger. Their lack of ethics and respect sickened me.

And then, I worked quietly—and urgently—with the anti-poaching team to bust a poaching racket run by employees from a photographic lodge; the same lodge in fact, that had hired the anti-poaching team. Something was just not right. My instincts had become fine-tuned and I had learnt to trust them. I could practically smell a poacher at 50 metres. Eventually we had all the evidence we needed: wire snares, blood in a freezer, and worse, blood all over the inner walls of an unused dwelling. I also had damning photographs of their shoe-prints, clearly visible in the Kalahari sand, beside snare lines, and we knew exactly who wore which shoes. Particularly gut-wrenching for me was our discovery of snares set high up in trees, to strangle giraffes.

*What would have happened if I'd already been gone? Would any of these things have been discovered? And if they'd been discovered, would they have been properly reported and followed up?*

I also knew that many years after elephant guru Iain Douglas-Hamilton learnt to know a clan of Tanzanian elephants intimately, he returned to undertake a survey of them, only to find that a disaster had befallen this supposedly safe population. Many elephants that he had known were missing. Because elephant carcasses aren't always seen, and no one else knew the family structures, this tragedy had gone unnoticed.

I just couldn't leave.

Before departing for Zimbabwe in 2001, I'd gone with a friend to a psychic—in fact, I'd gone to two—purely for a bit of fun. The first cut short his reading, leaving me nervous about what he'd seen that had scared the living daylights out of him. The second warned there would be many paths along my new road, and that I must always be sure to stay alert and to choose wisely.

My decision to stay doesn't seem all that wise, even to me. This can be a dangerous and brutal country and once again it is gripped by political violence. The Opposition leader, Morgan Tsvangirai, was recently beaten up in Harare. Journalist Edward Chikombo dared to release a photograph of the battered and bruised Tsvangirai in hospital. He lived for two short weeks after that. He was abducted and murdered, his body dumped.

Right now, this is not a country where you can speak out against the government and expect to stay alive.

Even if you can get past the brutality, there's often not a lot to admire in its leaders. There's been plenty of press about one of my contacts, Didymus Mutasa (still one of the most powerful men in the country), and other high-powered Cabinet ministers, falling hook, line and sinker for an elaborate hoax when a spirit medium claimed she'd discovered a place where diesel flowed from a rock. It's one thing to have your future told, but pure diesel flowing from a rock?

During this time of chronic fuel shortages, several Cabinet ministers and numerous officials set off in a convoy of scores of vehicles, and even helicopters, to investigate. The spirit medium (said to be a primary-school dropout) strung them along in a two-week con during which time she was reported to have been awarded a farm, a car, and cash from the government. The press published photos of the jubilant government officials watching diesel gush to the ground.

My contact in the President's Office earnt himself a new name. Now he's known as 'Diesel Rock Mutasa' or 'Didymus Diesel Mutasa'.

Am I really staying in this crazy country?

# TRYING TO CATCH DREAMS

## 2007

Miriam is the latest in my circle of friends to decide to leave Zimbabwe. She's lived here for ten years, and although she knows she will miss many things, she's tired of life in a crazy dictatorship. We share a final dinner with Carol in Harare, still managing to laugh together despite all of the tragedies. Two British tourists—a mother and her ten-year-old daughter—were recently trampled to death by a bull elephant while on a game walk in a part of Hwange National Park that we love. We all agree the aggression of this elephant is a reflection of the turmoil going on in wildlife areas around the country.

Miriam flies off to America, and I travel back to Hwange. I now have a can of pepper spray which I carry in the field with me, a gift from Miriam's one-time partner. It is not the elephants that I fear.

Zimbabwe is on its knees—no fuel, no bread, no meat, no eggs, few dairy products and empty shelves everywhere. My friends in the cities endure daily power cuts, often of eight hours or more, and constant water outages (if there's any water at all). There are power and water problems in the bush too; they're just less frequent.

It's difficult to imagine that at the time of Independence in 1980, the

Zimbabwe dollar was stronger than the US dollar. In 2001, 30 litres of petrol was costing me Z$1440. In June 2003, it was Z$13,500. In June 2006, 30 litres cost me Z$10,200,000 (that's 10 million and 200 thousand dollars). The exchange rate has now hit Z$150,000,000 (150 million) to one US dollar. To make matters worse, the government knocked three zeros off the currency overnight to try to make it manageable, so what was Z$750,000,000 (the equivalent of five US dollars) has suddenly become only Z$750,000 (the equivalent of nothing). Shaynie's life savings are worth absolutely nothing.

Immigration problems are my latest battle. I'm now required to travel the six-hour return journey to Bulawayo every three months to have my passport stamped. I feel like some sort of criminal on parole. I have not been issued with a new visa and can well imagine who is behind this. For now though, I just do as I'm instructed, unable to cope with anything more.

Shaynie knows that I need to somehow recapture my dreams. 'Hey, Sharon!' she booms while standing high on a rock during a weekend away in the Matobo Hills, pretending to throw a big bag of dreams my way. 'Catch!' she shouts.

Things in the field keep going from bad to worse.

Lady's closest sister, Leanne, is missing. When I last saw her, she was right beside my 4x4, looking healthy and happy, kicking the ground, loosening clumps of grass and stuffing them in her mouth. With perfectly symmetrical tusks, longer and thicker than those of most of the Presidential females, I always considered her to be a prime target for the hunters and poachers.

Every day I search for this favourite family so that I can work out what's going on. A week passes and I find Leanne's two youngest calves, Lee and Litchis, wandering together but otherwise alone. Lee is nearly six years old, Litchis is not yet three. In normal circumstances, they would never be roaming like this without their mother.

There is no body to be found, but I now know for certain that Leanne is dead. She was not sick as far as I could tell, so has very likely been shot. I am gutted by this knowledge.

Lee seems to be doing okay—but Litchis is growing thinner by the day. I fear for his life. Why aren't they with Lady and the rest of the family? I see them alone in odd places, and wish that I could follow them on foot, believing they might lead me to Leanne's bones. Jabulani and I try this one day, but it's soon clear that our presence on foot is freaking these little guys out. We retreat.

Although Litchis was still suckling from his mother, as the youngest calf does until the birth of the next offspring, he was no longer dependent on milk. Had he been, I would have tried to arrange for his capture, so that he could be hand-raised, but there are certainly times when it's best not to interfere. Two weeks later, Lee and Litchis join back up with Lady and the rest of the family.

Elephant families are deeply affected by death. When we meet up now, adults Lady, Lucky, Louise and Lesley stay close by my 4x4, and close by each other, as I sing the first verse of 'Amazing Grace' to them over and over again. They're quiet and withdrawn. Lee stays close by Lady, who frequently suckled him during the year of his birth, as she also did with Litchis. I take comfort in knowing that Lady will keep a close eye on them.

Outside my *rondavel* I join Last, a mechanic employed by the Painted Dog project, who works on my 4x4 in his time off. He was so named, he tells me, because he was to be the last born. (I'm sure Last is happy with his name. I'm less sure about the man I recently met whose mother had christened him Smelly!)

My resident vervet monkey troop is in a state of alarm. They sit high in the treetops; often, I suspect, to simply enjoy the view, but also always on the lookout for predators.

'Do you know there's a leopard there?' Last asks me, casually.

'A leopard where?' I query.

He points to the bush not twenty metres away.

I see the great cat lying on the ground, its beautiful patterned coat il-luminated by dappled sunlight. There is no movement though, and I catch a slight whiff of decay.

'Is it dead?' I ask.

'You'd better hope so,' Last utters straight-faced as he watches me walk towards it.

I certainly hope it's alive, but it's now obvious that it isn't. The young leopard had come close to human settlement only because it was injured and weak. Its body is emaciated. One of its back feet is broken. I can't help but wonder if it had escaped from a snare.

I immediately report the dead leopard to the management of the nearby lodge, and ask that the carcass be collected.

An hour later, nothing. 'These people really do need a boot up the butt,' I say to Last.

So I report it to the Parks Authority.

When the deputy in charge finally arrives early the next morning the body of the leopard is nowhere to be seen. 'A hyena must have dragged it off overnight,' he says while climbing back into his vehicle, happy to simply leave it like this.

'Will you please show me the spoor that indicates a hyena dragged this leopard off,' I demand indignantly, tired now of such blasé reactions.

There are no animal footprints—that is very clear to me—although there are definitely a lot of human ones. I am insistent. The police must now be involved, as taking a leopard—even a dead one—is a criminal offence.

Of course I'm seen as over-reacting. Why not just let it be?

The police track the human spoor, which matches *exactly* the shoe-print of one of my neighbours (another photographic lodge employee), and find a freshly dug grave, from which they unearth the skinned remains of the leopard. The skin, naturally enough, is nowhere to be found.

Despite clear evidence, no arrests are made and I face up to the fact that poachers live right beside me, while I do what I can to *save* the wildlife.

Soon afterwards, I awake to pitiful wailing. A baby bushbuck has somehow managed to get his head through one of the small, diamond-shaped holes in a chicken-wire fence and is stuck. He is kicking frantically and droplets of blood are trickling down his tiny forehead. I take off my jacket and wrap it around him. I have no wire-cutters but after what seems like an eternity I'm able to manoeuvre him free. Still wrapped in my jacket with his impossibly huge, handsome eyes looking up at me, I carry him to my garden. After washing the blood from his head, he declines a drink and bounds away. Next morning I open the door of my *rondavel* and find the ground resplendent with tiny hoof-prints of mother and baby.

I'm pleased when Christmas rolls around. With so many of my friends no longer in Zimbabwe it is quiet, but on Boxing Day I'm thrilled to meet up with the L family.

Orphaned Lee and Litchis are still coping okay, and everyone else is fine. Other Presidential families appear from the bush and by evening there are more than 50 elephants around me. White-faced ducks whistle their way through tufts of pink and purple cloud. Elephant silhouettes are reflected in puddles of rainwater, tinted a soft pink. As darkness approaches, the bulbous clouds become wispy and blanket the sky with bands of astonishing deep blue and orange. Other swollen clouds roll in like a moving canvas of fluffy marshmallows. I close my eyes for a few minutes, to sharpen my hearing. There is the soft rumble of elephants and the soothing gentle popping of champagne frogs, in glorious stereophonic sound. Egyptian geese honk and red-billed francolins cackle. Elephants slurp and splash their way through surface water, as dung balls thump to the ground. It all sounds as amazing as it looks.

The grand Lady stands motionless beside my door, and I revel in her company. She lets out a low, purring rumble every now and again, checking on her family. It is sad that Leanne is no longer here. Even so, as night descends, with an Amarula in my hand, I know that this is an extraordinarily beautiful place to be.

# DISORDERLY CONDUCT

# 2008

*Beyond this place there be dragons,* the early map-makers are said to have declared on reaching what they thought was the physical edge of the world— and it seems to aptly sum up my life in the Hwange bush. Although the first few months of 2008 have thankfully passed uneventfully, I'm forever fearing what awful thing might be around the next bend in the road.

And then, while out patrolling on Good Friday, I meet the dragon when I see Leanne's son, Lee. He is missing one quarter of his trunk, ripped off by a wire snare. The despair that hits me in the chest makes it difficult to breathe. He bends unnaturally to get water to his mouth, much of it spilling to the ground.

A research vehicle approaches. 'We're having an Easter *braai* tonight,' the driver slows to tell me. 'Come and join us.'

He hasn't noticed my distress. I point to Lee, and try to explain what has happened to the L family. 'Twenty-five per cent snared, in just one family,' I say.

But it's like water off a duck's back to the young people in this truck. 'Well, we'll be having a drink and a good time, if you want to stop by,' they say, before driving off.

That night, I choose to sit out alone under an exquisite full moon at Kanondo, on the rooftop of my 4x4. Hundreds of fireflies dance around me, to the music of elephant rumbles, the haunting howls of jackals and the frantic klink, klink, klink alarm call from a handsome blacksmith plover pair. They're trying desperately to protect their three eggs from the giant footfalls of the elephants, who are innocently wandering within centimetres of their nest on the ground. I can see the outline of the elephants clearly. The air is clean and crisp. Tusks gleam in the magical night light, huge ears flap, and the night birds sing.

Members of the W family join me, and I'm especially thankful for their company. The beautiful Whole gives me a trunk-to-hand greeting and I talk to her warmly. Little Winnie is suckling contentedly. Whosit, who is thirteen years old now and quite the cheeky teenager, decides to rest one of her small tusks, much too heavily, against my windscreen.

'Hey! Whosit!' I cry. 'I'll give you a smack,' I tell her.

Which is, I suppose, a pretty silly thing to say to a wild several-tonne elephant.

The parliamentary and presidential elections are never the best of times in Zimbabwe and they're upon us once again. Some people have chosen to leave the country temporarily. Although there have been ongoing reports of politically motivated violence, it's been relatively calm in the run-up to these elections. The dollar keeps losing value, though, now on an hourly basis. The exchange rate is more than Z$40 million to US$1 (which is actually 40 billion to 1, when you put the three zeros back on), and the inflation rate is over 200,000 per cent. People want change.

When the election results are not immediately released, everyone knows that it cannot be good news for Mugabe's Ruling Party. It is stalling for time. Votes are counted and recounted.

Finally, after more than a month, the results are announced. For the first time since Independence in 1980, ZANU-PF has lost its parliamentary majority, and President Mugabe has lost the presidential election. Opposition Leader Morgan Tsvangirai wins 47 per cent of the votes to Mugabe's 43 per cent, but because nobody has acquired more than 50 per cent of the vote, a presidential re-run is scheduled, giving the Ruling Party enough time to unleash a terror campaign. In fact, the state-sponsored campaign of violence, rape and torture has already started.

There are murders, beatings, gang rapes, genital mutilation of both males and females (all often reportedly done with relatives forced to watch), as well as disappearances. It's a blood-bath out there. The message is clear: if you vote for the Opposition, this is what will happen to you.

More than 10,000 people are reported to have been maimed and injured, and 200 murdered. Two hundred thousand people are said to have been forced out of their homes, and more than 20,000 homes destroyed. With a vote for the Opposition increasingly likely to cost even more lives, Tsvangirai pulls out, just five days prior to the scheduled run-off, as violence intensifies. He hands victory to Robert Mugabe, who wins resoundingly—against himself.

It is clear that Mugabe will never relinquish power. He is determined to be president for life.

Bowing to regional and international pressure, a power-sharing agreement is signed: a 'Unity Government' is to be formed with Opposition Leader Morgan Tsvangirai as prime minister, and Robert Mugabe as president. It will take months of negotiations to work out the finer details and for new ministers to be sworn in.

President Mugabe's supporters are not happy. I smell more trouble ahead.

And now I've become a 'Wanted Person' in Zimbabwe!

'Oh forgodsake! What now?' is all I can say.

I feel rather like Ned Kelly, and have visions of my mugshot appearing on lampposts with a reward for my capture. Am I wanted dead or alive?

In reality, I am fourth from the bottom on a list of names that is on display in a glass-fronted cabinet outside the public entrance to the Dete police station. The others are wanted for poaching, breaking and entering, theft, assault, fraud and rape.

The trumped-up charge against my name reads 'Disorderly conduct'. It's true I'd used a disparaging word in a private email, but how that could have been turned into 'disorderly conduct' is unfathomable.

Out of pure frustration, I had in fact called a woman working for the largest hotel in the area a bitch, in an email to her manager, after years of her spiteful, unreasonable and aggressive behaviour towards me, and her ongoing attempts to frustrate my elephant work. Just recently I'd success-fully initiated a trap that caught one of their employees red-handed with a poached impala, which only worsened my relationship with her.

With friends in high places, she managed to get hold of my email and then file a formal charge against me for using that word. But how on earth did that extend to me being on the wanted list and why haven't I been arrested? I am white-skinned, fair-haired, wear rimless glasses over blue–green eyes and I'm the only female matching this descrip-tion for at least 200 kilometres. I live a mere twenty kilometres from the police station in a sparsely populated district. I drive an easily recog-nisable 4x4 and spend my days with the elephants, but am home most evenings by nightfall. And the police can't find me, or leave a message for me?

Now, six months later, I hear that word on the street is that I'll 'be locked up' if I don't 'turn myself in'. One day in a Zimbabwean jail is certainly one day too long, so I finally drive into Dete. My situation is apparently amusing to the officer in charge (a mate of the ex-governor's family, I'm told), but I don't share his sense of humour. He demands that I either pay a fine or go to court. After nearly an hour of fruitless talk, I decide that they can go ahead and subpoena me.

I hear nothing more but I'm told by friends who pass by the police station that my name remains on the wanted persons list.

While the violence is now under better control, other conditions worsen in the country. A deadly cholera epidemic hits the capital Harare, and thousands die. Typhoid is also about. The risk of malaria is ever present. Shaynie tells me about a plump, wriggling putzi fly larvae that her mother once squeezed from her wrist. She reminds me to iron my clothes to rid them of this fly's eggs, otherwise they'll hatch beneath my skin into squirming flesh-eating maggots.

*What sort of country have I chosen to remain in?*

# MASAKHE

# 2008

Thank goodness for my elephant friends! By October, tiny babies are once again appearing in all of the families, and how wonderful it is when they're brought right to the door of my 4x4 by their mothers when they're just days old, the whites of their eyes still bright red, their ears still flat against their head. It's an enormous privilege that I'm trusted to this extent. I delight in recording all of these new births, and watching the family's loving and protective response to the new additions. It's the babies of those I know best who thrill me to the core.

'Hello, little guy,' I say, beaming at Misty's new baby boy. 'Welcome to this world.' I decide to give Shaynie the honour of naming him. He is a very special little elephant and Shaynie has already enjoyed some very memorable encounters with his mother. I know that she'll do him justice by coming up with a great name.

By now Zimbabwe is close to hitting rock bottom. It sometimes seems like there's no future for this country. I find myself in a Bulawayo gift shop, its shelves all but bare, as they are everywhere. What's available is over-priced. A young mother, no doubt a tourist, with a spluttering baby on her hip, turns to a fellow shopper and asks if she happens to have a tissue.

'A tissue? Do you know how much a tissue costs in this country?' the old lady fumes as she shakes her head and walks away.

I dig into my handbag and hand over a wad of scratchy green (practically unflushable) toilet paper, which is all that I'm carrying.

What a sorry state Zimbabwe is in. Nobody even has a tissue to spare.

We're now a nation of hunters and gatherers. If we find something and can afford to, we buy more than we really want, to trade with someone else who has a cupboard full of something that we can't find. Word spreads like wildfire that sugar or flour or salt is available somewhere and crowds gather like vultures to pick the shelves clean before nightfall. Even a simple loaf of bread is now a prized commodity.

Despite the hardships, most people do share the little bit they have. No one resents stirring two teaspoons of sugar into the coffee of a visitor, despite not knowing when or if it can be replaced.

Shaynie eventually chooses the isiNdebele name *Masakhe* for Misty's baby. It means 'to build' or 'to rebuild that which has been broken'. She knows that for me, for the Presidential Elephants, and for the country, it is a fitting name. So many things have been broken for all of us, and it's time to try to rebuild. A few days later, when I bump into the M family again, I lean out of the window of my 4x4 and, gently placing my hand on the head of Misty's baby, christen him Masakhe.

I'm absolutely thrilled too that there is another baby for Lady, just as gorgeous and special as Masakhe. This little one is named by a couple in Perth, who kindly assist me with replacement field equipment. They choose to call her Lantana. I just hope this doesn't mean she's going to grow up to be a noxious pest! I adore her little pink tongue as it closes in on Lady's breast as she suckles only centimetres away from me.

When Zimbabwe proceeds with an internationally approved one-off sale of ivory just one month later, the only thing that seems to be rebuilding is the disturbing ivory trade. CITES (pronounced sigh-tees)—the Convention on International Trade in Endangered Species, which is the body that regulates world trade in animal products—has controversially granted Botswana, Namibia, South Africa and Zimbabwe approval to sell a combined total of 102 tonnes of their stockpiled ivory to Chinese and Japanese 'accredited traders'. This represents over 10,000 dead elephants.

While Zimbabwe argues that it needs the money for elephant conservation programs (which, I imagine, we're unlikely to ever hear anything about), I simply cannot equate trade in ivory with the conservation of elephants. More importantly, I've lived among Zimbabwe's wildlife for too long to believe that corruption and greed can be controlled sufficiently for this sort of legal trade to work. I don't believe there is the capacity—or the will—to properly regulate the market. This sale ensures that the illegal black market is kept alive by making it so much easier to exploit the loopholes. An insatiable appetite for ivory, particularly in Asia, drives elephant poaching. I just don't understand anyone's desire to fuel that appetite further with 'legal' ivory. Although many people in Southern Africa support the legal trade, I agree with my East African colleagues that this sale will help only to worsen the continent's poaching problems. One way or another, every person who covets ivory carvings and trinkets has the blood of an elephant on their hands.

I don't believe either, as Minister Francis Nhema would have us believe, that most of the tusks in Zimbabwe's stockpile—from which they will sell to Asian countries legally—have come from natural deaths. How many elephants outlive all of the ration-hunting by Parks staff, and the poaching, and the sport-hunting, to die naturally of old age in their sixties? In eight years I have not seen the carcass of even a single elephant that has died of old age.

All this talk of a 'legal' ivory trade seems to also make it easier to forget how hideous the illegal ivory trade is—trafficking that has been linked to terrorist organisations and organised crime. Elephants die horrific deaths at the hands of desperate and oftentimes just plain greedy and uncaring humans. Conscious that their gunfire might be heard, and preferring to save the cost of another bullet if they can, these killers will axe the backbone of a fallen elephant before it is even dead to ensure that it can't get to its feet and kill them. Then they axe off the face to get to the ivory, unconcerned about whether the elephant is still alive. And that's all they take. Only the ivory. To see a fresh carcass with an axed backbone and hacked-off face once is to see it one too many times. It's abundantly clear to me, especially while so much corruption abounds, that all trade in ivory must end: the illegal and the so-called legal.

Yet it's a sad fact that the sight of a dead elephant is not shocking to many people here. It is, actually, exciting. A dead elephant is *nyama* (meat). Except that by the time the carcass of an elephant killed for its ivory is typically discovered, the meat is putrid and can't be eaten.

As Christmas approaches there is more sad news. Gavin, who so readily agreed to take in the snared calf Future, has been fatally tusked by one of his trained elephants in Victoria Falls. He was not much older than me. I can't help but wonder if distant gunfire, still much too prevalent across the country these days, may have rattled his herd. There are certainly people here who give the captive elephant industry a particularly bad name, but Gavin wasn't one of them.

Small, pleasant diversions, away from the Hwange bush, are increasingly important to me. For a few days at least, I can forget. Dinks, who has been living in South Africa for more than four years, is returning to Zimbabwe for Christmas. Shaynie and I are excited, and decide that we'll all spend some time together in Dinks' favourite place on earth, the Matobo Hills.

We also decide, with a wine in hand, that we need to do something about those 'Twelve Days of Christmas'. There are no partridges or pear trees here, so 'an el-e-ph-ant in a mud bath' it has to be. We end up with twelve shots of Amarula, eleven spiders biting, ten warthogs wallowing, nine kudus leaping, eight shrews a-chewing, seven buffaloes bellowing, six savannah sunsets, five charging rhinos, four lions snoring, three friends a-singing, two crimson shrikes—and that el-e-ph-ant in a mud bath!

We collect Dinks from the dingy bus stop in town and retreat to Shaynie's flat. With mattresses, pillows, wine and snacks quickly spread out across the lounge room floor, we watch *Mamma Mia!* and laugh and dance and sing along like teenagers.

We talk evocatively about our own lives and how different it all might have been. But there can be no regrets. Because no matter how we got here, we are three very different women who somehow became special friends, still sharing extraordinary times that we'll cherish forever.

There's not much frenzy to our preparations in the prelude to Christmas, mostly because there's so little available to buy, although Shaynie does splurge on a (very scarce) turkey and we eventually find one small pot of cranberry sauce. We decide that it'll be fun to dress formally and eat our Christmas Eve dinner on a white tablecloth, with champagne and candles, under the stars in the Matobo. Of course it rains. So we set up inside our rustic accommodation instead, looking out over the splendidly sculptured granite boulders and wooded valleys of this timeless place, breathing in the grandeur and the mystique of the Maleme Gorge, pretending to be classier than we really are. It's the first and only time I've seen Shaynie in a dress, and it's a long one at that. She's even clomping around in high heels, which, come to think of it, probably brought on the ill-timed rain.

'We're heading up that *gomo*,' Shaynie and Dinks announce on Christmas Day, their sights set on some horribly high rocky outcrop.

I followed them only once, years ago. That walk was long and agonising. I could barely breathe. Wheezing uncontrollably, I collapsed at the top, swearing never to do it again.

'You should have seen that view,' they croon after climbing down.

'I like the view perfectly well from the bottom, thanks,' I say.

After days of fun and laughter, there are tears and hugs as we put Dinks back on the bus, into the ever-growing diaspora.

# BILLIONS AND TRILLIONS

## 2009

Emails from Australia bring news of intense bushfires that have inciner-
ated entire communities in rural Victoria; Australia's worst natural disaster
in over one hundred years. February 7, Mandy tells me from Melbourne,
will long be remembered as Black Saturday. These firestorms killed 173
people and destroyed more than 2000 homes. Hundreds of thousands of
domestic and wild animals perished. With no television or internet access,
I'm pleased not to have images of it all.

Weeks pass and then I'm emailed a photograph of a gallant fire-
fighter, caked with grime and sweat, offering a drink from his plastic
water bottle to a thirsty and injured koala. Burnt koala paw on human
hand, pink tongue poking into the lip of the bottle, it's an image that has
touched the hearts of millions around the world. It has become an image
of hope.

In a similar way, it is Lady who has become my symbol of hope for the
Presidential Elephants. It's when I encounter her with baby Lantana and
the rest of her family, wandering among animals like zebra, giraffe
and antelope, peaceful and so very grand, that I feel 'Hope' returning to
the passenger seat beside me.

Yet in this mad land of Mugabe, a loaf of bread now costs 300 billion Zim dollars. That's six of the 50-billion-dollar notes that are now in circulation—but even these won't be of much use for long. It was only a few short weeks ago that our highest denomination note was 500 million dollars.

'How is that even possible?' Mandy asks me from Melbourne.

'I'm living it,' I exclaim, 'and even I don't know the answer to that!'

Zimbabwe's inflation rate will soon pass an absurd 230 *million* per cent. The government simply keeps printing more and more money to pay its debts. Some of the currency even has use-by dates printed on it, as if it's already known it won't be good for long.

The Reserve Bank has announced that 100-trillion-dollar notes are to be released. *100 trillion dollars* in a single note! That's a number with 14 zeros in it: $100,000,000,000,000. You go cross-eyed just looking at it. Calculators are useless; the numbers simply don't fit on the screen, even though the government has already slashed even more zeros from the currency, to try to make it more manageable.

When Andy was still alive and I travelled frequently to Zimbabwe as a tourist, I divided prices by ten to give me an idea of the cost in Australian dollars. Now we have Monopoly money. Million-dollar notes blow around the streets, nobody bothering to pick them up. *Find a penny, pick it up, and all the day you'll have good luck.* I bend to pick up a $750,000 note only because it's adorned with sketches of elephants. Beggars hold up crude cardboard placards declaring they are STARVING BILLIONAIRES. There are signs in public toilets in neighbouring South Africa and Botswana urging people to use only toilet paper and not cardboard, cloth, newspaper—or Zimbabwe dollars! As much as some people would like to, no one dares display such signs here.

Farm invasions continue. Thousands of productive white farmers have now lost their farms, with no monetary compensation—the best of the land grabbed by the Ruling Party elite and their families. Hundreds of thousands more people, some say in excess of a million, have been displaced as growing numbers of farm-workers lose their jobs. The commercial farming industry has all but been destroyed. Zimbabwe used to be one of the biggest exporters of beef to Europe and a top exporter of tobacco to the world. It used to help feed the Southern African region. Once known as the 'breadbasket of Africa', it has been reduced to a basket case, a begging bowl. Now, it has to import food to feed its own people.

Unemployment sits somewhere above 80 per cent, with a similar proportion of the population said to now be living in abject poverty. Electricity and water supply is either non-existent, or intermittent at best. There are alarming levels of poaching across the country, and rapidly increasing deforestation too, as new farmers cure tobacco with indigenous timber.

President Mugabe blames Western sanctions for it all, which he loves to refer to as illegal. How they could possibly be considered 'illegal' is baffling. Furthermore, sanctions and travel restrictions have only been on targeted individuals and companies; there have been no trade embargoes. Somebody has to be blamed for this mess, however, and the regime is never going to blame itself.

Eight long years now we've kept saying how beautiful Zimbabwe is, and how it will all come right. We carry eternal optimism around in our wallets, along with our trillion-dollar notes. It's starting to feel like we're all lunatics living in an asylum.

Zimbabwe's new 100-trillion-dollar note ends up being worth around 40 US cents. And then the Zimbabwe dollar is officially abandoned altogether. The US dollar becomes Zimbabwe's most widely used currency, along with the South African rand and the Botswanan pula. So, now, here I am in a country that loathes the West, using US dollars as its official currency.

The Unity Government has finally been formed and Morgan Tsvangirai is prime minister, sharing power alongside President Robert Mugabe. A new Cabinet has been sworn in. There's hope around the country, and indeed around the world, that some sanity might now prevail. I get indigestion just thinking about it. Where in Africa these days, no matter who's in power, is it not corrupt?

Although there are people 'holding thumbs' (as the saying goes here) for a change of wildlife minister, it's considered a lowly portfolio in Zimbabwe and ZANU-PF's Francis Nhema retains the position, despite the shocking levels of poaching and the unprincipled sport-hunting that has occurred over the last nine years on his watch.

'Mugabe is 85 years old. He can't be president for much longer,' people are still saying. But these ZANU-PF guys are here to stay. I have no choice but to try harder to work with them.

Shaynie and I enjoy a splendid weekend of wildlife on the estate. We search for Lady and her family, but they're in hiding once again. It's like Shaynie is destined never to meet them. We do bump into the Ms however, and Shaynie is thrilled to meet 'her' little Masakhe, who she immediately falls in love with. She is becoming much more relaxed around these elephants and better understands why I'm still here.

It's Anzac Day in Australia. After the undisguised threats on my life, and my ongoing conflicts and battles, I feel like something akin to a war veteran myself. Shaynie's supportive presence is comforting.

'Please explain this to me like I'm a three year old,' I beg her. 'How is it that I've remained on the wanted person's list for more than twelve months when I live right *here*?'

'The unscrupulous harass only those they fear,' Shaynie declares. 'If you were insignificant to them they'd leave you in peace. You must be doing your job better than you should be,' she decides.

By now I'm just tired of it all.

'You really must find out what's going on with that,' Shaynie urges.

The next morning I tuck my hair under a cap, keep my sunglasses on, and ensure that I have a reputable lawyer's phone number in my bag. We drive together in Shaynie's vehicle to the police station, knowing that if recognised I could well be thrown into jail. The camera on her mobile phone is ready for action; she just needs to stop shaking long enough to be able to take the photograph that I'm after. We are both uneasy, but I want a photo of the list.

After a nervous glance at each other and a deep breath, we nod our heads in solidarity and open the car doors. We walk together in silence towards the cabinet displaying the list. Shaynie nervously runs her finger down it. My name is there, with the charge against me. It is all still clearly legible. But a neat horizontal line has been drawn through the middle of it.

We share a sigh of relief. Shaynie glances around and, with nobody in sight, takes a photograph with unsteady hands. Only when we're back in the car do we shake our heads and laugh at last at the absurdity of it all.

We're nearly back at my *rondavel* when Shaynie's phone rings. Mobile phone reception is finally available, albeit sporadically, in these remote parts. It's her older sister, Caroline, calling from Bulawayo.

'It's all fine,' Shaynie declares, sounding upbeat, 'we've just left the police station.'

But there's been much more going on. Caroline's husband, John, is dead. He has died, suddenly and unexpectedly, from a suspected aneurysm, at 49 years of age. Shaynie is distraught.

I race around and throw a few things in a bag. I drive her the three hours back to Bulawayo. My own trials and tribulations are once again put in perspective.

While Lantana, Masakhe and their age-mates have been keeping me thoroughly entertained in the field, I've become a properly published author. I'd decided that I needed to raise the profile of these elephants outside of Zimbabwe, if there was to be any chance of keeping them and their land areas safe and secure. *The Elephants and I* has been published by Jacana Media in South Africa. I fly to Johannesburg to do television, radio and magazine interviews. It's a whirlwind trip, and interest is high. More and more people are falling in love with the Presidential Elephants of Zimbabwe, and that can only be a good thing.

If I want to remain in Zimbabwe and stay alive, there are limitations on what I can say and write. When the legendary Cynthia Moss calls my book 'brave and passionate' I hope that I haven't overstepped the mark. Delia Owens, another renowned American conservationist (and co-author of the international bestseller *Cry of the Kalahari*), writes of my 'courage . . . grit . . . pluck', which I attribute to growing up in Australia, 'the plucky country'. I'm honoured to read comparisons to Joy Adamson's 1960 book *Born Free*—with one newspaper editor calling me 'the Joy Adamson of Zimbabwe'—and try my best to forget the fact that both Joy and George Adamson, like Dian Fossey, were murdered in the field.

I'm also asked by South Africa's popular *Getaway* magazine to become its 'Elephant Ambassador in Africa'. I'll have my own page to write about the elephants and their Hwange surrounds. Although there'll be no payment, it's a superb way of sharing the uniqueness of the Presidential Elephants and an opportunity to make myself more visible, in the hope enemies might be less inclined to harass me. But in Zimbabwe, as I know only too well, anything could happen.

After eight years of leading a relatively solitary bush life, the attention feels incredibly foreign to me. But I know that by putting myself out there, I'm giving these elephants a better chance.

Mandy emails an offer to set up a basic website for me. I have no idea just how widely used the internet has become in the years since I've been in the bush, but she assures me it will be beneficial. I'm grateful, especially as I know how busy she always is. Once it's up I become inundated with kind and encouraging emails, all of which I endeavour to answer personally. It is Lady that people enquire about the most.

The Presidential Elephants of Zimbabwe are slowly but steadily finding their place in the spotlight.

After the publicity that the book and website generated, I'm in a better position to help promote tourism. I've come to believe that the return of tourists is crucial to the preservation of Zimbabwe's wildlife, including the Presidential Elephants. Without the tourists, sport-hunters and worrying land claims will determine the wildlife's future. But while the waterholes on the estate remain so degraded it's difficult to do this in good faith. With some goading, water is usually pumped satisfactorily into the lodge pans, but game-drives need to venture further afield. There's no animals for the tourists to see if there's no water out there. It's exasperating that estate operators charge tourists up to US$50 per person for one game-drive, yet put none of this back into the land and the maintenance of other pans. Neither the Parks Authority nor the ministry enforce any rules. In a country where precious wildlife is such a draw-card for tourists, this is simply unfathomable.

The local Ndebele people have a saying: '*Ithendele elihle ngelikhala ligijima*' ('Don't just sit there bleating, get up and do something about it'). I've been bleating about waterhole neglect long enough. Now I'm determined to get on and simply do something more myself. The elephants have suffered with lack of water for long enough.

I've been fighting the misinformed for years on this issue, since well before I organised the prior work using the Painted Dog project tractor and small scoop. Some of my critics, both black and white, mysteriously claim that the use of a bulldozer will break the natural seal of the pans so that they won't hold any water. This, they say, is why they continue to do nothing. I can see no logic in such a claim if the work is done properly. And what if a 'seal' is temporarily broken? The pans have held insufficient amounts of water for years anyway.

Shaynie works in Bulawayo for a company that has the right equipment to do the job, but I don't have enough money. The SAVE Foundation in Perth has generously offered some help, as have a few other groups including Wildlife Environment Zimbabwe (the official wildlife society), but this is a US$20,000 job. I decide to try to win over Shaynie's boss, Jim, regardless.

Talking to tuskless Cathy, the matriarch of the C family. (Photo courtesy of Brent Stapelkamp)

Sometimes while sitting in my 4×4, I'd look back over my shoulder and find a huge bull looking right at me.

There was always somebody outside my 4×4 wanting to say hello.

Arrhhh, but I can still see you.

Willa and I share a tender moment. My relationship with the Presidential Elephants was said to be one of the most remarkable ever documented. (Photo courtesy of NHU Africa)

The tall and
the tiny of the
elephant world.

Mr Baboon, were you the one who stole my potatoes?

My friend Lady.

Lady brought baby Lantana so close to my 4×4 that it was difficult to take a photo, even with the widest angle lens.

Ignoring my very close presence beneath them, Wonderful (left) is greeted by a bull.

The gorgeous new-born Ayesha, named by my kind donor Roby.

The lovable Whosit, with only the windscreen separating us. She loved to give me a fright, leaving me certain that elephants giggle in infrasound.

I spent hours every day sitting on the roof of my 4×4 recording the lives of the Presidential Elephants. (Photo courtesy of NHU Africa)

Esther doctors the awful snare wound on Adwina's leg. It took time, but Adwina recovered well.

(Left) My 'Mother Elephant' sign outside the cottage I moved to in 2011. The 'snake blocker', which didn't always work, is in front of the door with Craig's painting of Whole. (Right) Grace, who lost the fingers of her trunk in a snare, uses her foot to kick an *Acacia erioloba* pod on to her trunk before tossing it into her mouth.

(Left) Not that it did much good in the end, the Presidential Decree reaffirmation certificate was signed by President Robert Mugabe in 2011. (Photo courtesy of NHU Africa) (Right) Minister Francis Nhema (left) and Chief Dingani at the Presidential Decree reaffirmation ceremony. (Photo courtesy of NHU Africa)

The elephants loved their mascot, who I named Fearless.

Nothing beats sundowners in the African bush.

My favourite elephants always preferred to be centre stage. This is Willa desperate for some special attention.

Wilma loved to sleep on my bullbar.

Cecil the Lion near Ngweshla campsite inside Hwange National Park in December 2013, eighteen months before he was killed by a sport-hunter.

Members of the E family at Mpofu pan.

The gentle Misty. (Photo courtesy of NHU Africa)

Misty, Masahke and family enjoying the wet season.

Wahkuna (Whole's granddaughter) with a wire snare around her back right leg.

Wahkuna recovered well after her snare was successfully removed. She kept the wound covered in mud and dust to help it heal.

After arranging for waterholes to be scooped, I later had them de-weeded with the help of men from the nearby township of Dete.

(Left) During a 2013 fly-over to check on poaching activity, I spotted these elephants inside Hwange National Park dead from cyanide poisoning. (Right) Minister Saviour Kasukuwere in 2014 at the commissioning of the solar pump installation that feeds Mandlovu pan.

Who, really, is the king of the jungle?

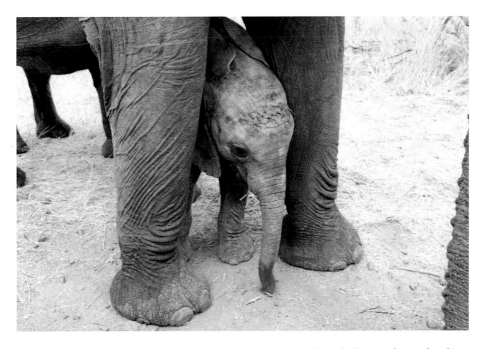

It was always such a privilege when mothers brought their babies right to the door of my 4×4 and stayed beside me for hours.

This is the last photo taken of Dad with my mum and his four daughters before he died in December 2015. From left: me, Deborah, Genevieve, Mum and Catherine.

Like my dad, Lady will live on with me, always.

I am one with the elephants. Still. (Photo courtesy of NHU Africa)

We drive out together onto the estate, surveying existing waterholes and other dry, cracked sites like antbears deciding where to burrow. I'm still trying to convince Jim to assist when Lady and her family unexpectedly appear on the road ahead: a gift from above. I stop our vehicle and call loudly to her through cupped hands: 'Lady! Lady girl. Come on, Lady. Come here, my girl.'

Mighty trunks swing rhythmically as the entire L family lumber our way. It's not long before Lady is holding my hand within the 'fingers' of her trunk, and fluttering her long, elegant eyelashes at Jim. The flapping of her huge ears is so near that we're fanned by a cool breeze.

Just like that, Jim will do this scooping for the couple of thousand dollars that I've managed to gather and will donate the rest. After five years of so much futile talk, it has taken me only five days and some flirting by Lady to secure a deal.

Five weeks later the job is under way. The bulldozer equipment arrives on a long flat-bed truck. From dawn till dusk I oversee the work with Jim's brother, Tom. We talk endlessly, and occasionally heatedly, about how each pan should best be scooped.

'We need to remember that all of the wildlife, including the giraffes, must be able to drink with ease. We need gently sloping sides, on three sides at least,' I insist multiple times every day.

Tom whistles loudly over the din of the bulldozer to attract the driver's attention and I motion with my arm in the air for a more gentle curvature. We need depth, but I'm insistent that there be no sharp edges or steep sides. There is a small amount of water in Kanondo pan, in the outer edges I had scooped four years ago. Given it's the only water on the estate, we unfortunately can't let this pan dry out to enable us to scoop it properly this time round. Instead we agree that we'll create another pan here, separate but connected to the original one.

One morning Wilma appears at the tree line. With the bulldozer operator and a colleague of his in my 4x4 with me, I call to her, and she lumbers straight to my door to say hello. Neither of these men has seen an elephant in the wild before, let alone one responding like this. One of them whispers with a half grin, 'Arrhhh, but now I am scared of you. You have very special magic.' From then on, they both bow their heads and pat their hearts whenever they see me.

I come upon Lucky and her tiny newborn baby one afternoon by the roadside and take photographs especially to show Jim. I give him the honour of naming this special little bundle of joy. He calls her *Langelihle*—Lunga for short—the isiNdebele word meaning 'good day'. I know that I'll take great pleasure in saying 'Gidday good day' every time I see Lucky and her wee one.

The days are awfully hot, glary and dusty. Every day by sundown we are bone-weary and grubby, our eyes irritated. My left one becomes blood-red and feels as if it's been sprinkled with glass fragments. Months later, when I finally see an ophthalmologist in Bulawayo, a minuscule piece of plastic is removed from the surface of my eyeball.

The scooping of three key pans and the creation of another three smaller ones (one of which I name 'Lady's pan') go off without a hitch. Not surprisingly perhaps, I don't receive any thanks for resurrecting these waterholes, at least not until I prompt the management of the group who should have organised and paid for this work themselves. Only then do I receive a thank you of sorts. For saving them tens of thousands of dollars, and in effect resurrecting the estate, I receive an email. It contains just two short sentences.

My battles are far from over.

After the arrival of new white management in the largest hotel in the area, sport-hunting trophies of all shapes and sizes suddenly adorn the walls, floor and shelf surfaces of every public area inside this lodge. This is supposed to be a *photographic* safari lodge. I had campaigned hard to get hunting banned and the ex-governor and his family removed from the land. I've just scooped the surrounding pans in order to help *save*

the wildlife and yet here we are, surrounded by a huge collection of dead animals, heads even appearing behind the game-drive booking desk!

It takes three long months, with repeated pleas that finally have to be escalated to board level, before the menagerie of hunting trophies is removed.

'You're still having wins,' Shaynie says to me. 'Keep remembering those eagles flying through that turbulent wind.'

# PIZZA AND ICE-CREAM

## 2010

It's been a generous wet season. The scooped pans have filled to their brims, and the wildlife has returned. My elephant friends roll and splash in the new expanses of water. Given that females within each family often give birth within a few months of each other, there are always groups of playful youngsters about. They cavort in the water, legs and trunks waggling in the air, then find a place at the water's edge to slip and slide in mud with their mothers, before tossing trunkfuls of sand over their heads and backs. And then they all come and share their dirty bodies with me.

'You're too clean,' I imagine Whole, Whosit and Willa saying to me, as they touch my arms with their mucky trunks, leaving me streaked with mud.

With the waterholes looking superb, I've started occasionally accompanying lodge guests who have a special interest in elephants, on game drives as my time permits. I do this on a voluntary basis only since there are plenty of people around who are indifferent to my project costs, and would immediately make it difficult for me if they thought I was earning any money on the estate. It's satisfying when visitors leave with a deep respect for elephants and a new-found desire to stand up for their welfare. Hearing that their game-drive has been a highlight of their trip, and often of their lives, is another reward, and I meet some wonderful people.

There's another good reason for me to occasionally climb aboard the game-drive vehicles: the safari guides need to learn more about these elephants. Having me there also means that some of my close elephant friends come to know and trust their vehicles more readily.

But problems soon start to surface. There are more game-drive vehicles out and about, and further failings in the estate management become glaringly obvious. Rubbish, including toilet paper, blows around; visitors are being allowed out of vehicles, wandering about, scaring off the animals for others; some vehicles drive off-road wherever they please and game walks come much too close to these habituated elephants. I write reports, flag problems and make recommendations, but rules and regulations are never enforced. It has become a free-for-all out there.

Eventually I resign myself to this indifference, and just get on and do what I can. I patrol daily, always on the lookout for signs of poacher activity and snared animals (while picking up endless amounts of rubbish). I check on water flow and pan levels. I help secure the expensive immobilisation drug for use in animal de-snarings and monitor the de-snared animals. My monitoring of each of the Presidential Elephant families continues too, of course, recording family interactions, new births, those in oestrus and musth, and anyone who is missing or injured.

At least currently there's good water in all of the pans. It's actually a fulfilling time.

Shaynie has changed jobs and moved to the bush, although she has kept her flat in downtown Bulawayo. She's now working in the back office at Wilderness Safaris, which has four luxury photographic lodges on two wildlife-packed private concessions inside Hwange National Park.

Carol, Miriam and I have all visited these camps and love the area where Shaynie is now based.

Uneasy with her new proximity to wildlife, she resorts to earplugs at night. 'Sometimes it's best not to know how close the lions are,' she shivers.

I can't understand it. Their deep-throated bellows are among my most favourite sounds in the world; the closer the better.

I still need to visit Bulawayo every three months to get a stamp in my passport. For these visits I have the luxury of the use of Shaynie's flat in town, even though she's rarely there.

Barbara and her daughter Dee live in the flat next door, with Frank the landlord downstairs and an assortment of single folk who come and go. It's a cosy little crowd where everyone looks out for one another. Shaynie's sister CJ comes into town occasionally, and we often find ourselves sitting together on the outside staircase when the power goes off—which still happens just about every day—enjoying a companionable drink and a lively chat in the darkness.

CJ and her partner Herbie live and work on an out-of-the-way gold mine, and we compete for the best bush tale. CJ tells me about snakes and scorpions and spiders, of frosts flattening her veggie garden and of pesky wandering goats. Stray dogs pinch her *braai* meat, while vervets pinch my bananas. We text each other when we're in the bush, now that I'm finally able to use a mobile phone there (although the signal is still not reliable). We fantasise about delicious morsels and make fantasy invitations to meet in an hour or two for cheesecake and cappuccino, which are both in agonisingly short supply unless you live in Harare, on the other side of the country. We share the ecstasy of our first shower of rain, and the misery of spotting our first 'Kalahari Ferrari' of the season.

Shaynie's neighbour Barbara is an alien, a bit like ET. She is in fact state-less. In 2001, the Mugabe government decided that children of parents who were born in another country had to renounce their foreign citizenship within six months if they wished to remain a citizen of Zimbabwe. Barbara's mother was born in the United Kingdom and her father in South Africa.

Barbara was born in Zimbabwe. She holds no foreign citizenship and there-fore had nothing to renounce. Regardless, aged in her 50s, she suddenly found herself classed as an alien, no longer a Zimbabwean citizen, ineligible to vote and unable to acquire a new passport. Several hundreds of thousands of people, both white and black, overnight became aliens in the country of their birth, the only country they've ever called home.

'I'm a citizen of nowhere,' Barbara tells me with a laugh—because if you don't laugh, you're going to cry at the stupidity of it all.

'And here I am, hoping that one day I might be granted permanent residency in this country, and then citizenship,' I groan.

Barbara, Dee and I regularly walk the streets in town, to the conster-nation of the well-to-do whites. It's not the conventional thing to do. We play 'spot the white', and might see two or three others over the course of several hours. I wonder what they think might happen to them if they were to walk around too.

There's always someone on the streets trying to tempt you with their wares, from bananas to batteries and pot scourers to pillows. I'm used to the recurring call 'makiwa, makiwa' ('white person, white person') as I walk by, as well as 'sister', or 'aunty' and 'mama'. Sometimes I'm called 'Mama Elephant', which always makes me smile. But when a teenage boy calls me 'gogo', I almost trip over the tree root just ahead of me.

'You think I'm going to buy something from you when you call me granny?' I shriek in mock dismay. Gogo! Ouch.

'We're going to the Bend-down,' Barbara announces one morning. 'Would you like to join us?'

The street market is known by this name because you have to bend over and rummage through the vast piles of clothing. It's another place that white Zimbabweans don't often frequent; it's clearly not the sort of place to be seen. It is, however, the reason why there are so many well-dressed folk around Zimbabwe, even in the middle of nowhere.

Massive bales of clothing arrive from overseas, bought cheaply by vendors who then resell them at street markets. Most garments are second-hand (I prefer to think of them as pre-loved), but many are barely worn. I'm astounded by the range of well-known Australian, American and European labels available, which mean nothing to the vast majority of Zimbabweans, but you have to be prepared to spend a lot of time bent over and digging deep to find the treasures.

I sit on a bulging pile and sift through it for items. I leave contented with a long Geoff Bade skirt and beautiful De Luca top, having spent a couple of one-dollar notes for what, in the First World, would have cost me a couple of hundred. I don't know where I'll wear them—although I do from time to time dress up for sundowners with my four-legged friends. With a bottle of pink bubbly in a cooler bag beside me, and the soundtrack from *Out of Africa* ringing out from my laptop, I sit decadently on an edge of my cut-out roof, with bubbles in hand, until well after the sky fills with dazzling stars, while my elephant friends doze off around me. They seem to particularly enjoy the glorious instrumental *I had a Farm in Africa*, opening and closing their eyes so very slowly in time with its rhythm. It's good for my soul to be dressed up among them, to feel just a little bit classy for a few hours. The fact that I'm sitting on top of an awfully battered and rusted old vehicle doesn't matter at all. Nor does the occasional wet splosh of bat poop that lands on my stylish outfit.

Barbara and I often walk more than forty blocks a day carting supplies for me to take back to the bush. I buy fresh fruit and vegetables from the ladies with little pyramids of produce at their feet, sitting shoulder to shoulder along a designated street. *'Bonsella!'* they exclaim—'Gift!'—handing over an extra piece for free, encouraging me to come back and buy from them again. When this fresh supply runs out I'll live primarily on pasta and tinned fruit as I've done for the last ten years, although I have progressed from locally tinned tomato-and-onion mix to actual pasta sauce imported from South Africa. Pepper grinders can now be found, as well as an assortment of tinned cheese sprinkles. A box of good South African red is usually available these days too, and so my recurring pasta days are now less likely to make me gag.

Bulawayo is a needed change of pace for a few days, and a welcome opportunity to enjoy a drink and a laugh with friends, but there are too many people in the city and far too much noise. Fat from pizza and ice-cream, I am, all too soon, longing to be back in the bush with the elephants.

# FINDING ADWINA

## 2010

I learn new things about elephants every day, and am sometimes left with more questions than answers. When in the field, I quite frequently come across sizeable chunks of ivory lying on the ground, broken off in a clash of tusks or when being used as a lever. Perhaps the mineral-deficient Kalahari sand contributes to the number of breakages. All pieces, if you choose to pick them up, must be handed in to the appropriate authorities. I always pick them up whenever I see them, not trusting what others might do if they get their hands on them. Earlier in the day I'd picked up a smooth twenty-centimetre-long piece, which had appeared overnight around a pan, and I'm still driving with it on my dashboard.

I spot the L family in the distance, and hurry to check up on them. Lady is more excited than usual to see me. I pat my heart, as I've learnt to do, in a gesture of respect for her. Her dexterous trunk slithers inside my window and she grasps my steering wheel with her fingers. They move to mine, then to my face, and back to the steering wheel.

'Do you want to *drive* my vehicle today?' I ask her with a big grin.

The gaping tip of her trunk worms back towards my mouth, exposing two enormous moist nostrils. I'm reminded of a big spongy sea urchin as she exhales a stream of warm air, flecked with mud particles, onto my face. She takes my fingers in the fingers of her trunk and gives me an elephant handshake. Her pull is powerful and I struggle for a moment to release her grip.

Never allowing her to get the upper hand for long, I push her trunk out of my window. But today she is persistent. Her trunk snakes back inside with increased urgency. This is unusual behaviour. Even after a lively hello, Lady typically stands good-naturedly beside my door. Today she's on a mission. Her trunk is slithering around in front of me. Quickly, she locates what she is looking for—the piece of ivory.

Impulsively, I grab it before she does, unsure of what she's planning to do with it, but in a flash she pulls it from my hand. It eventually falls to the ground, where she proceeds to touch and smell it. Does ivory have a smell? How did she know the ivory was on my dashboard? Could it be ivory from an elephant she's acquainted with? Can she tell? Initially, she had seemed anxious about it. But once she'd investigated it, she lost all interest. Had she established that it was just a broken-off piece, and wasn't therefore from a dead elephant? Would she have reacted differently if I'd been carrying ivory extracted from a carcass?

I'm still coming across snared elephants, although thankfully not so frequently. Most recently it is Adwina from the A family who has a horrific wound caused by a snare around her back right leg. The first attempt to remove it had failed when the immobilisation dart bounced from her hide. Some darters are still learning about darting elephants, and nobody with more experience had been available that day. Slowed by her horrific injury, Adwina and her youngest calf had been wandering alone. I haven't been able to find Adwina since, despite searching every day.

A very pleasant and helpful couple named Esther and Hans are currently attached to the nearby Painted Dog project, which Greg still leads. Esther's been darting some elephants recently, with Hans at the wheel. She's particularly skilled and is always concerned with more than just darting: she appreciates input about the family groups, always keen to know who she's darting, and later how the elephant is faring. I enjoy working with her. She's been on standby for weeks now to dart Adwina, once I manage to find her again.

I'm at Kanondo, where I often spot snared animals. The anti-poaching team doesn't typically find many snare lines here—the elephants and other wildlife pick up snares elsewhere—but Kanondo is a large open area and it's easier to catch a glimpse of snared animals as they wander by. It's why I spend time driving around this area every day, checking on all of the animals that show up.

At long last I spot Adwina's head protruding from the scrub. I can't see her leg, but I know immediately that it is her. She's completely alone, slowly making her way away from the pan. My heart pounds and my hands shake. I fumble with my mobile phone. If we lose her this time around, she may die from her injury before we find her again.

'She's finally here, Esther, at Kanondo,' I blurt into my mobile pretending to be calmer than I am. There's no time for more talk as Esther and Hans need to quickly pack their 4x4 and race the fifteen kilometres to join me.

A few minutes later, I'm back on my mobile. 'Esther, she's already moving off into thicker bush,' I warn.

I strategically position my vehicle in Adwina's path and try to encourage her to stay put. But she is restless.

I'm back on my mobile yet again. 'I'm not sure that I can hold her much longer. Please, we need a tracker,' I say. I know this will delay their arrival, but it will give us a better chance of success.

I circle around and keep herding Adwina back and forth, back and forth, trying to prevent her from crossing the road that I'm on and heading into thicker bush. In desperation I call for another vehicle to help me keep an eye on her.

That vehicle eventually arrives, but it's too late. Adwina runs across the road that I'm on. I can hear Esther's vehicle pulling up and I drive quickly towards her, needing to get to the next road to prevent Adwina from crossing that one as well. Hans is driving and Esther is as calm, cool and professional as always. Thank goodness one of us is so composed. She's about to start preparing the dart. The tracker with them is called Mkhalalwa. I leave them to get on with it and race off towards the next road.

By the time the dart is ready Adwina is still somewhere between these two sandy roads. But the bush is horribly thick. We're all looking in the wrong direction when an elephant eventually crosses. I catch a glimpse of it, and manage to confirm that it's Adwina. Mkhalalwa quickly leads Esther and Hans after her on foot.

I can hear sounds of elephants everywhere and the risk of them walking straight into one in the thick bush is high. Eventually, I see all three retreating back towards our vehicles. My hands cover my eyes in disappointment.

'We just can't miss her twice,' I whisper to myself.

It's not practical for this darting team to wait around, since the chances of Adwina returning immediately to the open area are low. We wait together for a while longer, but all we see are lone bulls.

I return to Kanondo alone, in the desperate hope that she will reappear. A game-drive vehicle with American tourists arrives, and so I show the safari guide the photographs that I've just taken of Adwina and ask him to keep a close eye out for her.

Meanwhile, the gorgeous Whole and her family have appeared in the open. There's a bateleur in the sky. A spirit messenger. I momentarily think of Andy. It seems impossible that he's been dead for ten years. 'Please help us find her,' I murmur, looking skywards.

I drive with the tourist vehicle to the mineral licks, where Whole, Whosit, Willa, Whoever, Wishful and others enjoy the minerals and then surround our vehicles. I share information about their family relationships and introduce the tourists to all of my favourites. I explain that the elephants are very familiar with me and my vehicle and know my voice well, but that as strangers they must sit in silence and never attempt to touch them. The Americans are visibly moved by this close encounter.

'I could just cry,' a middle-aged man whispers.

Then, suddenly, Adwina reappears in the open just a few hundred metres away. She's come back to splash soothing mud on her wound.

'Thank you, thank you,' I say, gazing once again towards the sky.

If I thought my heart was pounding earlier, it is now about to jump out of my chest. One phone call and Esther, Hans and Mkhalalwa are immediately on their way back.

Adwina does it to me again though. She starts to move off well before the darting team arrive. I dash back to the same road that I was on earlier, having asked the safari guide and his guests to remain still and to monitor her from there, which they do willingly. Once again I herd Adwina back and forth, back and forth, trying to keep her from disappearing into the dense bush. But it feels like I'm going to lose her yet again.

I hear Esther's vehicle roaring towards us and glimpse through the bush the safari guests waving coloured clothing in the air, to help guide them in. Hans can now see where Adwina is, even though there are by now scores of elephants in the area. Esther knows that I'm struggling to hold her at bay and, like me, fears that we'll lose her again if she crosses the road. She has one chance to successfully get the dart in but her distance from Adwina is awfully close to the limit of the gun's 40-metre range and thick bush is preventing them from moving closer. Adwina isn't staying still, but with calm skill Esther leans out the window of her 4x4 and fires. The dart hits, albeit a little precariously, on the side of Adwina's leathery rump.

Through the leafy bush I can see the pink-feathered dart protruding from her backside and I breathe a huge sigh of relief. My mobile phone rings. It's Esther, confirming that the dart's in, and asking me to keep up with Adwina to see where she falls. Adwina's head and trunk eventually start to droop while I peer at my trembling hands, thinking that I could do with a bit of sedation myself.

In a few minutes she's down. We hurry in our two vehicles towards her fallen body and the operation is immediately in full swing. There are elephants all around us, but fortunately none are close family members and so they're considerately keeping their distance. The injury is horrific. The length of copper wire is embedded deeply, the wound a great deal worse than it was a month ago. There's no skin left on the lower portion of her leg at all. Esther and Hans cut the wire and treat the wound. I tip water over Adwina's ear to keep her temperature stable and Mkhalalwa holds her trunk, ensuring that her breathing is not obstructed.

I invite the game-drive vehicle to come in quietly, to witness this life-saving procedure. The wound is soon treated and we all move off so that Esther can safely administer the reversal drug alone. My whole body is shaking; it's impossible for me to relax until Adwina's back on her feet.

And soon she is. The whole procedure took less than 30 minutes, from the time the dart hit to Adwina getting to her feet once again. Five long weeks of searching came to a close with just minutes of frantic, compassionate teamwork. Adwina wanders off, a little dazed, across the road that she's now welcome to travel without interference from me. Her family's still nowhere in sight, nor is her youngest calf, but I feel confident that she'll be okay. Once the wire has been removed, the chances of full recovery are high no matter how dreadful the wound.

It's a time for celebration and we all sit in our vehicles next to the recently scooped Kanondo pan, full of water from the wet season, surrounded by the W family who have chosen to stick around and help us celebrate. Esther's reward for the day's effort is the opportunity to meet the beloved Whole. It is however Whole's daughter, the cheeky Whosit, who insists on standing right beside Esther's open window.

I stay on after the others depart, alone under the almost-full moon, sipping a beer handed to me from the game-drive vehicle's cooler box. Whosit's firstborn, Wish, places his trunk inside my open window and proceeds to give my 4x4 a little shake. A tad naughty perhaps, but it makes me laugh out loud just the same.

I make my own forlorn wish: that we never have to do another snare removal.

A few days later I'm out with guests from Brisbane, who I've known for many years. We raised funds for elephant conservation together back when I lived there. We stumble upon Adwina, who is once again at Kanondo splashing mud on her de-snared leg. She is still apart from her family, but she is looking much better. One side of the wound is horribly deep and raw, and a little blood is still oozing from it, but she is now putting full weight on her leg.

It is another three weeks before I see Adwina again, and this time she's reunited with her four-year-old son, Ade. This is a very positive development; Ade no longer needs to be looked after by family members. Having lost so much skin on the lower portion of her leg, there is nothing to protect the flesh, and her wound is taking a worryingly long time to show signs of real healing. She bathes it in mud and dust continually, helping Mother Nature along.

The next time I see Adwina she is still limping, but she's surrounded by all the members of her family. She is going to be okay.

There's always one battle or another going on. Inside Hwange National Park, animals are being rounded up in pairs, reportedly as a gift for the president of North Korea, who is a close ally of President Mugabe. Once news of this shipment breaks, the press dub the operation 'Mugabe's Ark'. Two young elephants are among those who have been removed from their families, destined for a life in captivity.

I know that if I want to survive here, I can't be too vocal about this, although I quietly make my views known. Joyce Poole—with decades of knowledge and now head of a Europe-based NGO called Elephant Voices—gets involved to try to save the elephants from export. With all that is now known about elephant family bonds, intelligence and grieving, the abduction of elephants from their families is generally viewed as inhumane and unacceptable. Public outrage is widespread. A number of other animal pairs have already been captured, among them giraffes, zebras, warthogs, hyenas and rock hyrax. Conservation groups in Harare get involved, voicing their concern for all of these animals. Somewhat surprisingly, the director general of Parks (who reports to Minister Francis Nhema) eventually announces that the deal has been cancelled and the animals will be released. Zimbabwe is not known for bowing to public pressure, and so I'm pleasantly surprised. The two elephants can't simply be released back into the park, since they're too young to survive without their families, who can't be identified. Instead, they're transferred to the captive facility in Victoria Falls that Gavin had managed before his death (now renamed Wild Horizon's Wildlife Sanctuary), where they will be integrated into a makeshift family, and at some future time, hopefully, returned to the wild.

I'm heartened to know that, sometimes, Zimbabwe does the right thing.

A film-crew from Natural History Unit Africa is set to arrive to make a documentary about my work and relationships with the Presidential Elephants. The crew has successfully applied to the appropriate authorities for filming permits and it's all systems go. I'm not sure how I'll cope having a five-person film-crew with me every day for what could be several months, accustomed as I am to leading a relatively solitary bush life. I've only met Kira, the South African-based documentary producer, briefly once before. She was in Zimbabwe last year documenting the release of some rehabilitated elephants into Hwange National Park. These elephants had been captive and had been abused; a black mark on the already controversial elephant-ride industry. The SPCA (Society for the Prevention of Cruelty to Animals) had successfully intervened in that cruel debacle and managed to secure the elephants' release back to the wild. I was invited into the park with them, to witness this release. Following this happy event, Kira asked to interview me on camera.

An international documentary will certainly help with my mission to increase awareness of the Presidential Elephants. If I can entice an even wider audience to fall in love with these elephants, then their ongoing safety and survival might be more assured. There can't be any pre-prepared scripts to work to in such a wild environment, and how the footage will be edited is entirely out of my hands. I've obtained assurances however that neither Zimbabwe or my ongoing work with the elephants will be compromised, and I have to trust that these promises are honoured.

Once news of the documentary gets around, those dragons emerge once more.

I'm presented with a document from the group that currently owns the land where my *rondavel* is located. It announces they will evict me from my tiny home of ten years, and try to stop me from patrolling the estate, unless I sign what they have termed a 'partnership agreement'. They're demanding that I turn myself into some sort of unrewarded marketeer, contracted exclusively to them. If I don't agree to this, they say I will have to leave.

This is the same group that I scooped pans for only last year and who, despite having me on their doorstep for the past nine years, have never shown any interest in working with me to conserve, promote or market the Presidential Elephants. Now, suddenly, they're demanding exclusive, unpaid rights to my services.

The 'partnership agreement' insists that I promote their lodge as the preferred destination for all Presidential Elephant tourists. It requires that I must serve only their interests, and that I must never 'provide service', 'advertise' or 'promote' anybody else. It also introduces a clause allowing them to give me only 30 days' notice to vacate my *rondavel*, which they can do at any time. If I don't sign on to this 'partnership', they will try to halt my work altogether.

It is soon made clear to me that there's no room for negotiation. It's very evident that this group is trying to ensure that it alone benefits from the documentary, which I simply can't stomach. These elephants are meant to be the nation's flagship herd after all. I have seven days to sign their document or I must leave within 30 days.

I try to phone Ministers Nhema and Mutasa, but neither is available. And then like a bolt of lightning out of the blue, my decision is immediately clear to me. I email that I will not be signing their pathetic document.

'If they want a dancing bear,' I say to Carol over the phone, 'they'd do better to try the circus.'

As distressing and disheartening as this all is, it's the push I need to finally get out of the living conditions that I've come close to loathing over the past few years. I'm tired of living with constant booming voices and blaring music, filthy grounds and rubbish pits that I spend hours tidying and sanitising every month. There are light-fingered children, with items regularly disappearing from my 4x4 and garden. When there's no water, human faeces, topped with toilet paper, have been known to appear in the grounds.

'But that is baboon,' I'm assured by one lady.

'Baboon?' I ask gently, with my eyebrows raised. 'So baboons use toilet paper?'

It is people's indifference to all of this that disappoints me most of all. It is not the same place that I moved into so many years ago. You only have to look around to see that. Like much of the country, everything looks broken.

One lodge offers me a temporary option on its grounds, but the offer is withdrawn just days before I'm due to move there after it receives veiled threats from the same group who presented me with the partnership agreement, and who are now trying to ensure that I have nowhere to go.

Finding alternative accommodation isn't going to be easy. I have nowhere to move to, no way to transport what I own, and no clue about what I will do next. I give many of my things away, sell a few pieces of furniture for the pittance that I can get for them in the bush, and burn what is of no use to anyone else and can't be carried. I decide to store my 30-year-old 4x4—which won't likely make it to Bulawayo in one piece—at my friend Henry's property in nearby Gwayi. Henry lives in South Africa but runs a humanitarian project on this land. His wildlife-loving son, Caleb, was just eight years old when they cornered me soon after my arrival in Hwange, eager to hear about the elephants, and have been friends and keen supporters of mine ever since. Somebody is trying to claim their land too but hopefully my vehicle will be okay sitting there for a while. A new neighbour called Craig thoughtfully offers to help me transport what I can to Bulawayo to store in Shaynie's dining room.

I will never see my sausage trees produce flowers and fruit after all.

I let the filmmakers know that I have no choice but to pull out of the documentary. They make it clear that there's no story without me. Colleagues encourage me to stay on a little longer and participate, but my land access now needs to be sorted out by the ministers in Harare. And I don't feel confident that I can appear happy and positive on film under the current circumstances.

I'm not ready just yet, and I realise it will take time, but I know that I will eventually rebuild. I'm simply not going to give them the satisfaction of doing anything less.

# MUGABE'S CAVALCADE

## 2010

After spending weeks in Bulawayo at Shaynie's flat, I travel by bus to Harare to help Carol celebrate her birthday and to try and relax after this awfully unsettling period. I've decided that I also need to look for a replacement vehicle. My faithful 4x4, currently sitting under a tarpaulin in Gwayi, has served me well, but it's decrepit after a decade of field work. What's more, its fuel consumption has become a nightmare with the hikes in petrol prices, and it currently has no brakes at all and a shattered back window after I recently reversed, tired and distracted, into the low-hanging branch of a tree that I swear hadn't been there the day before. If I am to return to Hwange, I will have to purchase something else.

But first, Carol takes me back to the beautiful Bvumba Mountains, the hidden jewel in Zimbabwe's crown, which I visited previously with Dinks and Shaynie. A visit to Tony's coffee shop is on the itinerary. Carol loves this classy cafe, loves Tony, loves the scrumptious selection of cakes always on offer, loves the list of hot drinks that's almost a metre long and especially loves the truly divine hot chocolates.

'I am absolutely not going to pay US$10 for a single slice of cake,'

I declare. 'That's an awful lot of money to spend on one slice of cake, especially when I've earnt no salary for the past ten years.'

Carol decides that I simply must have a piece for her birthday. 'My treat,' she decides.

The slices we order are enormous. And absolutely delicious. It's many years since I've tasted anything quite so good. I unashamedly demolish my entire slab of chocolate-laden cheesecake, unlike the tourists at the table behind us, and am tempted to ask if I can take *their* leftovers home with me in a doggy bag! I contact both Dinks and Shaynie, bragging about what they're missing out on.

We waddle back to our cottage, nestled high on a ridge, with soothing water views below and luxuriant forest all around. I plonk myself down on a comfy chair outside, wrap a duvet around me to keep out the crisp air of the late afternoon, put my feet up and settle down with a glass of red wine to enjoy the changing colours of another mesmerising African sunset. Samango monkeys scamper unseen through the treetops and a red-chested cuckoo sings his 'quid pro quo' song over and over and over again. For the first time in two years I find that I want to write seriously again, and it is here that I draft the preface for another book. The Bvumba has managed to quieten the growing rage within me.

Life here would be just perfect, I think to myself, if only there were some elephants to enjoy . . . and if only I'd managed to get that doggy bag of cake.

During the weeks that I'm in Harare on the hunt for a replacement 4x4, Carol and I twice encounter President Mugabe's cavalcade. It is a display of utter extravagance. Everyone knows the telltale sounds of their approach and drivers scurry nervously to get off the road. Police motorbikes zoom past first, with lights blazing and sirens blaring, sending shivers down my spine, as traffic is halted at every intersection. Then a string of police cars rocket past, their sirens also blaring. Next comes a knot of speeding black limousines, with blackened windows, driving two abreast. One presumably has the president inside. A troop of soldiers in sturdy helmets, sitting alertly on the open back of a truck, their machine guns at the ready, zips past next. And finally comes an ambulance, just in case, emergency lights flashing. All of this at breakneck speed, and in perfect formation.

'And all I want is a vehicle that isn't 30 years old,' I groan to Carol, wondering if the president himself, sitting right there inside one of those posh black limos, remembers anything about the Presidential Elephants.

Before being evicted, I drafted a reaffirmation of the Presidential Decree in the hope that President Mugabe might agree to sign it. But I don't yet know what level within Minister Nhema's office and the Office of the President my proposal has reached, and if anyone there really understands its benefits. I figure that if we can get his signature on something reaffirming the Presidential Elephants' importance to the nation, the challenges besieging them might lessen. It's a long shot and I'm not getting my hopes up, but it's worth a try. Now though, I need to get my accommodation and transportation problems sorted out before chasing this up.

The end of 2010 is fast approaching, and there are power cuts almost every day, sometimes for as long as fifteen hours. This is even more frustrating than usual. To top off the year, reports of elephants being killed by sport-hunters *inside* Hwange National Park are now being openly acknowledged by some Parks personnel. Photographic tourists and hunters, together in the same areas, simply don't mix. The whole situation is shameful, to say the least. There is little festivity in this holiday season, and I spend time wondering if Hwange can even be called a national park while hunting is occurring within it.

'Santa clearly doesn't know where Zimbabwe is,' I text wearily to Henry in South Africa.

He responds as quick as a flash. 'Santa doesn't go to Zimbabwe anymore. He's scared somebody will shoot his reindeers.'

After no success at the second-hand car dealerships, Carol's mechanic sends out word to the local 4x4 club that I'm on the hunt for a reliable vehicle that isn't too expensive. I eventually settle on a 1989 Land Cruiser wagon. A slightly younger vehicle with a shorter wheelbase might have suited me better, but I console myself that at least there's plenty of room for me to sleep in the back, if I ever find myself homeless again. The engine has recently been rebuilt and it promises better fuel consumption. I decide that I'll get the roof cut out to give it a similar feel to what I'm used to. Every purchase of a used vehicle has to go through not only a change of ownership and a tax payment, but a new set of number plates as well. This process takes weeks, and it is indeed well over a month before all of my necessary paperwork is approved and returned, even with constant chasing.

Zimbabwean bureaucracy is incredibly frustrating for everyone these days, and no longer amusing. Once again I can't help but wonder why I don't just leave. Like me, Carol has been talking of leaving for years now and continues to assure me that she'll soon be on her way. But deep down inside we both know we love it, still.

Little is improving under the Unity government though. People everywhere remain poor and desperate, despite Zimbabwe's wealth of platinum, gold, coal, chrome and nickel. Diamond deposits, believed to be the second largest anywhere in the world, have recently been discovered. Yet little money finds its way to the Treasury.

'You know who the mines minister is these days, don't you?' Carol asks.

I do. The fabulously rich ex-governor, now cabinet minister—who accused me of being an Australian government spy—holds this post.

# GRANTHAM

## 2011

The new year arrives and I am still in Harare, finalising alternative accommodation in Hwange and the paperwork for my 4x4. I'm missing the elephants, but seriously wondering how much longer I can possibly stay in Zimbabwe. Then, news of a disaster in Australia reaches me.

On 10 January, floods ripped through the Lockyer Valley, where I'm from. A wall of water eight metres tall hit Grantham with deadly ferocity, smashing into homes in this small farming community where I grew up. This was no ordinary flood. It was described as an inland tsunami, arriving with deadly speed and fury. Some residents are reported to have been swept to their deaths.

Nobody has been able to reach my parents. 'Why haven't they evacuated Mum and Dad?' I blurt into the phone to my sister Deborah. 'Just because their house is still standing doesn't necessarily mean they're okay.'

Deborah is only 30 kilometres away from Grantham, in Toowoomba, although she may as well be in Africa with me. All roads leading into Grantham are closed. Phone lines are down. My eldest sister Genevieve lives closer, in the small township of Placid Hills, on a hill right next to Grantham. She can see helicopters making rooftop rescues, hampered by pouring rain, but the magnitude of the tragedy isn't yet understood by anybody.

'There are obviously others in more urgent need,' Genevieve texts.

Far away, and not comprehending the enormity of the situation, this makes little sense to me. The torrent of water that levelled the town had hit on Monday afternoon. A second flood hit on Tuesday. On Wednesday afternoon we still don't know if our parents are okay. Genevieve can see that water levels have receded in some parts of the cordoned-off town, but still has no information. Finally, in darkness, at 10.30 p.m. on Wednesday, rescue personnel reach my parents' home, which is built on stilts, and confirm that they're okay, although they're without electricity, drinking water or plumbing. They will be evacuated by boat the next morning.

It has been an emotional and nerve-racking time. Compared to others, my parents have been relatively lucky. At the height of the flooding there had been two metres of raging water underneath their house. The violently swirling floodwaters were full of huge trees, concrete water tanks, vehicles, whole houses and masses of other debris. Their own house could easily have been knocked from its stumps, with them inside. But with tall hedges and trees all around their home they couldn't see much of this. Only now do they learn the fate of their friends and neighbours, and of the many houses that were destroyed or floated away, of the myriad vehicles thrown through the water like matchsticks, of people stranded inside these houses and cars screaming for help, of precious lives lost.

A convoy of army trucks rolls into Grantham to join the police and other emergency services already there. The town is designated a crime scene while the gruesome search for bodies gets underway.

Nine days after this catastrophe the 350 or so residents are finally allowed into what is left of their homes, but it will be many more long weeks before my parents can return to live in theirs. The once-picturesque town resembles a war zone, smashed to smithereens. On 26 January, instead of celebrating Australia Day, a memorial service is held in Grantham.

A week later I fly out from Zimbabwe and arrive in my hometown, which is still in lockdown. After weeks of cleaning and clearing by hundreds of soldiers and emergency-services personnel I still can't believe what I'm seeing. The scale of the devastation is shocking. It looks like a bomb has gone off.

The Lockyer Valley is now being referred to as the valley of lost souls. My parents' house is indeed still there, perched high on the wooden stilts that saved their lives. A kilometre away where there was once a general store, a fuel station and a pub, there are piles of rubble, deserted buildings and eerie spaces where homes had been. It feels like a ghost town, especially at night when dark shells of houses haunt the road through the forlorn little town. I'm not sure how people will recover from this. Politicians remark on the community's 'toughness' and I'm thankful to have grown up in this neighbourhood.

My parents are still taking stock of their losses and their good luck. They'd received a warning phone call just ten minutes before the floodwater reached Grantham. Not realising the fury of what was heading for them, my 77-year-old mum jumped into her car to take it to higher ground; another vehicle was organised to bring her back home. But by the time she was making her way back, the initial stages of the raging torrent had arrived, and she found herself waist-deep in wild water before managing to get safely back to the house. Had she been just a few minutes later, it would likely have been tragically different.

Nor was I spared the devastation. My entire pre-Zimbabwe life was stored underneath my parents' house in a shed my dad built for me, with a raised cement floor. Everything was stored above the highest flood level he had ever known but this was a flood like no other. All of my possessions had sat drenched in filthy water and stinking, thick sludge for nine days while no one was allowed into the town. They were sodden, ruined and broken. Genevieve and Deborah had collected what was salvageable and painstakingly washed and scrubbed the little that could be saved.

Scores of beautifully framed photographs and original prints and paintings were destroyed, along with hundreds of books and thousands of photos spanning nearly fifty years of my life. And then there were the thousands of enlarged photographs of the elephants stored here too, along with years of video footage. Yet a half ream of useless printer paper was untouched and still gleaming white. I couldn't even work out why I'd packed it. Also perfectly intact was an envelope full of insurance photos of my household contents for annual insurance that I'd paid religiously over the last 25 years. I'd cancelled it just three years ago, when donor funds had dried up and buying fuel to enable daily patrols of the estate seemed a better use of my ever-dwindling savings.

I pick up a gleaming black mug and stare at it with a sinking heart. It reads LIFE'S A BITCH. THEN YOU DIE.

I hadn't actually lived in Grantham for 30 years, and hadn't used any of my household items for the ten years that I'd been in Zimbabwe. And I know that there are lots of people worse off than me. During my years in Hwange, material possessions have become far less important to me, but I still feel a very real sense of personal loss. It's the thought of all those irreplaceable photographs and video footage, and books and letters and diaries and journals, that pains me the most, along with knowing that I now have very little to fall back on.

The debris around my parents' house had been so thick that the tall back staircase was completely blocked and there'd been deep, thick, stinking silt everywhere. Before I arrived, a 30-strong Army contingent was assigned for a day to help my parents with their cleanup. In Africa, the word 'army' often evokes fear, but in Australia, I have to remind myself, these personnel are admired as highly trained soldiers and peacekeepers who expertly assist with search-and-rescue and disaster relief. They helped my parents greatly in their efforts to return to some degree of normality. But dramas continued for my family. My mum, attempting to get her beloved garden back to some semblance of order, dropped a lump of concrete onto her foot, smashing three toes. My niece, Rebecca, who had only recently moved to north Queensland, found herself directly in the path of Cyclone Yasi, which devastated the township of Tully. My nephew, Matthew, in flooded outback Queensland, was stricken by a waterborne disease associated with cattle and found himself recovering in hospital.

Karen, my hippo friend, emails that perhaps the flood is a sign that Zimbabwe is where I'm meant to be, where I'm meant to stay. But I am not nearly so sure, despite struggling with First World life. I can't get the microwave to start; I can't work the iron with its strange steamer attachment; I don't know which button to press to answer the phone, before realising that I don't have to press any button at all. I feel unsure of so much, and strangely insecure.

Then comes news of more shocking devastation. On 22 February, just five weeks after the Grantham catastrophe, Christchurch, New Zealand, home to my friend Eileen's family, is hit by an earthquake. Close to two hundred are feared dead and much of the city is in ruins. When I lived in Auckland I travelled often to Christchurch on business and knew it well. Eileen's family are shaken but unhurt. Even so, my emotions are already too close to the surface and, especially while watching news reports on television, I find myself struggling with a dreadfully heavy heart.

I need to go and walk on a beach.

When I arrive in Maroochydore on the Sunshine Coast it is raining. It doesn't matter though. I don't need sunshine, I just need some peace.

Standing still in waist-deep water, letting the foamy waves wash over me, I breathe deeply and feel months of stress roll off my shoulders. For a few minutes an incredibly bright and beautiful double rainbow envelops the rolling ocean. I'm startled when the head of a cormorant pops up in front of me. For a second I imagine it's a sea snake. He's trying to fish in these choppy seas, his sleek, agile form ducking and diving under the waves. The name Maroochydore comes from the Aboriginal word *Muru-kutchida*, meaning 'home of the black swan'. I don't see any black swans, but the graceful black cormorant won't be forgotten in a hurry.

As I walk the beach, I find it difficult to even recollect my life in land-locked Zimbabwe; a life a million miles from this peaceful beach; a life that I'm not feeling particularly keen to return to. I recall the words of a poem I once read. They described the *dash* between the dates of birth and death inscribed on a gravestone as all that really matters. This rings more true now than ever before. Is Zimbabwe where I want to continue to spend my dash? I really don't know. I certainly don't want my life to pass me by feeling constantly unsettled. Yet despite everything, I do know that what is still most important to me right now is my elephant family in Hwange.

The week after I leave Grantham and fly back to Zimbabwe, my little devastated hometown is once again in lockdown. This time its residents are being treated to a right royal visit. Soon to marry in spectacular style, Prince William arrives in this tiny town to lift their spirits. Known to have a soft spot for elephants, Prince William is royal patron of a UK conservation group called Tusk Trust. If Zimbabwe and its president weren't so widely condemned, I'd have tried to make a plan to get a letter of introduction into his hands.

# STARTING ANEW

## 2011

I fly from Brisbane into Harare, wondering what the rest of the year might have in store for me. I need to collect my recently purchased Land Cruiser from Carol and drive it to Bulawayo, and then on to Hwange. Call me crazy, but I'm going back to start again.

Not everything has gone to plan in my absence. The cruiser's roof has been cut out nicely, but the roof-cover is a disaster. When it's raining, it is like Victoria Falls inside my vehicle. I'll have to completely redo 'my hat', as my indigenous friends like to call this fitted tarpaulin.

The lodge that Val once owned has been through several changes of ownership over the past ten years and is now called Miombo Safari Camp. It's where I'm heading back to live. Although more uncertain now than ever about what might lie ahead, I feel a sense of déjà vu as I drive back. I pass a beautiful big baobab by the roadside, which signals that my turn-off is close. There's a bateleur in the sky. I like to think that it is Andy, encouraging me on.

I'm incredibly fortunate that the lodge owners have offered me this cottage free of charge, so long as I make it liveable. Nobody (at least nobody human) has lived in it for many years. I mean, how bad can it be? Right?

A couple of attractive pot plants have thoughtfully been placed at my front door. When I open it though, a pungent smell of urine hits me right between the eyes. I involuntarily wrinkle my nose and walk in. It's a proper little house, nothing like the tiny one-room *rondavel* in which I'd lived for so many years. For that, I'm extremely grateful.

A sizeable white bucket, almost half full of water, is sitting ominously on the floor. High above it, perched under the A-framed thatched roof, sits an old geyser (the Zimbabwean name for a hot-water system), and a 44-gallon drum (which is the water tank). One or both of these is sending frequent fat drops of water down into the bucket below.

There's another worrying puddle of water around the base of the toilet and yet another underneath the nearby sink. I peer into the shower. I can't imagine ever feeling clean after bathing in there.

'Easily fixed,' I reassure myself, looking around for something a little more encouraging. I glance up, and cringe. Patches of sunlight are visible through the rotting thatched roof. I breathe deeply, and tell myself that all will be fine, eventually.

As night falls, an army of giant praying mantises flutter in through a broken window. I generally like these gentle insects, but this is a winged invasion. I decide to shower and take refuge under a mosquito net. The hot water is cold, and while dancing a jig under the chilly flow I manage to stand on a scorpion. It's a tiny little fellow and as I grasp the soft ball of my foot, cursing, I remember that it's the small ones that are usually the most lethal.

I flop into bed—a real bed, in a bedroom that is mine, for the first time in ten years (even if it doesn't have a door). I tuck my mosquito net in especially tightly all around me. My throbbing foot, combined with the continuous drip, drip, drip from the peculiar geyser setup, and a horde of overly active rodents, means that sleep does not come easily.

Craig is still around and has thoughtfully offered to help me settle in. He collects Amos, his odd-job man, to help too. First, they disconnect the geyser and drum and lower them to the ground. There are hoses and pipes everywhere. It eventually becomes apparent that it's the drum which has been leaking steadily onto the wooden support rails and down onto the floor.

'Arrhhh, this drum, madam,' Amos announces, 'it is dead.'

Drums are incredibly difficult to come by right now. 'There are no other drums, Amos. You need to try to fix it,' I insist.

'But you can't fix dead, madam,' Amos declares.

Well, how can I argue with that?

I encourage him on regardless. He uses a soldering stick, straight out of the red-hot coals of a fire he has made in my front yard, to apply silver solder to hole after hole after tiny hole.

'Arrhhh, but there are too many leaks, madam,' Amos keeps muttering quietly as he works away at it for hours.

'Let's get this all back up in the roof,' Craig ultimately urges, visibly tired after a day of similar challenges in my bathroom.

The next day Amos goes off to the township called Hwange (a polluted, rather smelly, coal-mining settlement 70 kilometres away, which I try to avoid) to purchase a pane of glass to mend the broken window in my living room. It's just a standard size but before leaving, he measures and re-measures it methodically. He reappears carrying a compact parcel. Craig walks in front of him, shaking his head.

'You don't want to know what's in that package,' Craig mutters.

I glance down at the parcel wrapped sturdily with both cardboard and tape. If that's the window glass it certainly isn't the right size.

'That's the glass?' I ask tentatively.

Of course it is the glass! Amos decided that it would be easier to carry if he had it cut in half.

'Amos! How does this glass fit my window nicely now?' I challenge.

'You just put putty across the middle, madam,' says Amos. 'And also use Trinepon glue.'

I close my eyes, and bite down hard on my tongue. Yes, I am now certain that I'm back in the Hwange bush. I think of John. Trinepon—Trinepon glue, Trinepon putty, Trinepon plastic steel—had been his universal fix-it-all too.

Soon it's time to move on to the roof problem. I need a young man named Thabani, a thatcher who lives just down the road in Dete.

'Please Amos, will you ask Thabani to come and talk to me tomorrow?'

'Yes, madam. That is no problem, madam.'

All of this 'madam' stuff makes me feel 200 years old. When I ask Amos to call me Sharon, or better still *Mandlovu*, he insists that it's much more polite to call me madam and that's what he continues to do.

After yet another night of busy rats and mice (my rodent intruders come in so many different shapes and sizes that I can't help imagining that I'll succumb to bubonic plague), Thabani arrives, bright-eyed and hopeful of some well-paid work.

'This roof, *Mandlo*, it needs to come off. It is rotten,' Thabani exclaims.

'No, Thabani, for now you just need to patch it for me, please.'

It'll be another two months before the local ladies begin their annual ritual of cutting thatching grass in the *veld*. There's little thatch left in the area from last season and certainly not enough to cover my entire roof. Right now, still unsure of what might lie ahead, I'm not prepared to invest in a complete rethatching job anyway.

'But *Mandlo*, this roof it is very little all over,' Thabani insists.

'Yes, Thabani, I know. It's rotten and it's thin. But for now we have to just patch it, even though there are giant rats in it too.'

'Rats?' Thabani queries, his eyes shifting skywards.

And then, precisely on cue, the performance commences. There we all are, Thabani, Craig, Amos and me, standing in the living area and gazing up, watching a huge rat cavorting on the wooden beams.

'Look at the tail on that thing,' Amos urges.

'I think it likes to be looking at the stars up there through those holes,' offers Thabani.

By now I can only roll my eyes and groan. 'Please, Thabani, get a thatch cap on this roof by tomorrow afternoon,' I plead.

Craig's early morning arrivals are becoming routine. It's no longer 'Sit back, relax, pull up a spider' or 'Sit back, relax, pull up a snake'. Now I welcome people with 'Pull up a rat'!

Craig comes armed with tools and paint and putty and cement . . . and rat poison.

I've bought clay birdbaths from the roadside in nearby Gwayi. Craig helps me place them in my front yard. Why am I not surprised when neither of them holds water for longer than an hour? I also bought a couple of new owl- and elephant-shaped clay planters. I wander over to the lodge, bucket in hand, to collect a little soil since everything around my cottage appears to be pure sand. As I use my hands to scoop up some dirt, a wriggling baby cobra slithers right beside my fingers.

It's 2 p.m. on my sixth day back in Hwange and I badly need some red wine. Forget the glass, by now I'm ready to drink straight from the bottle.

My cottage still smells of urine—rat urine as it turns out—so in desperation I go with Craig to Hwange town to buy disinfectant, air freshener, and more rat poison. On the way back we stop to buy watermelons by the roadside. In Australia you might find honesty boxes beside crates of produce on the roadside. Here, before your engine is even switched off, you're mobbed by half a dozen or more dishevelled folk, frenzied by lack of business, all desperate to sell a single melon, a handful of baobab fruit, or tomatoes from enamel dishes. I also buy a hand-made wooden chair with a classy elephant carved into its back, hoping the wood has been legally obtained.

By Day 10, my cottage is looking more liveable. Poor Craig and Amos are exhausted, and I'm thrilled. I now have mended windows and locks, a tiled shower tray and hand-built towel rack, a welded gate and security bars, a painted front door and shower, a cemented doorstep, functional power outlets, a working geyser, a working toilet and sink, not to mention birdbaths that don't leak. I also have a tidy thatched roof and polished cement floor.

Life is good. Even the rat population is gradually declining. I decide to keep my rubber thongs that have deep rodent teeth marks all around their outer edges as a souvenir of what I arrived to.

It's a full moon, and I sit on my doorstep with a glass of red wine feeling a deep sense of satisfaction. After all of these harrowing, and often hilarious, days, I no longer feel compelled to drink straight from the bottle.

But at two o'clock that morning I'm sitting bolt upright in bed. 'Oh man. Are you kidding me? What now?' I mutter.

Bats. Now I have bats. Two of these pint-sized creatures fly overhead, around and around and around. (Perhaps I'll end up dying of rabies instead of bubonic plague!)

The next day is décor day. I welcome Craig with, 'Sit back, relax, pull up a *bat*.'

There's not much relaxing going on here though. We set to work and use buckets of crack-filler and paint, and then drill holes for pictures and curtains. I arrange brightly coloured African fabrics and cushions, dust on layers of Doom Blue Death insecticide (I can't imagine anything surviving a name like that), make 'snake blockers' for my doors, dig and cement a *braai* pit and some birdbaths and ponds outside in the rock hard earth, and attach my *Thandeka Mandlovu* signs to the outside wall. Craig also sets to work on painting an elephant—Whole, my favourite W family elephant—on my front door.

Now that all of my home improvements are complete, I long to get out in the field with the elephants. Sitting outside planning how to tackle my land access hurdle, all of a sudden there's a thunderous explosion, followed by ominous crackling, from my cottage. I race inside to find the electricity distribution box, mounted on a wall in my bedroom, on fire. (Now is not the time to wonder why this electricity box is above my bed.) Long orange flames are licking skywards, towards the thatched roof.

I let fly with a four-letter word and then yell 'Help!' and 'Fire!' while frantically moving my bed. My attempts to extinguish the flames with a blanket don't seem to be doing much good, and I dash outside to holler again, hoping that the lodge gardener might be close enough to hear me. Sprinting back inside I do the only thing I can think of. Not fully appreciating the risk of electrocution, I put my hand through the flames and flick off the switches on the distribution box, before bellowing some more. I sound like a wounded buffalo. The flames are out before help arrives, and I'm not too badly burnt.

My blackened bedroom wall tells the tale. The flames have reached extremely close to the very dry, highly combustible thatched roof. Had my roof gone up, so would have my whole cottage with all that I owned inside it, and then the surrounding bush, and possibly even the lodge as well.

Is somebody trying to tell me something? For months now I've been feeling as if a hex has been cast on me. I imagine a *tocholoshe*, a mean little gremlin-like creature sometimes said to be only ten centimetres tall, creeping around me. The locals believe that an *inyanga* (a witchdoctor) can, for a fee, craft a *tocholoshe*. This often-bearded little goblin is said to execute dastardly deeds as instructed by its master. The lodge staff hope one hasn't taken up residence in my house.

For now I just need to get rid of all the thick smoke inside. I borrow a fan from the lodge, and open wide the windows and the front and back doors. Somebody is already attempting to fix the electricity box.

By nightfall power is finally restored, but I'm feeling decidedly uneasy. Although everyone seems to have an opinion, nobody has properly determined the cause of the fire. Will this scenario repeat itself while I sleep? Smoke still chokes the air, and although I do shut the doors, I keep the windows open, planning to close them before I drift off to sleep. The security bars that Craig has repaired mean I don't feel too vulnerable. Exhausted, I lie on my bed for just a moment, and promptly fall fast asleep.

At 2 a.m. I awake with a start. Somebody is creeping around inside my cottage. I can hear movement, and strange sounds that I can't identify. I pluck up the courage to climb out of bed. It's pitch dark and I use my hands to feel my way. I stand at the doorway and listen. I hear nothing. So I inch a little further towards the kitchen area.

All of a sudden I collide with something unknown; my leg brushes against some sort of strange, furry being, much bigger than a rat. I let fly with another four-letter word.

What the heck is in my house now? A baby hyena? A baby lion? A *tocholoshe?* I dive for a light switch. And there she is: Chloe the lodge cat, looking up at me and meowing innocently.

'Chloe,' I sigh, bending down to pick her up, and now laughing wildly. 'You crazy cat, you scared the living daylights out of me. Don't you ever do that again!'

It's actually been a fun time settling into my new home. I'm so grateful to have had the help and company of Craig and Amos. I just hope my elephant friends will be grateful for all that we've been through, on their behalf.

Visitors pop in over the course of the next few weeks, curious to know where I'm now living.

'It's a shame it's so small,' one South African colleague declares.

'Small?' I frown. 'Compared to what I lived in for the past ten years, this is a palace!'

'Well, it's got . . . character,' he decides.

'Let's be honest,' I laugh. 'It's got rodents and a rotten roof!'

Even so, I feel more at home than I have in a very long time.

# MEETING CECIL

# 2011

It is with trepidation, rather than excitement, that I finally venture out onto the estate, after more than five months away from the elephants. I desperately want to find out how they're all faring but at the same time I feel waves of anxiety, deep in the pit of my stomach. What dragons are awaiting me now, I wonder?

We had a good wet season and there are still gratifying amounts of surface water lying around. Now that the rains are over, though, the water in these depressions won't last for long. Water should already be pumping into the main pans, but it is not. There's still no one making any effort to keep fresh water flowing for the wildlife, which is disheartening to say the least.

I drive around searching for the elephant families. Lol, from Lady's family, was due to give birth to her very first calf while I was away and I'm keen to know how she is coping. Of course I long to catch up with Lady too, and indeed all of her family. Echo from the Es should have given birth to her first calf too, around the same time that her own mother Eileen was due to deliver another wee one. Assuming all has gone well, Whole should also have a new little baby beside her. There will be many births (and I will soon learn, some disappearances as well) to record.

From the moment I stumble upon my first family I am overjoyed. All the residual stress of the past few months instantly lifts.

It is the adorable C family with matriarch Cathy that I come upon right away. Tuskless Cathy has an incredibly strong bond with her sister Courtney. They're the friendliest of the Cs, along with Courtney's son, Court. He's a lovable and somewhat bold boy who simply doesn't want to leave his relatives. He's taller than both Cathy and Courtney, which puts him in his very late teens. (From Cynthia Moss's Amboseli project I learnt that a male of seventeen stands taller than every female in a population, which helped greatly with my age estimates.) Males typically leave their natal family, either of their own accord or when they're pushed out by the older females, at around thirteen or fourteen years of age, leaving just the girls to stay together for life. Yet here's Court, approaching twenty, and he's still with his mum. His trunk is frequently dotted with war wounds, most likely from brief encounters with independent males which must have convinced him to stay at home with his mum and siblings for as long as possible.

Courtney recognises my voice at once and comes trotting over to investigate, looking a little confused. She stands right beside my door. 'What are you doing in *that* vehicle?' I'm sure I hear her say. While I stand up through my open roof, the Cs investigate my bonnet and back window, apparently satisfied that it is indeed *Mandlo*, back with them once more.

I find the W clan milling around together. All five sub-families are present—Whole's, Wilma's, Wanda's, Wide's and Wiona's. I hold back, and search through my binoculars for Whole. She's not here. But members of her immediate family are. I call to Whosit and Willa, to Wilma and Wonderful, to Why, and to all of my special friends. They come bouncing excitedly up to my 4x4, huge heads waggling, not caring at all that I'm in a different vehicle.

'Where on earth have you been?' I'm sure I hear them ask. They poke their trunks inside my windows, rest their tusks on my bonnet, nudge my bull bar, touch my side mirror, peer in through my open roof, and squeal and rumble.

I'm thrilled to be among them once again. But where is Whole? Has she died in childbirth? Is she sick? Has she been snared? Not every elephant from each sub-family is here in the open, and so I desperately hope that Whole is already in the bushes somewhere, preoccupied with her new baby. I look at Whole's grandson, Wish, and feel another rush of concern. He doesn't look at all well. He is thin and much smaller than he should be. He tries constantly to suckle from his mum, Whosit, but she isn't moving her front leg forwards to allow him to do so. He is only a year old and isn't getting sufficient milk. Whosit, it seems, isn't a very good first-time mother.

A few days pass before I bump into Whole. And I breathe a huge sigh of relief. She has an adorable baby girl beside her, and I am on another Hwange high. A lot of trunk-sucking is going on beside my door, which is the equivalent of a human baby sucking a thumb. This little one will be named Will-be because, as a supportive friend says, 'She WILL BE our new hope for the Presidential herd and a beginning of a better time with less poaching and threats, and freedom for you to do your job.'

Whosit decides to help celebrate the arrival of her baby sister by according me a memorable encounter. I'm sitting in the driver's seat of my 4x4, focused on Whole and Will-be to my left. Whosit clearly wants some attention focused back on her. As I turn, her huge face is unexpectedly right there in front of me, glaring in at me through the windscreen. Mere centimetres separate us. I jump with such fright that I whack my knees on the bottom of the steering wheel. 'You wicked woman!' I laugh aloud.

A few days later when some of the As materialise, I search for Adwina. It's almost a year since Esther removed the ghastly wire snare from her leg, and I'm keen to check on how she is doing. She's still not walking as well as she could be and the wound is very obvious even now, but she looks healthy and happy. She too has a gorgeous new baby girl beside her, who Esther names Antje.

There were two successful snare removals from elephant bulls in my absence. No one had taken identification photos though, and while I've seen photographs of the sedated bulls lying on the ground I wasn't able to identify them from these angles. I've been constantly wondering who was snared.

One afternoon I find myself with tuskless Debbie, who now leads the D family after the sad and mysterious disappearance of matriarch Disc; Disc's body, like that of numerous others, has never been found. I notice Dempsey, a teenaged bull, with a snare wound. The wire is thankfully off, but he is still limping quite badly. The wound on his back left leg matches one of the photographs I'd seen.

'I'm sorry you had to go through that, Dempsey boy,' I whisper.

While the snaring isn't as bad as it used to be, it still occurs and probably always will, despite the anti-poaching efforts. At least I now know who one of the recent victims was, and can monitor his progress.

Try as I might, I just can't find Lady and her family. I worry, wondering if they're alright, and hope none of them have been snared. I drive around, desperate for them to materialise from the bush.

Eventually I catch up with the Ms and the Es. These two families are closely related and often move together. I'm thrilled to see Misty again. She comes when I call to her, but hangs back a metre or so, not ready to offer me her complete trust again just yet. Masakhe is beside her, happy and healthy, now two and a half years old. As expected, Eileen has a fine-looking little baby beside her. He is later named Elvis, a true king of the savannah. But Echo has clearly been through a sad time with her first pregnancy: she no longer has any breast development, and there is definitely no baby. Did she miscarry? Was her baby stillborn? Did it die after birth? That information has been lost forever.

After weeks of dedicated field work, Lady and her family are still nowhere to be found.

I need to find out what's happening with my proposal to reaffirm the Presidential Decree. I've already emailed Minister Francis Nhema directly, but despite frequent phone calls and faxes to his office, I still haven't managed to speak to him. Subsequent correspondence with the always helpful Minister ('Diesel Rock') Mutasa seems to have an effect and a meeting is scheduled for me in Harare, not with Minister Nhema, who seems intent on avoiding me, but with his second in command.

'Do those elephants still exist?' I'm asked in the first few minutes of our meeting. It's immediately clear Minister Nhema hasn't passed on any information at all, and I have a lot of work to do. The original decree was never formally documented by the ministries, and I yearn to see a certificate this time. It turns out to be a long, productive meeting.

Once I'm back in the bush, I continue to send extra information. This isn't as simple as it may sound, since printers, photocopiers and fax machines are few and far between, and the ones I can access are often broken. There are also frequent phone-network outages. All of this drives me to distraction. Weeks fly by and I hear nothing in response. I don't even know for certain whether or not the minister is supporting my request. I'm considering making the tedious sixteen-hour return journey back to Harare for another face-to-face meeting.

Then, completely unexpectedly, I receive a text message out of the blue that reads in part, 'Am pleased to advise that His Excellency the President signed the reaffirmation decree.' I read this three times before I leap to my feet, let out a boisterous whoop of joy and do a little dance. I grab a bottle of pink champagne from my fridge, pop the cork, and drink straight from the bottle! I grab my mobile phone and contact those who I know will share in my excitement.

'He signed it. He actually signed it!' I gush.

I'm beside myself, giddy with astonishment, gratitude and deep satisfaction. And champagne tastes so much better when you drink it straight from the bottle!

Now, I have to make sure that it really does mean something.

A few weeks pass before I manage to see the signed document. Alas, somewhere along the line, the words 'Hwange Estate', as they appeared in one sentence in my draft, have been altered to read 'Hwange National Park', a reflection of how removed the Harare people unfortunately are from the realities on the ground. They probably don't even realise it, but it's a blatant mistake. Although the text has been substantially shortened too, the overall sentiment is still there, loud and clear. Perhaps I shouldn't be so picky, but I can't help myself; I ask if the president could possibly sign a corrected, and professionally typeset, version (which is what I'd been planning all along). I'm told sternly that no one would be game to ask him! At least what we have is signed by the president and further sanctioned with his seal. And it was a coup to get it at all.

To be perfectly honest though, I'm not convinced the signed decree will mean all that much in the long term. But I'm determined to try to *give* it real meaning. I wonder if the president would have signed it, in the current prejudiced environment, had he known it was proposed and drafted by a white person. I'm quite sure that he knows nothing about me, despite my decade-long battle on behalf of his flagship herd.

My next mission is now clear: I need to ensure this reaffirmation gets as much publicity as it deserves, especially as there are now rumours of methane gas and coal-mining licences being issued within the key home range of these elephants, very close to photographic safari lodges. The South African film crew are still in touch, and will soon start working with me to make the previously planned documentary. Minister Francis Nhema has finally taken a personal interest and has agreed to be filmed reading the decree reaffirmation on behalf of President Mugabe. I have to trust that his interest will endure, after the cameras are switched off.

Things are finally moving in the right direction.

Sadly, things are not going so well for one of my close friends Down Under.

While my Kiwi friend Eileen was celebrating her fiftieth birthday recently, across the ditch in Australia, she discovered a lump. Cancer had come calling. This is another harsh reminder of what an absolute bitch life can sometimes be and makes me question again what I'm doing back here. Eileen has no choice other than to deal with her cancer, but I have a choice. I don't have to be here fighting so many battles in this crazy place; life throws us enough curveballs without seeking out more. For Eileen, it's going to be a long bumpy ride, down a path that she did not choose. My own despair here in Hwange has been more or less self-inflicted. I take strength from Eileen's determination, and resolve to send her only bright and hopeful vibes—along with a little angel, to sit on her shoulder. She is stubborn, like me, and I know that she will get through this.

Shaynie's settled well into her new job at Wilderness Safaris and has, along with her bosses, invited me to spend a week in their part of the national park. If I was a tourist with only one trip to Hwange likely in my lifetime, this is where I would spend my time. It's what the Presidential Elephant areas on the Hwange Estate *used* to be like, with abundant water pumped into fourteen pans early in the dry season. I secretly want to take the Wilderness Safaris directors home with me in my duffel bag.

Wildlife encounters are more spectacular than ever on this concession. Prey species are abundant and so it follows that predators are abundant too. The big cats typically go out of their way to avoid each other, yet in less than a kilometre—an impossibly short distance in the wild—we encounter three different species. There are three cheetah cubs on a termite mound by the roadside, a little further on in the low branches of a tree two leopards are feasting on an impala, and just around the corner, there are seven lion cubs. The patron saint of pussy cats is looking down on us favourably!

The father of the seven cubs, our expert guide Lewis tells us, is called Cecil. The face of one of my favourite uncles, who shares this name, flashes in front of my eyes as we catch up with this magnificent, big, black-maned lion and his lustrous pride of ladies, out hunting. *Why would the lion researchers call such a magnificent beast Cecil?* I wonder to myself. I love my Uncle Cecil but the name doesn't seem nearly powerful or masculine enough for a lion. Then Lewis reminds us the founder of Rhodesia (renamed Zimbabwe at Independence) was Cecil John Rhodes. I'm surprised, but evidently there's no resentment of colonial times here. As Cecil bellows unforgettably to the waxing moon and the myriad stars above, I decide that I would rather think of him as Astro: astronomical in more ways than one.

Then one evening, after enjoying some G&Ts while soaking up the breathtaking sunset colours and the rise of the full moon, I squat behind the game-drive vehicle (as one has no choice but to do).

'Lions!' Shaynie yelps.

'Yeah, right, Shaynie,' I say, by now very used to the never ending jokes about what is about to eat you.

'No, man, really! Lions, right there,' she blurts out, letting the spotlight guide the way to a pride of lions just ten or so metres away.

'Oh shit,' I squawk, swallowing my distrust. 'Those lions just watched me pee.'

'I bet that makes you want to pee again,' says one of the tourists on our game-drive vehicle as I scramble back on.

The four lionesses intermittently bellow, and hyenas howl, under the glorious full moon. We sit savouring every moment before making our way back to camp.

It is quite by chance that in this remote part of Hwange I meet up with an American woman and her companion who are thrilled, but confused, to see me. They'd paid extra to a Hwange Estate operator who had assured them that they would be spending time with me while at their next lodge, only to be told at the last minute, when it was too late to change their booking, that I was unavailable. I knew absolutely nothing of this, or of them, or of the donation they'd made towards my work.

'What are they doing with the premium paid by these guests, and the donation?' Shaynie wonders aloud.

'Certainly not putting it towards the Presidential Elephants,' I say, dejectedly.

That my name was now being used without my knowledge came as a shock to me, even though I knew this had already happened to someone else. Although I'm actively encouraging elephant tourism, I'm not here to help any estate operator line their pockets in unprincipled ways.

I also know that in some neighbouring countries a set percentage of profits from photographic (not just hunting) lodges must go back into assisting the wildlife and the surrounding communities, and although some do this routinely in Zimbabwe, it isn't compulsory.

Deceitful advertising and giving back. These are now on my ever-growing list of things to discuss with Minister Francis Nhema when I soon have him captive beside me in my 4x4 for an afternoon of filming among the elephants.

Shaynie, as always, manages to lift my spirit. After dinner one night she presents me with an extravagantly iced ball of real elephant dung to belatedly celebrate my 49th birthday.

# AN ELEPHANT KISS

## 2011

Now that I'm settled back into Hwange, it doesn't take long for old trouble-makers to try and stir up more trouble. Those fire-breathing dragons are back once more.

The group that was insisting I sign their 'partnership agreement' has now mysteriously claimed that I'm attempting to sabotage their business. They've lodged a formal complaint with the Dete police to try and have me charged. The fact that I've had nothing to do with them since peacefully leaving my *rondavel* last year doesn't seem to matter. The police decline to let me read what has been filed against me.

My relationship with this country is starting to feel like an abusive marriage. I just keep going back for more, unable to break the cycle of harassment.

I email Mandy, who I know will share in my bafflement. 'So guess what this little elephant-loving girl from country Queensland is now?'

'Your capabilities are mind-boggling!' she replies. 'Do people actually believe all of this stuff? A saboteur?'

It is Zimbabwe's way. If something is repeated often enough by those with powerful connections it doesn't matter how untruthful, crude or incomprehensible, it's likely to become fact. People are generally bullied into immediate and silent submission.

'So what have you got to say about this?' the local CIO agent asks me when he eventually appears on my doorstep. 'Are you trying to sabotage their business?'

'They don't need any help from me, or anyone else,' I declare to this man, whose involvement in Zimbabwe's secret police isn't very secret. 'They're doing a fine job of sabotaging themselves. Do you seriously believe this drivel?' I ask.

'You need to come down to the police station,' he declares.

'Excellent,' I say. 'A five-person film crew has just arrived from South Africa to start filming with me. Let me just go and get them, so they can come with me.'

He leaves pretty quickly, without me in tow, but predictably soon reappears demanding all sorts of things that I am never going to agree to without a fight.

'Do you and your people really have nothing better to do with your time than sit and doze on a filming vehicle all day long, for the next month or two?' I ask incredulously when he tells me that he—or a fellow police officer—must be on the filming vehicle to oversee what is being taped, every single day without fail, despite all of the approvals already in place. 'How about you spend your time investigating those who continually report me? Then, perhaps, you might actually find some bad guys.'

If nothing else, at least this has given the film crew a first-hand glimpse into the frequent attempts to hamper my work. They don't, however, risk turning on their cameras when these confrontations are taking place. They know their equipment would be confiscated in a flash.

I've painstakingly arranged a small function at one of the lodges, during which Minister Nhema will read the Presidential Decree reaffirmation on behalf of President Mugabe. The crew will be there to film. Chief Nelukoba Dingani, who is the area's traditional leader (akin to a tribal king) will also be in attendance, as will representatives from Parks and the media. Ingonyama, an exceptionally talented dance and drama group from Dete, will also be there to help welcome the minister, as will the Forestry Protection Unit, who are involved in snare destruction in the Presidential Elephants' key home range.

Of course there is a problem. There's always a problem! Just two days before the function I unexpectedly find myself talking to Minister Nhema on my mobile phone.

'Air Zimbabwe's just gone on strike. I can't make it to Hwange,' the minister says to me.

*No way, I think to myself. You're not getting out of this that easily!* There are no commercial flights to Hwange these days. To save the time it takes to drive from Harare, he'd planned to fly to Victoria Falls, before driving on to Hwange.

'What if we can charter a plane for you?' I offer as a last resort, despite having absolutely no idea whether we can pull this off.

'That would be okay,' he says.

I hang up, feeling faint. The film-crew leaps into action. They check to see if they can get approval to pay for this flight, and to see if a suitable plane is even available to fly from Harare into the Hwange airport. Half an hour later I ring the minister back. Everything is in place; he just has to get himself to the airport.

This new plan actually comes with an upside: the film-crew can now request to record the minister's arrival on the Hwange tarmac. No filming is generally allowed at any airports in Zimbabwe, purportedly for security reasons. It certainly doesn't happen quickly, or easily, but we're finally granted approval.

Minister Nhema arrives the morning before the official function, and I greet him at the airport. He doesn't remember that he's met me before. I'm surprised when he casually invites me to climb into his awaiting vehicle beside him, to talk. His eyes are no longer downcast. He is charming and friendly. In fact, I feel that he is very much on my side.

It is planned that I will take him out in my vehicle after lunch, with the film-crew in tow, to meet some of the Presidential Elephants. As I walk towards my 4x4, I see that it's being combed by the CIO and police.

'What is that?' one of them asks me, pointing to what is clearly a brick under my seat.

'It's a brick,' I say.

'What do you plan to do with it?' he asks.

I just can't help myself. 'I plan to hit Minister Nhema over the head with it.'

They can't help but smile and then ask me again. I explain that I frequently drive in soft Kalahari sand and that if I get a flat tyre—which I do often—I need chocks for my wheels, and something to place my bottle-jack on so that it doesn't sink into the sand.

'Oh,' they say.

Then they find the hollow iron bar that John gave me for loosening tight wheel nuts. They look up at me, heads cocked to one side.

'Just think about it,' I whisper.

Once they're finally convinced that I have no intention of assassinating Minister Nhema, he climbs into my vehicle next to me. It's unusually windy and cold and I worry the elephants might be in hiding. For the first hour we drive around and see very little. It's a chance to talk however, and in this more casual environment, the minister happily answers many questions. But I'm getting anxious now. What if all of the elephants really stay away today?

Thank goodness for the Ms and the Es, with whom we eventually catch up. Misty saves the day, being her gorgeous friendly self, as always, relaxing with her family just centimetres from the doors of my 4x4, as if I had magically placed them there myself. Minister Nhema stands on my battered passenger seat (after first, very politely, asking my permission to do so), and soon he's up through the roof gazing into Misty's eyes, visibly astonished. He has been Wildlife Minister since the year 2000 but has never met the Presidential Elephants before.

'Amazing!' he eventually says, flashing an impressive smile. 'So that's why you sing "Amazing Grace" to them.'

We are laughing and smiling and talking together easily. I want to get out of my 4x4 and give Misty a huge hug.

The documentary director, Richard, prompts me over my radio to ask Minister Nhema what his 'totem' is, a question I'm also really interested in knowing the answer to. The various clans in Zimbabwe are linked to different animal totems (elephant, lion, crocodile, monkey, zebra etc), which are sort of like a mythological ancestor. They're a form of identity and a way of tracing lineage. It is said, for example, that people of the same totem shouldn't marry, as this would be akin to marrying a relative. More importantly to me, it's said that you shouldn't eat your own totem, as this is considered similar to eating your own flesh. I find myself hoping that Minister Nhema's totem will turn out to be the elephant, so that he feels more connected to them, and might take an extra special interest. But his is the lion.

Back at the lodge late in the afternoon, the minister excitedly recounts his experiences to staff who've respectfully gathered to greet him on his return. I can't understand what's being said but there are wide eyes and lots of laughter and broad smiles. One senior Forestry Commission staff member later says to me, 'Minister Nhema told me three times about his afternoon with the elephants, each time showing me exactly the same photographs.'

I'm thrilled this experience has touched the minister so deeply, and hope that his interest in the elephants doesn't end up being short-lived. I've been warned that he has a reputation for being unpredictable and changing his mind. There are recent stories of him openly speaking of banning sport-hunting in Zimbabwe altogether, which he has the power to do, and next minute emphatically denying he'd ever said this.

The official function the next morning goes off without a hitch. I introduce Minister Nhema, who passes on best wishes and congratulations from President Mugabe—although I'm quite sure the president doesn't have the faintest idea that the minister is here on his behalf. Before reading the decree reaffirmation, Minister Nhema very clearly goes off-script, speaking from the heart about families, Presidential Elephant families. Among other things, he admits to 'a rude awakening', saying that yesterday he 'met families that show love, respect and good attitude probably better than human beings', and that the 'wilderness is perhaps more civilised than what we call civilisation'. He concludes that lessons learnt from the elephants may 'be the answer to mankind'.

Tears well up in my eyes. I want to believe that Minister Nhema now understands the love and awe of the elephants that I have.

Chief Dingani speaks too. Traditional leaders are supposed to be politically neutral, but these days the Ruling Party 'encourages' them—with gifts of houses and cars and goodness knows what else—to mobilise their communities at election times and ensure the vote goes the 'right' way. I try to forget this as Chief Dingani delivers his speech in isiNdebele.

Given that I still have little grasp of this complicated language, I don't understand why everyone erupts into laughter. 'The chief says he's going to find you a husband', the woman beside me whispers. Minister Nhema seems to find this particularly amusing, while I chortle along too, swept away in the pride of the day. Marriage is the last thing on my mind, but I'm told I should consider this an honour.

It's been a humbling few days for me. I am overwhelmed by the gracious words and camaraderie, although I know it's unlikely to last. While I doubt that the chief—who has frequently called for elephants to be shot—is genuine, I dare to hope that if ever there is another fight to save the Presidential Elephants, Minister Nhema will be on my side. In an attempt to keep his interest high, I later name a new little baby boy in the C family Comrade Nhema and he is touched by this gesture.

'Anyone who shoots at the Presidential herd is as bad as someone shooting at the president', he is later quoted as saying in a newspaper story. 'When you shoot at these animals, you can expect to be shot back at. If you kill them, you will also be killed. No one should compromise the Presidential herd.' And I feel a warm glow, deep in my heart.

We start filming in the field in earnest. I find myself laughing a lot, and exclaiming just as often 'I sure hope you don't include *that!*' as inquisitive elephants grab at microphones and at my clothes. One steals my jacket! There are cameras on my windscreen and occasionally under my 4x4. There's always a camera in my face. I'm also asked to sit completely motionless for 45 minutes at a time, for time-lapse photography. We're fortunate to be able to frequently film the families of Whole, Misty and Cathy. There are action-packed snare removals during which everything moves at a frantic pace. The darters and I don't delay even for a second during these life and death situations and there are deep groans from the crew when they're not in place quickly enough to film the cutting of one wire.

Then one day I'm worried when Willa unexpectedly lies down beside a mineral lick, under the blazing sun. I don't often see adult Presidential Elephants lying down, unless they're unwell, although I'm aware that other elephant populations are observed asleep on their side quite frequently. I hadn't recorded when she was last in oestrus but I think, based on the age of her youngest calf, and her own inter-birth intervals, that it will be at least another four months before she has another baby. So if she isn't soon to give birth, perhaps she is sick? The days are hot, so maybe she's simply exhausted.

Willa gets back on her feet and wanders over to the shade of a teak tree to lie down on her side once more. I wait for her to rise, and then drive towards her, stopping a few metres away.

'Hey, Willa girl. Are you alright, my Willa?'

She wanders towards me, coming to a halt just centimetres away, as she always does. I talk to her, as I always do. And then something exceptional happens. Willa rests her trunk on the ground, and puts what feels like her full weight against my door. I feel my 4x4 shift, and understand that she could toss it on its side like a matchstick if she wished to. But I know this isn't her intention. She wants company. She wants comfort. She wants me to reassure her that everything will be alright. While talking to her and tenderly touching her trunk with the back of my hand, I put my face against the long leathery nose of this wild giant and kiss her gently.

This is not a hurried encounter. This is two beings, totally at peace with one another. It is a bond forged over years and years with love and patience and understanding, from both of us.

We must make an incredibly perplexing sight for the film-crew and the guides who are watching this extraordinary display of trust unfold.

I look up over the rim of my glasses, into Willa's eyes, and hold her gaze. I kiss her again, and again. She stays just as she is, looking down on me with kind, wise eyes. This intelligent being, gifted with conscious thoughts and emotions, is clearly thinking. She may not be able to speak my language, nor me hers, but she has chosen to commune with me none-theless. We understand each other and she knows that I'm concerned for her. I recognise her own genuine warmth.

This encounter with Willa leaves me feeling euphoric. To have gained such trust from an enormous wild animal—one that has been through many difficult times—makes everything worthwhile. No human could thank me so well.

'That was one of the most remarkable things I've ever witnessed,' Richard declares.

Later, when I share one of the film-crew's photos of me kissing Willa with my hippo friend Karen, she weeps. And that's because she under-stands it all, because to people like her this isn't just a photo. It's a whole, revealing story in itself.

We keep searching and searching, but I simply can't find Lady and her family. There have been so many disturbances in these areas and gunfire is still heard far too frequently. With the entire family missing, I'm quite confident they're all together, somewhere else.

Then one morning, with a lone cameraman, Riaan, in tow, I look up from my notebook and all of a sudden I see her in the distance.

'It's Lady!' I cry. 'Is it Lady? . . . There's Lesley and Lucky and Louise . . . Yes! It's Lady, Riaan, I have to go!'

'Well, you can't go yet!' Riaan shouts while he's, quite by chance, attaching a camera to the underside of my vehicle. 'I'm only half done.'

'Riaan, it's Lady! I have to go. Now, really, I have to go. If you don't get away from my wheel, I'll be forced to run right over you.'

Through binoculars I can see that Lady and her family are muddy and have obviously already been to another pan. They won't stay here for long. Soon they'll disappear into thick bush.

'Riaan! I've *really* got to go,' I demand.

Within seconds he's finished, and is on the crew vehicle filming me.

I just need to get to her. I roar off to the other side of the pan. I stop and call to her, and she responds immediately. It turns out the camera under my vehicle is capturing exceptional footage, and Riaan races to catch up to us with his professional gear, but none of this matters to me as Lady comes and greets me for the first time in almost a year. I am so unbelievably happy to see her.

'My girl. Hey, my girl,' I croon with tears in my eyes.

Lady knows what I feel for her, of that I am certain. After taking my fingers in the fingers of her trunk, she puts her trunk on top of my head, and then over my mouth and nose in a sand-filled elephant kiss! She continues to touch my body, as if she can't quite believe it's me. I rub her long rough nose over and over again. All that matters is that she is fine. Her family is fine. And there is Lol, with a little baby boy cavorting beside her.

Rumbling excitedly, they all surround my vehicle before relaxing right beside me. I've missed them so much. This family in particular never fails to fill my heart with joy. I'm instantly at one with them all. I wonder where they've all been. What has made them start venturing further afield?

I wish Lady could tell me. They've been through so much trauma here, but out there is even less safe. I desperately hope that they'll now return to their old haunts.

Lady has always been such a comfort to me and has taught me so much over the years about her kind. I just love her to the moon and back and more, and treasure this meeting. When she finally rumbles to signal that it's time for her family to move off, I tell all of them to stay safe, as I always do.

I've been so busy with the film-crew that the days and weeks fly by even more quickly than usual. I haven't found time to wash my sheets or towels for weeks. Because baboons were constantly wreaking havoc with my thatched roof, I'd had to urgently arrange repairs. Thatching is always such a messy job and my home is in disarray. I've also resorted to ordering rolls of chicken wire to protect my roof from the primates, and this now needs to be fitted. I'll be pleased when filming is over and I can set my home right again.

'Only five more sleeps to go, and I'm freeeeee!' I text Barbara and CJ. Then, 'Only four more sleeps to go.'

When the last day of filming finally arrives, the crew has some two hundred hours of footage that somehow has to be cut into a 52-minute film. Less than half of one per cent of the footage will make it into the documentary. I'm sorry to think of all the footage of my beloved elephants that is destined for the cutting-room floor. But the crew has filmed some remarkable stuff.

'Okay everybody, it's a wrap!' Kira finally declares.

I'm surprised to learn that Lawson Mabhena, a journalist from the *Sunday News*—a newspaper that's a mouthpiece for the government—prepared a feature on me while we were filming, since few newspapers carry stories on whites, especially not the government press.

'When I first heard that Ms Sharon Pincott, an Australian wildlife enthusiast living with elephants near Hwange National Park, could talk to the jumbos,' he wrote, 'I thought: well that's a load of rubbish. Living with elephants, I could imagine as something easy for anyone with a passion for wildlife, but talking to them—that was a claim worth proving false.'

I can't help but laugh.

Like Minister Nhema, Lawson admitted to 'a rude awakening' and concluded: 'Seeing Pincott talk to elephants as one would have regular talk with humans, was indeed amazing, but even more amazing was the fact that no Zimbabwean I know—myself included—has such passion for our wildlife.' I am taken aback by such candour in the government press.

Lawson had enjoyed his brief close encounter with the elephants after the decree reaffirmation ceremony. It's something that still relatively few of his countrymen get the opportunity to experience, a situation that I hope to help change.

Everything still seems to be heading in the right direction.

With filming over, I take a few days off and try to relax in Bulawayo. During the spring months of September to November, before the rains, Bulawayo's unusually wide, dusty and littered streets are transformed by the stunningly beautiful mauves of flowering jacarandas and the flamboyant red of flame trees. In among these, Australian silky oaks with dark-yellow blooms add an extra splash of colour.

'It's much less dreary and drab in town when all of these beautiful trees are flowering,' I say to Barbara.

'I hate those jacarandas,' Barbara moans. 'They're messy and they smell.'

*Why is it that city folk so often fail to notice nature's beauty?* 'Oh, get a life,' I tell her with a grin.

When the first rains fall in town, after the seven-month dry, people hardly seem to notice. Windows and doors are quickly shut and everyone races inside. There's no getting away, though, from the rank odour of piles of wet garbage and the grease slicks on the roads. When the first rains fall in the bush I've been known to dance around in joyous thanks, arms raised skywards, soaked to the skin, inhaling every last particle of the wonderful earthy fragrance. There is so much to celebrate in Hwange when the rains come.

# VISITORS

## 2012

As the months pass, it becomes clear that we're not heading in the right direction at all. Lady is missing again. This time, it is different. Her youngest calf, Lantana, is missing too. All other members of her family are around but they're visibly stressed and anxious. Lady's adult daughter, Lesley, usually friendly and welcoming, stays with me for only a minute or two, before moving off into dense bush. All of the elephants are agitated.

I need more encounters with this favourite family to determine what is really going on. Based on my knowledge of Lady's last known mating session with the bulls, she should have a new baby by her side by now. If she lost her baby before it was full-term, she could have found herself quickly in oestrus again, and she might be temporarily off with the bulls. But I've seen the family several times now, over the course of a few weeks, and Lady and Lantana have not returned.

I'm desperately worried about them. I have never been so afraid for a life.

Then, inconceivably, Dee's best friend, Stephanie, dies just a few weeks short of her twenty-first birthday after a night-time car accident on the way to Hwange. Stephanie survived the crash and was taken to the nearest government hospital, but Zimbabwe's rapidly declining health facilities let her down terribly.

Dee raced around buying what Stephanie needed, which the hospital did not have. In fact the hospital had next to nothing. Pain medication, drips, bandages, gauze, cotton wool, plaster of Paris, none of it was available until it was privately sourced and paid for. Stephanie was lying naked on a bed, without even a screen around her. There were no hospital gowns, no pillows, no blankets. The ward was overcrowded, with eight beds where there should have been four. There was an awful smell of dirty toilets. Dee brought in a clean bucket to wash her friend.

Stephanie also needed blood, and at the back of everyone's minds was the nagging question: in this country where so many people are HIV-positive, were blood donations properly screened? Even blood had to be paid for in cash before it could be administered.

When Dee merely questioned why they had nothing at all to ease her friend's pain, the matron responded, 'Why don't you go back to England? Ask for what you want there.'

Thanks to a company's financial generosity, Stephanie was transferred as quickly as possible to a more reputable hospital in Bulawayo. Tragically, she died from complications a few days later. It is no surprise to any of us that the president chooses to fly overseas to have his own ailments treated, at the expense of the Zimbabwe people.

While I watch my friends reeling from this trauma, I am silently convinced that Lady has met a similar fate but I'm not yet ready to talk about it.

My next book, *Battle for the President's Elephants,* is released in South Africa and supportive correspondence and words of encouragement flood in. Yet more people now know and care about these elephants.

The documentary is also finalised. It's been quite a challenge getting this far. Over the last few months I've had to keep reminding the South African filmmakers that I still live in Zimbabwe, and that they'd agreed not to compromise my work here—or my life. This wasn't a documentary about President Mugabe and his government but rather it was about some of Zimbabwe's most extraordinary wildlife, and it shouldn't be political. I couldn't understand why some footage made the final cut while segments I considered so important were discarded. I was also surprised to discover that my own words were used as the narration. And why the cameras had to be *so* close to my face I just couldn't understand at all!

But, the filmmakers knew exactly what they were doing. *Screen Africa*, Africa's leading broadcast and film publication, describes *All the President's Elephants* as 'unforgettable' and 'touching and profound'. *Intrepid Explorer* magazine calls it 'riveting' and 'graphic and powerful'. It's selected to premiere at South Africa's Durban International Film Festival. I get no royalties from it, but increased awareness, as always, is my top priority.

I post a copy on DVD to Minister Nhema. His part has been beautifully edited. The world will now see a completely different side to this man, a side that I'm starting to believe really does exist.

My Kiwi friend Andrea and her friend arrive for a visit in June. After sharing my triumphs and tragedies for so many years via email, Andrea can hardly believe that she's finally here. I'm waiting for them at a crossroads, where Andrea greets me in tears. They've already encountered their first family of elephants crossing directly in front of their car and she is overcome with emotion. When we review her video we discover they'd seen members of the A family, including her namesake Andrea and daughter Alessandra.

Andrea has helped with editing my books and so I've pre-arranged (not without some hassles) that they be permitted out with me in my own 4x4 as a thank you. We leave their hire car on the side of the road and race to sit by a pan for sundowners. Within minutes we're surrounded by some twenty-five members of the P family, with matriarch Priscilla. What Andrea had dared hope to experience at least once during her visit has occurred within half an hour of arriving. She's unable to stop her tears of happiness.

During one of our outings I need to 'find a bush'. It's a hazard of spending hours in the field. Sixty seconds beforehand there wasn't an animal in sight but at the most embarrassing possible moment I'm suddenly surrounded by elephants, as I pull up my pants and try to shield myself behind a termite mound.

'Oh my goodness! It's the Ms with Misty and Masakhe,' I call out, much to Andrea's delight. I manage to return safely to my vehicle before greeting these shining stars of the documentary.

Over the next few days, we spend time on the estate and inside the national park. So many elephant families inside the park have far too many youngsters for the number of adults. I choose not to share my fears about what has happened to their mothers, and instead we enjoy the spectacle. We're also fortunate to have some splendid encounters with many Presidential families on the estate, but there is no Lady. And I am much more worried than I let on.

The full moon is more beautiful than ever as we sit out on the estate and watch it rise, Baileys in hand, to the magical sounds of the *Out of Africa* soundtrack that is echoing from my laptop. Andrea refills my glass as the sky fills with stars. I had no idea there were so many different flavours of Baileys! I'm a decade behind everything now.

I go on with my friends to the breathtaking rocky outcrops of the Matobo Hills, and we spend a night at Shaynie's flat on the way. Barbara and Dee cook up a delicious traditional *sadza* meal for us and we walk the streets of Bulawayo, and visit the street markets, so Andrea can get a feel for day-to-day African life.

I'm able to pretend that everything is okay. After just a few days in this country, tourists always manage to leave thoroughly enchanted. Even though Andrea understands more than most, she too leaves on a high.

So much looks grubby, barren and broken, yet it's still a beautiful country to visit in so many ways.

Soon I'm back in Bulawayo, struggling with permits yet again. There is so much inefficiency and corruption in the Immigration Department, but I refuse to pay them more than I'm already forced to. When I'm told that if I leave the country I may not be allowed back in, I decide not to go to Durban for the premiere of the documentary.

Instead, I relax with CJ and her partner Herbie as they watch the documentary for the first time on DVD. 'Right now, you should be washing the sand from your toes, and getting ready for its public debut,' Herbie says to me, with a note of regret.

But I'm happy to be here with friends and am thrilled to eventually hear that there's standing room only at the premiere. Dee breaks into floods of (mostly happy) tears every time she watches this DVD. I'm not sure whether to laugh, or to cry with her.

CJ and Herbie will soon be off to live in South Africa. Another two bite the dust. They don't quite know what they'll do there, but they've decided they at least need to give it a go. Nothing is improving very much in Zimbabwe, despite the Unity government. My friends always seem to be on the move, searching for a better life.

At least Shaynie will soon be returning to Bulawayo, back at last in mobile phone range. If nothing else, working in the bush at Wilderness Safaris has helped her overcome her fear of lions. She got her own back at the big black-maned Cecil, with whom she'd had many scary moments, when he was recently immobilised so the battery in his satellite collar could be changed. 'I squeezed his balls, just to let him know who's boss.'

She also discovered that he is longer than she is tall. His paw is twice the size of her hand. She's brave when he's knocked out!

Land-owners and operators continue to not even try to pump sufficient water on the estate, and the elephants suffer. My hippo friend Karen arrives to see a young Presidential Elephant dead, stuck in mud that should have been a water-filled pan.

One night shortly after Karen leaves, I hear twelve gunshots from my cottage. A few nights later, I hear another six. No matter how many times I report these incidents, they never stop, even around these photographic lodges.

My friends are visiting all of a sudden, moved by the documentary and book interest. Mandy, from Melbourne, decides to visit too. Her time in Zimbabwe doesn't begin well. She travels with her friend to Hwange on a pre-paid road transfer from Victoria Falls. Their driver is made to stop at one of the many roadblocks and then disappears with a policeman. They're left sitting alone in a vehicle, in a country known for bribery and abductions, wondering what the hell is going on.

Things improve dramatically once they finally reach their Hwange lodge and head out with me to the bush. 'Holy shit,' Mandy exclaims, when my elephant friends come when called. She instantly feels connected and fully appreciates why I'm still here.

But there is still no Lady.

When Mandy hands me a small rectangular gadget as a gift, I have no idea what it is. 'It's an mp3 player,' she tells me.

I look at her blankly. 'I still don't know what this is,' I say. Remembering that I was once the head of information technology for Ernst & Young in Australia, we laugh as Mandy gives me lessons on how to use it. 'That was as bad as teaching my mother,' she later smirks. She also bequeaths me her old mobile phone, and my model, discontinued more than a decade ago, is finally abandoned.

Uncharacteristically, Mandy sheds a tear as she leaves and for days I notice the silence of her not being around.

More and more now, I also notice the terrible silence of Lady not being around. The L family has split and is in disarray. Happily Lantana, Lady's youngest, has shown up and now wanders with her adult sister Lesley. But this is bittersweet. If Lady was alive, Lantana would be with her. It is still too distressing for me to face.

# BECOMING BRITNEY SPEARS

## 2012

Soon to be 89 years of age, President Mugabe is at it again. 'Trust white people at your own peril,' he has now publicly declared. In 1980, on the eve of Zimbabwe's Independence, he had said: 'The wrongs of the past must now stand forgiven and forgotten,' and, 'Oppression and racism are inequities that must never again find scope in our political and social system.'

Lest he forget.

A few years ago, the Mugabe government signed into law the Indigenisation and Economic Empowerment Act. The controlling interest (51 per cent or more) of all businesses of a predetermined net value, owned by either foreigners or white Zimbabweans, has to be disposed of, within a set timeframe, to black Zimbabweans. The desire to empower black Zimbabweans and have them benefit from their own natural resources is a commendable concept, but surely this is not the best way to achieve this goal. Not surprisingly, new investors are scared off and the economy continues to plummet. Western governments continue pumping hundreds of millions of dollars into Zimbabwe in food, educational and developmental aid regardless.

'*Trust whites at your own peril.*' It's enough to make my eyes roll so far back in my head that I don't know whether I'll ever see straight again.

My email runs hot. 'What are you still doing there, with *his* elephants? He's become a ranting racist.' I have no answer—except that the Presidential Elephants are supposed to be a flagship herd for the nation, regardless of who the president is. What I do have is a sense of growing unease.

After Mandy returned to Australia, she thoughtfully set up a Facebook page for the Presidential Elephants. My internet connection in the bush is still too slow, unreliable and expensive to do this myself. In the towns, where the signal is better, Zimbabweans are starting to embrace social media at last. But it's not easy yet, in the bush. (Mobile phones though, are here in profusion in back pockets, despite their owners struggling to feed children and pay school fees.)

Overall, the Facebook page turns out to be a really positive development. I sincerely appreciate the interest and moral support from so many people all around the world, happy my enthusiasm for these elephants is so contagious. It's great to hear more people are enjoying my books and the documentary. I decide to also use the page as an educational tool, to share all sorts of general elephant facts and observations. Within a few weeks followers swell to over 5000 and I try my best to personally reply to all of the messages received.

One message in particular really touches my heart. It's from a young black Zimbabwean named Faith, who was my neighbour ten years ago. Sometimes, she'd come out to the elephants with me. All these years later, now living elsewhere and having given birth to two children, she writes with love and passion about her encounters with the Presidential Elephants: 'I wish I had followed to the elephants' watering hole every day.' In a country where many people care so little for wildlife, it is special to me that she has never forgotten her encounters with Faith, Freddie and Fantastic. She still calls me *Mandlovu* ('Mother Elephant') and I take comfort that President Mugabe has not succeeded in segregating blacks and whites. Faith and I are just two people, separated now by distance, and not colour.

It's only after strangers start turning up on my doorstep, unannounced, that I realise all of the exposure is a mixed blessing. Eventually I become a little resentful of being viewed as public property.

'I don't understand this. I'm not Britney Spears or anybody, and heaven help me if I was,' I moan to Mandy. Knowing just how out of touch I've been, she is simply impressed that I'm aware of who Britney Spears is!

Strangers on holiday drive their cars right into my yard, parking just metres away from my open front door. They expect me to be pleased to see them. Some are lovely of course, and want nothing more than to say hello and thank you, and then they leave. Others are not quite so gracious.

I consider putting NO ENTRY signs on the short sandy road leading to my cottage, but this just seems ridiculous. Things eventually settle down. As always, I spend as much time as I can in the field, which is better, I think, than being at my home with uninvited strangers—and uninvited snakes.

I glimpse what I think is only a *small* slithery thing heading behind my couch. I am beside myself nonetheless. I grab my mobile phone and call the lodge gardener.

'Abson,' I yell. 'Please, there's a snake in my cottage.'

'I'll come soon,' he promises, in that laid-back African way that I'm now accustomed to, but which regularly drives me insane.

'No Abson, not soon. You need to come *now*, please,' I plead.

He arrives quickly, moves bits of furniture, spots my intruder and then jumps back, eyes wide. He phones for reinforcements.

Austin appears in a flash, and he and Abson chatter together in isiNdebele.

'Please, you need to tell me what's going on. What type of snake is it? It's small, isn't it?'

'*Mandlo*, this snake is … *big*. And it is a spitting cobra,' Abson announces.

I put my hands to my eyes, massage my temples and shuffle outside to leave them to it. There are vervet monkeys swimming the length of one of my ponds, fully submerged. They're having a ball, unaware there's a snake not far away.

The men soon emerge with something that is unnervingly thick, quite deadly, and as tall as me. The vervets scatter, sounding their alarm calls. What I'd seen inside had been only the tail end. I have a 'snake blocker' that Craig and Amos made for me when I moved in, which leans against my open door. This giant must have slid right over the top of it and had probably been inside for some time.

'Lucky it wasn't in your toilet,' Abson says in consolation.

It's not unheard of to be bitten on the bum by a venomous snake. Suddenly, I long to be living back in New Zealand, the land of the long white cloud and absolutely no snakes! Nor creepy black scorpions, the size of small lobsters, that have been known to crawl up my walls. Perhaps I should invite some of those strangers in after all.

# LADY

## 2012

One morning in November, as soft rain falls outside, I simply can't make myself get out of bed. I've known it for most of the year, but now I have to finally face the reality.

Lady is dead.

I lie under my mosquito net, curled in the foetal position, unable to move. I ignore a knock on my door, and reach over and switch off my mobile phone before it has a chance to ring. I am numb with grief, eyes swollen with tears. It is time to say goodbye.

I can't bear that she is gone. Her absence is devastating to me. She had kept my heart alive. For so long I could not—would not—accept that she was gone, but now it is time.

My heart is broken, my mind is tired. There's a screaming in my head. Surely it's time. Time to get out. Time to leave for good. This place has been devouring me, little by little, one piece at a time. There is now something missing from my bush life that is so unbearable I know it can never, ever, be the same again.

In the early evening, I finally get up and make myself a snack of Vegemite toast, which always brings comfort. I carry it back to my bed, and hug a big brown bear that I bought at the street markets. I want to sleep, even though it's what I've been doing on and off all day. I need to escape from this grief and despair. I need all of the turbulence to end.

I wake during the night, haunted by thoughts of what Lady likely went through in her final moments. I lie there for hours, wishing her back to life. And I stay in bed for another day, reliving the ups and downs of the past twelve years. I feel trashed, smashed and ripped apart. I so desperately want the rain that is falling outside to wash away all of the bad things.

I wish there was somebody to make me a cup of hot chocolate and to tell me that everything will be okay, but I really need to do this alone. Even the thought of climbing into my 4x4 and going out in the field to be with my elephant friends fills me with anxiety. I am burnt out. And truly frightened. Frightened that over time these elephants will all be picked off one by one.

I haven't been able to really talk about this loss to anybody, not even my closest friends. Inside Shaynie's flat in Bulawayo, I've secretly moved around photos of Lady so that she's not staring me in the eye.

I feel not just grief. I feel guilt. Guilt that I had not been able to keep Lady alive. Guilt over all that has happened to her family: the deaths and snares. Why had I not been able to do more for my friend?

The next day I drive into Hwange National Park and sit by Makwa pan, where a long time ago I scattered some of my dog Chloe's ashes, and where I've enjoyed many happy times with just the silence and beauty of nature. Now that the rains have arrived there are few elephants, but there are giraffes and zebras and antelopes and baboons and an assortment of birds to keep me company. I think back over it all once more, trying to put things in perspective.

All I know about Lady's death is that there is no body. And that perhaps is worst of all. Privately run anti-poaching teams had searched extensively in areas where I'd seen distraught members of Lady's family, but the bush is thick and vast and they had found nothing. I have no proof that she's been shot, but a natural death is unlikely. She certainly didn't die of old age.

When elephants die naturally, or when they've been killed just for their ivory, a body is more likely to be found. But when the skin and the meat are taken—which happens during ration- and sport-hunts (sport-hunters also take the head and the feet)—the carcass breaks down quite quickly. Even though some big bones remain, they can be hard to locate, including from the air. When Lady's sister Leanne disappeared for good in 2007, her body was also never found. With her beautifully symmetrical tusks, she'd been a prime candidate for sport-hunters. But Lady had broken one of her tusks and serious trophy hunters were unlikely to have been interested in her.

Over the years, local Parks management have never allowed me to visit their ivory storeroom to ascertain—in conjunction with my elephant identification photos—if a specific elephant's ivory is there. Ivory in this storeroom comes from elephants who die naturally or who have been ration-hunted by Parks staff. Or it's ivory that has been confiscated from poachers. This time I couldn't face being dismissed again, and didn't ask to see the stockpile. It was already abundantly clear that they didn't want to help me pinpoint how any Presidential elephant died, especially a prominent one.

I've known first-hand for more than a decade that death, despair and disappearances tear elephant families apart, and now I have my soundest evidence. Since Lady's death, her family has been in disarray, ultimately splitting into three small groups. What has been most heartbreaking is seeing Lady's adult daughter Lesley. She still often stands with her head drooping against a tree trunk, aloof and detached. She and her own calves, moving together with Lady's calves, were the first to leave the others. And then the remaining adults, Lucky and Louise, split up too. Only occasionally have I seen them all back together in one cohesive group.

During the time I knew her, Lady gave birth three times, to Lucy, Libby and Lantana. One of her older sons is Levi. He became an independent bull seven years ago. What has become woefully intriguing to me is that he sometimes now returns to be with his family. I've seen him with both his adult sibling, Lesley, and one of his aunties, Louise. Bulls that have been independent for years don't normally hang around their natal family. And they usually wander far. Is it possible that he came back because he knows of his mother's death? Were members of his family able to send out an infrasonic call specifically to alert him? Or is this just coincidence? There are still so many things that we don't understand about these remarkably intelligent and sensitive creatures.

There is also a sad misconception that elephants are safer fearing humans. Lady was calm and friendly, like I'm sure all elephants used to be, before we changed the balance and started terrifying them with weapons. But Lady is dead not because she didn't run away from humans. No elephants, whether fearful of human beings or not, can escape skilled marksmen.

I've brought with me to Makwa pan a photograph of Lady, her image alive on a three by five. Looking at it, I think back to the many extraordinary times I shared with this remarkable elephant, and all of the people who'd met her. I was her voice during these past twelve years, and I'm so very happy that she was heard, bellowing with the best of them.

I pull my little folding camping shovel from the rusty tin trunk in my 4x4 and dig a small hole under a bush, where a giraffe has just been standing and where balls of elephant dung lie. I secretly bury Lady's image there, in tiny little pieces, knowing this is a place that I will always feel happy coming back to. The rains and the insects will take care of her.

I sit on the sandy ground, leaning against the front tyre of my 4x4, and look out over the pan. I've always appreciated how unique my life is here and have never taken for granted all that's going on around me. But when you give so much of yourself it is exhausting.

I feel sure Lady wouldn't want me to give up though. She deserves more people to know who she was, and how important her life was too. If she could talk, I think she'd tell me to keep going; to at least give it one more go.

One more go. Geez, how many goes is that? I've been giving it one more go for the past ten years.

Nevertheless, this is what I will do. I still can't walk away.

During this time of grief, other disturbing events have taken place. A few months ago I wrote to Minister Nhema when I discovered there were mining pegs marking out coal and methane gas licences, right in the key home range of the Presidential Elephants. I reminded him of the reaffirmation of the Presidential Decree and requested that a no-mining zone be put in place with haste within a sensible radius of Hwange Main Camp. While the minister hasn't responded to me directly, I've found out that he asked, 'Why do I have to hear this from her?' It worries me dreadfully that as the responsible minister, he doesn't appear to have even known about this.

Not nearly enough was said aloud by others either when two rhinos were senselessly murdered on the estate. I used to love watching cheeky young elephants mock-charging these pointy-horned beasts, sparring playfully before being forced to turn on their heels and make a hasty retreat in a puff of dust. The rhinos had wandered onto one of the grabbed hunting concessions, where they were shot and their horns hacked off to be powdered for their supposed medicinal properties. Now there are no rhinos to be seen here, and poaching has decimated their population inside the national park as well.

There are always plenty of bizarre goings-on too, including a story that one of the Dete schools, just down the road from where I live, has been closed because goblins are terrorising its teachers. The teachers deserted the school, leaving hundreds of students stranded. According to a newspaper report, government officials have instructed the villagers to cleanse this school of the goblins. A spirit medium has been engaged to do this.

My own reputation for possessing 'very special magic' when it comes to wildlife has grown. I actually quite enjoy being thought a little bonkers because I choose the company of wild elephants over that of humans. Perhaps a goblin has taken over my body too.

Lady certainly has. I still see her every day, hurrying towards me. Her magic lingers in the air. And although my voice falters, I sing 'Amazing Grace' to her, certain that her spirit is still here.

# SPLITTING APART

## LATE-2012 AND 2013

Run by a white Zimbabwean named Johnny Rodrigues, Zimbabwe Conservation Task Force is a Harare-based group loathed by the government. During the past decade Johnny has been the only person inside the country who has been brave enough to distribute regular bulletins about the plight of the wildlife. He has endured extreme criticism, death threats and the attention of the dreaded CIO.

Without Johnny, even those of us inside Zimbabwe would be aware of far less going on around the country. He has now reported news that's particularly disturbing. More young elephants have been ripped from their mothers inside Hwange National Park. Four have already been airlifted to Chinese zoos, while five others are captive in enclosures known locally as *bomas*, awaiting departure.

I am alarmed to read this, especially in light of the previous Mugabe's Ark fiasco, which was overturned. Did they learn nothing? The world understands so much about the complex lives of elephants these days, and even neighbouring South Africa announced a ban on the capture of elephant calves just a few years ago, declaring it unethical. This was despite CITES (the international controlling body of world trade in animals) having deemed this practice legal. But what is legal, and what is ethical, is sometimes two very different things.

It is not quite 7 a.m. when I read Johnny's report. I pick up my mobile phone immediately and ring Minister Nhema, not apologising for the early hour. He claims to know nothing about this. Again.

'How is it that the world now knows about this, and you don't?' I ask boldly, but gently. I get nothing but silence. 'Surely your signature has to be on the export permits?' Still there is only deafening silence on the end of the line.

I know that I've probably said too much but eventually the minister asks me to confirm my information. I do. Others already know about this, they just haven't been game to say anything.

I simply cannot believe that Minister Nhema could know nothing as he claims.

As a foreigner working with elephants here, there is little I can do publicly. But that doesn't mean I do nothing. Joyce Poole once again gets involved from afar. So does the SPCA and a few others in Harare who meet urgently with Minister Nhema. Australian-based activist Jude Price creates a petition to CITES, and lobbies extensively online under the banner 'Elephant E-ctivism' (later renamed 'For Elephants International').

A heartbreaking photograph of one of the forlorn little elephants, languishing in a concrete cell at a Chinese zoo, eventually surfaces. I can tell at a glance that this youngster is not even three years old—ripped from its mother while still suckling. It's deeply distressing to look at this photo. One of the other three elephants imprisoned in China has already died.

By late January, the ministry and the Parks Authority bow to local and international pressure and cancel the deal. I would like to believe that Minister Nhema has seen the light; he does after all, have the final say. The five remaining elephants in *bomas* inside Hwange National Park are too young to be simply released back into the wild, now that they've been separated from their families. They're taken to a fenced Parks facility outside Harare for rehabilitation, where they're integrated with other elephants.

This, though, doesn't help the three already enduring awful conditions in China.

Johnny believes that we haven't seen the last of this. He's convinced that more elephants will ultimately be ripped from their families, and transported to Chinese zoos. The Parks Authority has reportedly stated that it has outstanding orders from zoos in the United States, France and the Ukraine.

I am again questioning why I'm still here.

I have, however, with Minister Nhema's assistance, finally been granted a two-year residence permit. It has only taken me *twelve years* to get this. Yet the immigration department still can't help itself. The permit has been back-dated: in just eighteen months I'll have to fight for yet another permit and dish out more money. For now at least it's better than having to report to Bulawayo every three months, as I've done for the past six years.

'It's like he wants to keep you just close enough to ensure you keep your mouth shut, but not close enough to actually help you in any substantive way,' a colleague says.

I know that Minister Nhema could have done much more, had he really wanted to. An authority letter he promised, to stave off those still trying to make trouble with my land access in Presidential Elephant areas, has never materialised, despite numerous reminders. In the end I figure I have nothing to lose, and request the authority letter directly from the office of the president.

I receive it immediately. It is in my hands within 24 hours, kindly signed by Minister Didymus 'Diesel Rock' Mutasa, who is currently minister of state for presidential affairs. Minister Mutasa is pleased to hear of the continued success of the documentary and appears genuinely delighted that it's been nominated in all four wildlife categories in the 2013 South African Film and Television Awards: Best TV Wildlife Program, Best Director, Best Editor and Best Cinematographer. We talk of inviting the president to come and meet the most special of the elephant families, in an effort to raise more local awareness. Minister Mutasa assures me he will speak to President Mugabe.

But it isn't long before the most disturbing news of all reaches me. The area of Kanondo has been claimed—*again*—following the ex-governor's eviction in 2005. I cannot believe it. I phone Minister Nhema immediately. He says he knows nothing about this. Yet again. He advises me to gather further information. Yet again.

The claimant says she's inherited this land from her recently deceased mother. *Why have I never seen or heard of the mother before?* The fact that nobody, including the minister, is admitting to recognising their names is even more perturbing to me. And I can only imagine the nightmare involved, given local spirit beliefs, in intervening in land purported to have been owned by a dead person.

At first I wonder if there could be some benefits to this claim; new faces could perhaps improve processes. But having private individuals actually owning the land, in such key Presidential Elephant areas, isn't the way. And everything I learn only increases my concerns. It's reported that this land claimant inherited 'a business empire' from her mother and there are no doubt powerful connections in play. Later it's also discovered that this family is in the sport-hunting industry. The claimant is personally named in a post on a sport-hunting website, in which she is directly linked to her brother, offering hunts. It's also reported that the brother has already been in court for hunting illegally. After this information becomes public, the claimant's name quickly disappears from this hunting website and she denies that she will attempt to hunt.

Is this the ex-governor—or his accomplices—simply back in disguise?

I point out to Ministers Nhema and Mutasa that this land encompasses all but one of the waterholes recently scooped out by my donor. I stress that the Presidential Elephants are supposed to be a resource that benefits the nation and that any private claim is bound to have a negative impact on accessibility and therefore on tourist game drives, too. The key home range of a flagship herd simply can't be treated like agricultural land and split into small plots owned and controlled by individuals. I also remind them that the previous claim, on this exact piece of land, was overturned eight years ago.

'Do you recall the precise area I'm talking about?' I ask Minister Nhema over the phone.

'I've known Kanondo since you were in diapers,' he says to me.

I bite my tongue. Minister Nhema is only a couple of years older than me. What I really want to point out to him is that he should know this land area incredibly well since he put his signature on a quota allowing it to be sport-hunted in 2003. That's how well he knows this land. Instead, I remind him of what he said to the press after the decree reaffirmation ceremony: 'Nobody should compromise the Presidential herd.'

He assures me he will deal with it.

He doesn't. Instead, it gets worse. Chief Dingani, who also participated in the decree reaffirmation ceremony, then grabs the land adjacent to Kanondo, also claiming it as his own private property. A wildlife conservation project was actually the first, recently, to lay claim to land in this area and now everyone wants a slice. It is out of control.

I am back on the phone to Minister Nhema. He tells me, again, that he knows nothing; that he will deal with it. But an election is looming and I know well where his priorities lie. I'm also not in a position, nor do I have any desire, to provide a 'facilitation fee', which I know is what's usually required to make things happen in this country.

Once again, there are people who are not happy that I'm speaking out about these latest land grabs and more trouble is brewing. I throw my hands up in the air, and message Barbara in Bulawayo.

'I need a break from all of this. Look out for me in four hours,' I write, just in case I find myself in an 'accident' along the way.

Barbara, Dee and I walk together towards a bakery, where I plan to treat myself to goodies in a small white cardboard box tied up with string. It is always little things that help to make the big things bearable. Inside the box there will be a chocolate éclair, a milk tart, an apple strudel, and a jam donut—all of which I will devour like a hungry hyena.

'Sharon, hello! How are you?' someone shouts at me with a huge smile as we walk along, his hand now extended towards me.

'Fine. I'm fine, thank you. How are you?' I ask.

My hand is held for a moment while we both smile broadly at each other, as I continue to walk along.

'Who was that?' Barbara asks.

'I have no idea,' I admit.

And then it happens again. '*Mandlovu*! How are you?' And the performance is repeated once more.

When this happens a third time Barbara simply whispers, 'You don't know who that person is either, do you?'

'No. I really don't know who any of these people are.'

When an old 4x4 passes by us with hands waving frantically out the window, Barbara decides this is now getting a bit creepy.

And then we pop into a tiny specialty confectionery shop where a young man sidles sheepishly up to my side and says politely, 'Excuse me. You're from Hwange, aren't you?'

'Okay,' I mutter to Barbara, 'you're right. Now this is just plain weird.'

This time, we ask questions. It seems that copies of the documentary have been circulating around Bulawayo and the surrounds. With white skin and blonde hair, I am apparently very easily recognisable walking the streets of Bulawayo.

These people are clearly interested and proud to be associated with me despite President Mugabe's rants against whites. More and more I'm known as *Thandeka Mandlovu*, the much-loved elephant woman. In the bush though, hunters such as Headman Sibanda and other ex-governor cronies just know me as 'fucking white trash'.

The story is different again in Harare where, as far as I know, the documentary has never been mentioned or shown to more than a handful of ministry employees close to Minister Nhema. There is no real desire to make it more widely known that a white person is involved in all of this.

'Keep remembering *Mandlo*,' I am told, 'with these ZANU-PF men, one day if it suits them they'll try to make you feel like you're the cock of the walk, the next day, if it suits them, they'll make sure you're nothing but a feather duster.'

My teeth ache. It's all those chocolates and bakery goodies, and years of neglect. I've only been to a dentist twice in the past twelve years (and to a doctor just as infrequently). Spending money on such things hasn't been a priority and so I put up with the sharp stabs of pain as I eat and long periods of dull aching. I look at the black throw-top I'm wearing and realise it's one that I brought with me to Zimbabwe twelve years ago. It's time for another visit to the street markets.

Barbara looks terrified. 'So long as we don't get accosted by your groupies,' she grins.

# FINDING TIM TAMS

## 2013

On my way back to Hwange I encounter *seven* police roadblocks. More often than not I'm simply waved through, but when I'm stopped in the township of Gwayi, close to Hwange, I smile broadly at the policeman as I always do, and immediately hand over my licence without waiting to be asked.

'I know you,' he declares. 'You are the one who works with elephants.'

Given that I have PRESIDENTIAL ELEPHANT CONSERVATION PROJECT signs prominently displayed in both rear windows, this isn't difficult to figure out. With everything that's happened over the years though, perhaps he does genuinely recognise the name on my licence.

'How are the elephants?' he asks me, in the polite way of the Ndebele.

'Fine. They're fine,' I lie.

Many of the 'new farmers' around this area are in fact hunters, and they loathe me. I'm not interested in getting into a conversation with this cop, who no doubt is well acquainted with them. He knows that I'm aware that commodities like ivory get through these roadblocks far too often—presumably with the help of corrupt police.

I smile again broadly and present him with the palm of my hand, ready to take back my licence. But he tightens his fingers around it and wanders around my 4x4.

He's searching for a misdemeanour that he would expect me to bribe my way out of. 'Headlights!' he barks, indicating I should turn them on.

Oh dear, this isn't good. I never drive on public roads at night because I know that one of my headlights doesn't work properly. Luckily, the sun is shining directly on to them, and he doesn't notice that one's out. He continues his slow waltz around my vehicle and eventually arrives back at my window.

'Thank you,' I say with another encouraging smile, my open palm extended once again towards him. And I have my licence back, before he has a chance to search harder.

On my way home I travel through the estate and run into Whole's and Wilma's families mingling together. They rush to greet me, their temporal glands streaming in excitement, welcoming me as one of their family. Willa is here with her youngest calf, Wobble, and I think back to our kiss when she was pregnant with him. The adorable Wilma has fallen in love with my bull bar and chooses to stand with her trunk curled on top of it, her eyes closed. I can't bear to disturb her, despite the sun beating down on my perishable supplies. I feel uneasy though; I'm constantly wondering if any land claimants will turn up to harass me.

When the documentary screened in France recently, its name was changed to *La Gardienne des Éléphants* (*The Elephant Guardian*). Here I am, guardian over these adorable elephants as they all now snooze around me. *But who is my guardian?*

I continue to liaise with my ministerial contacts over the land claims, and I'm assured that all will be resolved. Chief Dingani is staking his claim, measuring up John's old house, having decided it is now his. I thank the heavens that John is long out of this never-ending mess. I send him a text. He still desperately misses his homeland.

Keith, a white Zimbabwean and chairman of the Farming Dining Club, gets in touch to organise a screening of the documentary in Harare. He and his wife Raynel recently had a particularly memorable encounter with the Presidential Elephants with me on their game-drive vehicle, and are keen to help broaden awareness. I catch a bus to the capital, where it's a full house. 'An exceptional evening, and one of our best ever,' Keith tells me. There are a lot of white farmers in attendance, many of whom have lost everything. I tell them I desperately want to believe that both Ministers Nhema and Mutasa are behind these elephants, and that they'll reverse the land grabs, the same sort of grabs that are achingly familiar to these farmers.

While I'm in Harare, Carol surprises me with the offer of a wonderfully big fridge. It will be the first time in all these years that I can actually freeze and store a reasonable amount of food, and make lots of ice for the long hot hours in the field. The problem is getting it to Hwange, but Keith arranges it all. He and Raynel have quickly become ardent supporters and I'm thankful to have them in my life.

Finally, I have a decent fridge alongside the little microwave that I recently splurged on, an old oil heater of Carol's for the freezing winter nights, and a fan to ease the sizzling summer ones. My thatched roof is covered with wire to shield it from the monkeys and baboons. And I have all the problems with my 4x4 fixed, including the unreliable starter motor which has been getting me stuck in the bush, and the jarring suspension. With the kind help of others, I feel like I'm settled and living a little more comfortably at long last.

What's just as extraordinary is that Tim Tams have become temporarily available in a couple of supermarkets in Harare! I just about fall over myself, prattling on to Carol about how these iconic Aussie biscuits came into the world just two years after me.

But not even Tim Tams can lessen the heartache of the ongoing tragedies.

All too soon there's a horrific snare injury in Whole's family. Greg, Esther and Hans are now based in other parts of the country, so Brent, who works with lions, agrees to help. He'll attempt to dart, but it will be several hours before he can get to me.

The young snared elephant is Wahkuna, Whazup's daughter and Whole's granddaughter. For the next three hours—which is an awfully long time to keep an elephant in one place—I sing and talk to Whole. If I can keep her with me, the rest of the family will stay too.

It's after five o'clock when Brent arrives. After the first dart hits its target, I have to rev my vehicle, bash on my door, and charge at Whazup, since she refuses to leave her daughter, now lying sedated on the ground. I'm unsettled and feel as if I am betraying their trust. Whazup is eventually darted as well (after an earlier misfire, which resulted in Wahkuna being darted first). When she falls some distance away, Whole and others come racing back to help her. And then I have to do it again, aggressively chasing off my beloved Whole.

With a Parks scout standing guard, Brent removes the wire and treats the wound. It is getting dark when Wahkuna and mother Whazup are both finally back on their feet. They're still groggy from the drugs and wander in different directions. There is no sign of Whole and the rest of the family. In darkness and alone now, I pray to the god of wild things that they'll find each other quickly, and will then catch up with the rest of their family. Lions are known to be in the area.

Three days later, Keith and Raynel are in my 4x4 with me—a thank you for all they've recently done—when I encounter this family for the first time since the snare removal. I've been searching for them every day. I recognise Willa in the distance heading into thick bush. I yell to her, 'Come here, Willa. Come here, my girl. Come on, Willa girl.' She turns towards us immediately.

I call to Whole. 'Come on, Whole. Come on, girl. Come here, Whole,' I yell, over and over again. Keith and Raynel must think I'm nuts, since there are no other elephants in sight. I'm simply yelling at the bushes. But I keep calling, knowing that Whole must be there somewhere. All of a sudden she's coming back out of the bushes, moving quickly towards us, her huge head bobbing from side to side. The entire family follows her. Soon, they're all right beside us. Whazup and de-snared Wahkuna are among them, and doing brilliantly. I am just about in tears, and Keith and Raynel are thrilled to have witnessed this reunion. Wahkuna's injury to her back right leg is already looking so much better, and she's putting weight on it.

Surely the authorities will not allow anything to ruin all of this. We talk at length about the private land grabs and what this will mean in terms of sensible access and monitoring of this flagship herd. Keith has some good contacts, and he promises to try to help.

The next afternoon we're surrounded by more than one hundred Presidential Elephants, all of them intensely inquisitive about the strange people I have with me in my vehicle. It is a spectacle to behold and together we savour every minute. And then, without warning, every last one of the elephants race away from us at high speed, their ears flat and tails extended. We have heard absolutely nothing. But the elephants have; distant gunfire audible to their ears only perhaps, or a desperate infra-sound alarm call from other elephants.

I'm back on that same old roller-coaster ride of highs and lows. What's more, I feel like I'm trapped in my own personal adaptation of *Groundhog Day*. Year after year after year, it's the same gut-wrenching problems over and over and over again. It's just a different day.

# BULLDOG WITH A BONE

## 2013

In late July there is another election. This time it's unnervingly calm across the country. ZANU-PF sweeps to a resounding victory. Commentators say there was no need for violence, since ZANU-PF had cooked the electoral roll (which was scandalously unobtainable by the Opposition) so well that it was never going to lose. Voters were turned away, their names supposedly not on the roll, while others were reportedly bussed in to cast their vote. Stories abound of non-existent and long-dead people on the roll. There is no doubt, though, that confidence in the Opposition has certainly dwindled. There are plenty of people who really did vote for ZANU-PF willingly, even if it was in return for nothing much more than a bag of grain. And for the continued downfall of the white man.

Prime Minister Morgan Tsvangirai is out. ZANU-PF rules the country alone once more. I wait with baited breath to see if Minister Francis Nhema remains as wildlife minister.

For the first time ever ZANU-PF have won overwhelmingly on my side of the country, where the Matabeleland massacres took place at their hands, in the early years following Independence. It's difficult to fathom that all of a sudden they seem to have forgotten what the Ruling Party did to them in the 1980s. 'There was the Nazi genocide of the Jews, and the ZANU-PF genocide of the Ndebele, but you didn't see Jews in Adolf Hitler's Germany later becoming Nazis, yet now we have the Ndebele overwhelmingly joining Robert Mugabe's ZANU-PF. Something is not right. There must have been some big bribes,' I hear people say.

In rural areas, the chiefs are said to have frog-marched villagers to polling stations, warning that they will know who to blame if the vote goes the wrong way. Chiefs are well rewarded by ZANU-PF for their efforts. Like with land in Presidential Elephant areas.

In response to international outcry about vote rigging, President Mugabe declares, 'The Western countries holding a different view of our election, we dismiss them as the vile ones whose moral turpitude we must mourn.'

*Who on earth writes his speeches, I wonder? Turpitude? What is turpitude?* 'We think using big words and having great oratory skill, speaking English better than the English themselves, will somehow hide our ignorance,' a black Zimbabwean commentator once wrote. I have to open my laptop's thesaurus to discover that it means 'immorality, wickedness'. Yet again, it is *the West* that is immoral and wicked.

I need more light-hearted relief. I've acquired a cute little bean-bag elephant that I decide to introduce to my elephant friends. And they absolutely adore him! It is just the most amazing thing: wild elephants standing by the door of my 4x4, staring curiously at this little fellow. Some try to steal him, and others look as if they'd like to eat him. He keeps getting himself into extraordinary predicaments but continues to go back for more. I name him Fearless. Whole and Wilma love him most of all. Fearless sits on their tusks, and snuggles up to their long noses. He's an instant hit on the elephants' Facebook page.

He has become the Presidential Elephant mascot, capable of making tens of thousands of people smile with each post.

I don't smile, however, when an email arrives from Carol. 'Now you are really fucked,' is all that it says.

*Oh no, what now?*

In a second email she tells me that President Mugabe has finally announced his new ministers. Francis Nhema has been assigned to a more powerful ministry and Saviour Kasukuwere is now wildlife minister. I've heard his name bandied about, unfavourably.

'Kasukuwere was previously the Minister of Youth Development, Indigenisation and Empowerment,' Carol tells me. 'He's long had a leadership role in the ZANU-PF youth wing and is said to have been instrumental in rallying the youth, and personally driving a lot of the farm invasion and election violence. He's ex CIO, a former bodyguard of Mugabe, and big with all of the anti-white policies.'

Nervously, I search the internet. There are plenty of entries. The first one I read says that Saviour Kasukuwere is known as 'Paraquat' for endorsing the use of this highly toxic herbicide on the torture wounds of Opposition party activists. He's better known as 'Tyson'—after US heavyweight boxer Mike Tyson—for his bulk and aggressive style. One journalist refers to him as 'a thug in a suit'. There are first-hand accounts of him having wielded an iron bar himself; not just simply directing the violence. He's described as one of the most violent ZANU-PF ministers. In one newspaper article he likens *himself* to Hitler.

I take a deep breath and pour myself a glass of red wine, resisting the urge to drink straight from the bottle. I can't believe that after all I've been through with Minister Nhema, I have to start all over again. With this.

I understand enough about Zimbabwe to know that not all of this may be true. But I decide that I should probably fear him. Not yet 43 years old, he is the baby of Mugabe's Cabinet, where the average age is around 70. (Old age is relative when your president is nearly 90 years old. The head of the *youth* league is reported to be 61!) Officials are rarely appointed on merit. Kasukuwere is too young to be a liberation war hero and isn't reported to be related to anyone special. I decide, therefore, that he could well be a thug of note.

But then I decide that I'm not going to fear him after all. I will try to work closely with him. My opportunity comes soon afterwards. He's on Facebook, taking questions about his new portfolio. I post a comment, introducing myself. His reply is a one-word command: 'Call'.

But I have no idea how to call this man. The next day he phones me. 'Sharon, this is Saviour,' he says in a surprisingly friendly, happy and pleasant tone. I'm taken aback. Straight away he's on a first-name basis with me, which is unusual. He is polite and well spoken—but then so was the ex-governor when I first met him.

Over the course of our first long conversation later that day, I tell him about absolutely everything. He probably already knows most of it, but I want him to hear it directly from me. I tell him about the allegations of spying levelled at me by his mate, the ex-governor, and the harassment and intimidation I've endured, including being on the wanted persons list. I speak at length about the land claims, stressing that this needs immediate resolution. And I tell him about the debauched hunting fraternity who continue to try to make trouble for me. I also remind him that I am white—which gets a little laugh—and I tell him, as I'd previously told Minister Nhema, that if he can find a black person who is prepared to work for no salary as I've done, and who can secure accommodation, and buy a 4x4, and fund food, fuel, a computer and field equipment for themselves, then I will be more than happy to hand over to this person immediately. Which gets another little laugh.

In response, he tells me that he is a businessman, first and foremost. The bush is not really his thing. But while he may have been dumped into this role, it's clear to me that he's determined to make an impact regardless.

And he does, almost immediately.

Johnny Rodrigues reports that hundreds of elephants, perhaps more than three hundred, are dead from cyanide poisoning in an area just south of Hwange. Their ivory tusks are gone. Poisoning elephants is not new in Africa. For centuries, tribal people have used natural toxic ingredients from trees on their spears to kill a few. But now ivory has real value, and commercial poisons are being used here to kill en masse. This had started—but had not been publicly reported—under Minister Nhema's watch. Minister Kasukuwere springs into action.

A delegation of ministers flies into Hwange to discuss this catastrophic poaching case and Minister Kasukuwere invites me to meet him at the airport, to chat during his chauffeured drive into Main Camp. He is indeed a big bear of a man. Without a line on his face, he looks like he's been Photoshopped.

A few weeks later, after more poisoned elephants are discovered even closer to Hwange, I contact Minister Kasukuwere again and suggest we urgently need to see what is really going on from the air. 'If we can arrange a plane and a pilot, prepared to fly for free, will you provide the fuel?' I ask.

'Absolutely,' he says, without hesitation.

And instantly we have an agreement. I speak to a contact in Wildlife Environment Zimbabwe, whose assistance will be crucial, and then to a white Zimbabwean in Harare named Pat Cox, who will pilot his own plane, a Cessna 206, which has room for five pairs of eyes in addition to the pilot. Minister Kasukuwere does exactly what he said he would, and the fuel is paid for and ready for collection. I've never experienced such efficiency here when dealing with a government department.

I urge vigilance since we don't know who is involved in this poaching racket, and how much our presence will ruffle feathers. The fuel, and also the plane while it's on the ground in Hwange, is subsequently secured against sabotage. We don't manage to secure against hyenas, however, and overnight one chews the tip of the tailplane (a small wing which provides stability). We awake to fragments of plane scattered on the ground.

'Do you have any duct tape?' Pat asks.

'*Really?*' I screech.

I loathe light aircraft, and now I'm flying in one patched with duct tape after it's been chewed on by a carnivore! Pat gives me motion sickness tablets and I suck away on his boiled sweets, as six of us fly in previously plotted, tight transects, scanning for carcasses. Pat flies as close to the ground as he dares. What we see over the course of several days confirms that a tragedy has certainly unfolded here, but thankfully the number of elephants dead from poisoning is less than half that reported.

There is, however, an additional alarming find. 'It may just be rocky boulders, but there's something way out to the left,' I shout over the roar of the engine. 'You need to circle around.' Simion, a National Parks scout who I respect, sees something too. Unlike some of his colleagues in the plane, he never nods off. We are all anxious as the aircraft banks around.

And there they are: another eight elephants dead. Fresh carcasses, with tusks already gone, lying quite close to a key Main Camp tourist spot inside Hwange National Park. Simion is immediately on his mobile phone, calling in ground forces, ensuring that they're ready to get into the field immediately upon our return to base. Pat takes coordinates and I take photographs to show the Parks warden.

When we land, I phone Minister Kasukuwere with the disturbing news.

I don't even want to think about what this new bout of poisoning would have escalated into, had these flights not happened at once. Minister Kasukuwere is quick to demand further action and answers from his men on the ground. No Presidential Elephants have been affected, but it's all now far too close for comfort.

Simion is back in the field without delay, where he and other rangers discover three additional carcasses and uncover buried ivory. They track a lone poacher and show him no mercy. But it is the Mr Bigs of the poaching rings who continue to evade capture.

These poachers are poisoning mineral licks with cyanide, a substance that is supposed to be strictly controlled. Even a creature as mighty as an elephant doesn't get more than 50 metres or so before the poison takes its toll. It's a simple way to kill. There is no telltale noise from rifles. There's also no need to hack off the face with an axe, which is a time-consuming and messy task, since the poison causes the bodies to decompose rapidly, and within just a day or so the tusks slide out of their sockets effortlessly. There are ancillary deaths in the animal kingdom but thankfully not as many as might be expected. This type of poison not only quickly turns the meat putrid, making it generally unpalatable, but it also very quickly detoxifies. Hungry animals that get to the elephant carcasses *swiftly* however, most notably flocks of vultures, are certainly poisoned.

Minister Kasukuwere and I have kept in touch every day. While Pat is flying back to Harare, I suggest to the minister that he might like to personally thank Pat for his time and generous use of his aircraft. He invites Pat into his offices for a cup of tea. Then he goes one better, and thanks him on social media. He thanks me publicly too, which is a first from any official here.

After it is admitted that poisoning has been going on for some time, the Parks warden on the ground in Hwange casually describes his lack of reporting as 'an oversight'. Minister Kasukuwere, on the other hand, publicly acknowledges serious problems not only with out-of-control poaching, but with tree-felling, abuse of wetlands (for development), and also the contamination of waterways. He may be a thug, but perhaps a thug is what we need right now.

'He's like a bloody big bulldog with a bone,' I say to those who ask about him.

# THE LOG WITH TEETH

## 2013

*All the President's Elephants* is still gathering acclaim around the world, winning 'Outstanding Contribution to Nature' at this year's Japan Wildlife Film Festival. 'It is very moving to see how closely people and elephants can be mentally connected,' the judges commented, while expressing respect and appreciation for my work. I'm still not used to this sort of public acclaim but am pleased the elephants are in the spotlight. It was also a finalist for an International Gold Panda award at the Sichuan TV festival in China, nominated for 'Best Nature and Environment Protection'. This is somewhat ironic given all that's currently going on with the Presidential Elephants and their land, and also taking into account China's love of ivory. But it's so important that documentaries like this one are shown and appreciated in countries like China, where instilling a love and respect for elephants, and not their ivory, is paramount.

I've broadened my work area to include adjoining Forestry Commission land, where I know the Presidential Elephants also roam, since this protected property surely won't ever be claimable under land reform. I've secured for them a very generous donation of a solar-powered water pump, plenty of solar panels, and a tall robust stand so that the panels are out of the elephants' reach. Water for the wildlife is an ongoing problem in these areas just outside the national park boundary (where most operators still care only about their own lodge waterholes), so I'm eagerly anticipating this delivery.

I make plans to remove the mass of weed from some key waterholes, even though they're in the claimed areas. An unpalatable, invasive weed is smothering the surfaces of two of them, including one of those at Kanondo. Parks staff don't often venture here, but given the ongoing land claim mess I drag the head warden out with me for a site inspection so he can see the problems first-hand, and give me permission to proceed.

Together with the men I've employed, we search hard for crocodiles before they start the heavy, dirty work. But we haven't searched well enough! There's a splash, and suddenly the men are hollering and dancing around in the pan.

'I thought it was a log,' Chrispen says frantically, still trying to extract his feet from the muddy bottom. 'I was kicking it with my foot, and then I bent down to pick it.'

'Arrhhh, that log has teeth,' Costa shudders. 'That one, it is too clever,' he decides.

The croc is about a metre and a half long; big enough to do some damage. I phone the head Parks warden to organise a team of skilled men to come and capture it.

'There's no crocodile in there,' they all declare after first looking around for spoor, and running their huge net through the pan once.

We know better! It takes time and there's a lot more hollering and dancing about, but the cunning croc is eventually caught.

Always, when times are tough and my spirit runs low, new people pop into my life. I like to imagine that the 'spirit messengers', the soaring bateleurs, are helping to make this happen.

I'm glad to now know Ayesha Cantor. She runs a Facebook page focusing on life in Africa that's very popular and a lot of fun, which she also uses to raise awareness for rhinos. She adores elephants too, and is fortunate to live close to Addo National Park in South Africa. We chat frequently online about conservation issues. After a power surge blows up one of my laptops and damages the other, Ayesha secretly puts out a plea for a replacement, and a man named Roby Sabatino obliges. I am floored by this kindness. Others cooperate, in a string of compassion, to get the laptop into my hands. When I ask Roby to name the latest addition to the Presidential herd, who happens to have been born into the A family (the daughter of Aya, granddaughter of Anya), he calls her Ayesha. And I have another extra special little elephant to keep track of. I'm not as alone in all of this as I sometimes think that I am.

Which is good to know, especially when Chief Dingani turns up on my doorstep, brandishing his official 'offer letter' that declares him to be one of the new land-owners in the key home range of the Presidential Elephants. 'I don't care about the President's Office,' the chief barks at me after I try to explain why this land should never be subject to individual claims.

*That will be interesting for them to know, I think to myself.*

'They have rewarded me with this land,' he tells me.

*That's even more interesting. Why doesn't he just go ahead and call it a bribe?*

'Nobody can tell me what to do. I am the Chief. I am going to the police, you are not allowed on my land,' he declares as he leaves. 'You are not even a Zimbabwean.'

I feel his piercing, parting shot hit my heart. Yet, I can't argue with this. Try as I might, I still can't even get permanent residency here, let alone citizenship, even after nearly thirteen years of working with the *president's* elephants.

His visit has rattled me. He's already threatened to make trouble for anybody who helps me, including the lodge where I'm based. I immediately text Ministers Kasukuwere, Mutasa and Nhema. I know that all of them will take my calls.

Minister Kasukuwere phones me immediately. His concern for me appears so genuine that for the first time while speaking in a professional capacity, I momentarily break down in tears. 'Rest assured that I will resolve this matter,' he immediately confirms to me in writing. And later he writes, 'I will get you permanent residency. Trust me.'

At a Cabinet meeting in early December, a document from the Parks Authority is tabled recommending that all offer letters in the area of the Presidential Elephants be withdrawn.

'All of the offer letters will be withdrawn,' Minister Kasukuwere confirms to me after the meeting. This gives me some renewed hope, but knowing what I do about how things work in this country, I'm still hesitant to believe it will actually happen. I admit to feeling increasingly nervous driving around by myself, especially on the one-way bush roads where there's no possibility of escape if approached. He assures me that I have no reason to feel anxious, and that the land claimants will soon be gone.

Two days later, I join the world in mourning the death of Nelson Mandela. The differences between Mandela and Mugabe, both freedom fighters in their own countries, is glaring. As South Africa's first black president Nelson Mandela championed racial reconciliation. He was unwaveringly patient and widely revered. By contrast, Robert Mugabe is generally viewed as a dictatorial leader of a brutal regime. But he, too, has many admirers, especially in Africa. At Nelson Mandela's memorial service in Johannesburg, President Mugabe is greeted by thunderous applause. I wonder what Mandela would think of that, given he once said, 'I detest racialism, because I regard it as a barbaric thing, whether it comes from a black man or a white man.'

From Nelson Mandela's homeland, my friend Henry and his son Caleb arrive, and insist that I join them for a break of a few days before

Christmas. My old trusty Range Rover was sold for a song, after sitting under a tarp for several months on their Gwayi property. This family has been so kind to me over the years. Caleb is now a striking nineteen year old, who prides himself on having met all three of my favourite elephants, Lady, Whole and Misty, and has developed an intense love of all wildlife. They're booked for two nights at Ngweshla campsite, inside the national park, where we enjoy a fantastic few days. It's a terrific campsite for wildlife sightings, but is renowned for its perilous-looking wire fence, which is low and full of holes.

Their tent leaks in the pouring rain while I snuggle in my sleeping bag under an ominously open-sided, roofed structure, with a picnic table in its middle and my mosquito net draped from the wooden beams above.

'Come and join me under thatch,' I urge. 'It's nice and dry out here.'

'No ways,' they say, while listening to the roaring lions.

'Listen to that,' I tease. 'Is that a roar? Really? A roar?' I have to admit that with all that grunting, a lion's roar always sounds more like a cross between constipation and orgasm to me!

Caleb is over the moon the next day as he photographs two of the sleek, nimble cats as they make a kill right in front of us. For me, it is heart-wrenching. A lioness springs into action and brings down a baby wildebeest, but skilfully keeps it alive so she can teach her adolescent offspring how to kill. She toys with it, waiting for her daughter to arrive for her vital life lesson. Then they play a game of catch and release. I wish it had ended much more quickly for the tiny wildebeest calf. But it is nature's way.

The dominant black-maned lion named Cecil also graces us with his presence. We sit and watch him and his big blond-maned friend as they snooze, stretch and yawn. One of these boys will be the father of the cub. We laugh at how lazy they are, and enjoy their regal company for an hour or so. Cecil is still as 'astronomical' as ever.

We laugh too at the African-print shirt I have on. I happen to be wearing it every time I see these guys. It's another top I brought with me from Australia way back in 2001 and I've worn it regularly in the field over the past thirteen years. In photographs with the Presidential Elephants, no matter what year it is, I'm frequently seen in this shirt! I really should allow myself to splurge on a few more items at the street markets, I decide.

'You should auction that thing online on eBay,' Caleb declares. 'You could make a good dollar—that shirt has history!'

After a wonderful few days full of fun and friendship they drop me back at my cottage. Henry knows that he won't likely be able to hold on to his Gwayi property for much longer. Odds are he'll very soon become yet another victim of the land reform program. Not even humanitarian projects are safe these days. 'These land grabs will be the death of Zimbabwe if they don't get things under control,' he laments, and I couldn't agree with him more.

'Santa's even more unlikely to visit you now,' Henry jokes as he drives off. 'He used to be scared that somebody would shoot his reindeers. Now he's terrified that somebody will poison or capture them!'

The air is thick with mosquitoes. I'm having to contend with leaking water pipes, both inside and outside my cottage. My geyser and water-reserve drum have also sprung new leaks. What's more, everything from my refrigerator to my hot water taps is giving me electric shocks. 'Always wear rubber slops (thongs)' is the only solution I've been offered thus far. It'll take weeks to get this all properly sorted. But once it is, I know I'll be set for at least a couple of years, without having to outlay more time and money.

Later, when I drive into Dete to get a flat tyre repaired, I bump into a black Zimbabwean named Jerry who used to work for the Parks Authority. We don't see each other very often these days. Years ago, I took him out with me to meet the Presidential Elephants and we had an extraordinary encounter with Whole, which he has never forgotten. Initially, he'd been terrified of this enormous elephant right beside him, but soon he was so moved that he asked if he could bring his family to meet her one day.

When I tell him about the latest land grabs, he hugs me tightly and says, 'If they take that land, then it's all over.' All I can do is blink back the tears that spring from nowhere and threaten to spill down my cheeks.

# A FOOL'S ERRAND

## 2014

The new year doesn't begin well. The land claimants are digging in despite the Cabinet directive: erecting signs, diverting water, and becoming more abusive to me and lodge game-drive vehicles full of tourists who report their 'ranting and raving'. One afternoon at Kanondo, where I'd been observing a snared elephant, a hand suddenly comes through my window and my locked door is flung open. My arm is grabbed by a male who flings his other arm across my body in an attempt to snatch the keys from the ignition. Then he has a shot at grabbing my mobile phone from my hand. I manage to dial and speak to Minister Kasukuwere, which unsettles this man and his land-grabbing companion enough for them to back off and leave. Despite having been ordered off the land, I remain in the area until nightfall.

That evening the local CIO agent phones me to advise that the land claimant has demanded I be arrested for trespassing on her private land. After I report this, Minister Kasukuwere emails me with just one word: 'Calm'. When I speak to him again, he assures me that everything is under control. 'With all due respect, minister,' I tell him, 'I think you need to come into the field and see for yourself that this is absolutely not under control.'

When I speak to Minister Mutasa, he assures me that the Cabinet directive still stands and I shouldn't be impatient. I certainly know that things take time in Zimbabwe. However, I also know that the more entrenched the claimants become, the more difficult it will be to remove them.

For safety's sake, I'm advised to collect a National Parks scout from Main Camp every day, to accompany me in the field. This is not realistic however. Not only do Parks not have the spare resources, but collecting and dropping off a scout each day would add several hundred dollars a month to my fuel bill. And there is no donor covering my costs.

I decide to travel to Harare to speak with Minister Kasukuwere in person. I know that he already has one of my books, and I bring to our meeting a copy of my latest one, along with a DVD of the documentary. When he asks me to sign the book, above my signature I write that I can't keep doing this without his help.

But I am on a fool's errand.

When I attempt to discuss the land claims, Minister Kasukuwere dismisses the topic immediately, waving it away with his hand. 'That must be fixed by now,' he says brusquely, and requests that our conversation move on. I persist for as long as I can, but get nowhere. I move on to my visa problems and ask about the permanent residency that he'd assured me he would secure. He says it is done, that I just need to get to Immigration with my passport. The reality, sure enough, turns out to be vastly different.

'I can never be certain what's going on with anything anymore,' I lament to Carol over a glass of white wine in her garden. 'Not that I've ever been sure of anything. But now I'm sure that I just can't keep going through all of this, time and time again.'

'I don't know how you've put up with it all for so long,' Carol sighs. She's been a friend and supporter since soon after I arrived in 2001 and can see that I'm well and truly at my wits' end. I'm not the only one: there are signs tacked to tree trunks around the streets of Harare that scream, IF YOU'RE NOT OUTRAGED, YOU'RE NOT PAYING ATTENTION. I *am* paying attention to what's happening in this country, and I am certainly outraged.

There is some happy news, though, that we delight in: Wilma has had a new baby, as gorgeous as can be, and Worry, whom Carol named as a day-old calf way back in 2002, is pregnant for the very first time. Despite it all, another generation has begun.

When Carol drives me to the bus stop in the city centre, both of us wonder if this might be the last time that I am here in the capital.

I overnight in Bulawayo, and decide on the spur of the moment to stock up on food supplies. I need to feel grounded and normal again, I need to feel like I'm going to stay put. I've been delaying restocking my fridge and pantry, always so unsure of what's happening from one day to the next.

'Come with me,' I urge Barbara. 'I'm going to do a big shop.'

'If I was you, I wouldn't even be buying green bananas,' she says.

'Imagine having this great big fridge and being too scared to fill it. Come on, I'm going to do it,' I laugh.

Back in Hwange, it isn't long before it becomes increasingly clear that something is seriously amiss. It's been two months since the Cabinet directive, and things on the ground have only gotten worse, despite Minister Kasukuwere even now assuring a South African journalist that all offer letters have been withdrawn.

The police are threatening to throw me in jail, for trespassing on grabbed land. I can't help wondering if this actually has more to do with the poaching case I'm pursuing, after two very well-connected men from Dete were caught with elephant tusks last year. Month after month after month their court date is postponed and they're allowed to walk free. The system is so corrupt and broken, even ivory poachers manage to keep going about their lives, knowing it could well be years before any real action is taken against them. If this happens at all.

What's more, the land claimants are now publicly declaring that I've made myself rich out of these elephants! Somehow, of course, they have to try to discredit me. I look around at how frugally I've been forced to live for all of these years.

My oldest sister, Genevieve, makes contact to tell me that our Uncle Cecil—my mother's brother—has died. I look skywards and an image of the big black-maned lion also pops into my mind. Since first meeting Cecil the lion, I can't seem to think of one without the other. As a Lutheran pastor Uncle Cecil had seen a lot over the years, including when he was based in a developing country. Every time we'd seen one another over the last ten years he told me he thought it was time I left Zimbabwe. I wasn't aware that family had been called to his bedside, but his words had been ringing in my ears.

Genevieve had been planning to visit me this year, but I tell her now this is not wise, and that maybe Uncle Cecil is right. Maybe it really is time. My dad, now in his eighties, thinks it's past time. My parents have grown old while I've been in Africa; my dad's body has been in severe decline since the Grantham floods. He's basically immobile now, being cared for in the family home by my mum, with help from my sisters when they're able. A high-care nursing home will eventually become necessary. He's mentally alert though, and frequently insists that I'm '*verruckt in the kopf*' ('crazy in the head', as his German-born grandfather taught his father to say) for staying in Robert Mugabe's Zimbabwe.

I try for more assistance from Minister Mutasa, my faith now wavering in Minister Kasukuwere. He has fallen ill however, and has been out of the country. Some of the Parks Authority management are still doing what they can to ensure the Cabinet directive is enforced, but there are others clearly trying to frustrate the process, and nothing changes on the ground. A couple of government officials, I'm told, have been sent to Hwange to investigate. They talk to Parks staff, land claimants and hunters. It is surely significant that not one of them tries to speak to me.

It is increasingly clear that deals have been done by local officials, deals that even the Harare heavyweights are not fully aware of. I know that none of this is actually about elephants. It is all about politics. And I am more and more distressed by this knowledge.

There has been talk that the chief has had his offer letter withdrawn, but I'm also hearing that he is determined to make more trouble for me. Sometimes I awake to unknown footprints around my cottage. I've been warned I should check my 4x4 each morning for evidence of tampering.

I hold my breath now as I start my engine, silently hoping that it doesn't explode in a ball of fire. Five friends are checking on me daily.

'You must drive back to town *now*,' Shaynie begs.

'Not yet, Shaynie. I need to see this through,' I say, giving her instructions on what to do if I don't answer my phone.

'One day,' she says to me in an email, 'I think I'm going to kill you *myself*!'

Which for a moment at least, makes me smile. She insists on making contact *twice* daily.

By now a fourth Cabinet minister is involved, Minister Sylvester Nguni from the Vice-President's Office, trying to find out why the Cabinet directive has not been enforced. 'We are trying to find a permanent way forward,' Minister Kasukuwere assures me again—but by now his words are as ephemeral as the wind.

Recently released reports reveal that over 100,000 African elephants were slaughtered for their ivory between 2010 and 2012, more than 40,000 of them in Southern Africa. Last year, another 30,000 elephants were massacred. Not only is this one every fifteen minutes, it's almost the equivalent of Hwange National Park's entire population of elephants wiped out in just one year. It would certainly appear that the CITES-approved (legal) sale of ivory in 2008 has fuelled the illegal trade.

As a result of escalating poaching in Zimbabwe, the United States Fish and Wildlife Service (USFWS) has announced a suspension on the importation of sport-hunted elephant trophies from Zimbabwe into the United States. The Wildlife Ministry and local hunters are livid about this, since most of their sport-hunting clients come from America and will now likely choose to take their hunting dollars elsewhere.

Predictably, Minister Kasukuwere starts referring to this ban as 'illegal sanctions on our elephants'. Just as predictably, the local hunters consider that I am partly to blame for this ban. I hear that they are, once again, out to try to crucify me. USFWS made its own decision based on concerns about the long-term survival of elephants in Zimbabwe, its questionable management practices, lack of effective law enforcement and weak governance. I am certainly not the only one who knows that there's uncontrolled poaching and unethical hunting going on here. I'm pleased the Australian government has already banned the importation of any elephant trophy, from any country, including Zimbabwe—although this is yet another thing that some Zimbabwe hunters choose to blame on me.

Meanwhile, the ex-governor's relations have managed to get their hunting quota reinstated for the land they've retained, between the two photographic lodges, despite Minister Nhema's declaration a few years ago that they must never again be allowed to hunt this area. Equally concerning, local Parks Authority staff try to justify their reissuing of this permit, stating these men no longer hunt on their own land; they shoot their quota on *other* people's land (where a quota has already been issued to *that* land-owner). How is this sustainable hunting? Now I'm expected to sit back and accept two hunting quotas on one piece of land! What's more, Parks is also issuing quotas to other people in areas where they should not be allowed to hunt at all, and certainly haven't been in the past.

I am absolutely bone weary of the harassment but I don't sit back quietly. Some people are furious that I continue to question what is happening. It is those who don't openly or publicly threaten me that I fear the most.

With Minister Nguni now involved, I still hold out some small hope that the land claim issue might at least be resolved.

On 21 February, President Robert Mugabe turns 90. 'What happened to "He won't be around for much longer"?' I mumble to myself.

In ten days time Minister Kasukuwere is scheduled to be in Hwange for World Wildlife Day. I've committed to have the recently delivered solar-powered water pump up and running on one of the Forestry Commission waterholes for him to commission during the afternoon. I enlist the help of Gary from 'Friends of Hwange', who looks after numerous pumps and boreholes inside the national park and has the expertise and equipment I need, to work alongside the equally competent installation team from Grundfos South Africa who donated the rig. All that can go wrong does, despite their combined skills, but eventually Gary pulls this monstrosity of a contraption upright with his 4x4 tractor. I can barely watch, fearing that this gigantic stand will topple right over, smashing all of its 24 solar panels. We fudge a few things at the last minute, to do with the troublesome borehole, in order to make everything look 100 per cent complete.

A whole swag of officials, and guests and reporters arrive on the afternoon of World Wildlife Day. The head of the Forestry Commission is Darlington Duwa, who was actually in my 4x4 when Minister Nhema first met Misty and the Presidential Elephants. He remembers Misty emphatically, and still has her photo on his phone.

Darlington's speech contains a surprise. The waterhole to be filled by this solar-powered pump is called Mdlawuzo (a name that few whites, including myself, can pronounce). 'Now we will know it as Sharon's pan,' Darlington declares.

I am not only shocked by this but also embarrassed. 'Sharon's pan' sounds truly awful! I thank him graciously and remind him that the local people call me *Mandlovu*. Perhaps the pan could instead be known as '*Mandlovu* pan' in celebration, too, of 'mother elephants' like Misty.

I celebrate with the installation team in front of the dignitaries and beneath the towering solar panels, by cracking open some bubbles. We all take a swig, straight from the bottle.

And then I'm hit by a devastating low. During drinks at the Forestry Commission's Ganda Lodge, Minister Kasukuwere finally admits that the land grabbers will not likely be removed. 'After everything, you're now going to leave them there?' I ask him, bewildered. 'Why did you put me at risk over all of this, for so long, checking on things and passing on information, if you're going to just leave them there? What has happened to the Cabinet directive?' Minister Kasukuwere storms off without another word and climbs into his chauffeured vehicle.

The land claim saga is not over yet, however, and Minister Kasukuwere emails me again about 'a permanent way forward'. These guys are known for keeping their friends close, and their enemies even closer. The trouble is, I don't know any more whether I'm considered friend or foe. It's a dangerous place to be, if you're on the wrong side of these men. As Minister Francis Nhema once told me: 'You only exist there because I allow you to.'

# THE LITMUS TEST

## 2014

It's now nearly four long months since the Cabinet directive and there is nothing to indicate that the situation with the land grabs will ever change. All there's been is more useless talk. This uncertainty, combined with all of the endless harassment and frustrations, is hard to bear. The documentary is screening once again in parts of Europe, showcasing my work to even more people, raising much-needed awareness and generating a lot of positive vibes for Zimbabwe. But I simply cannot ride this roller-coaster anymore.

I snap.

It's been another year of constant battles. I realise now that no matter how much I contribute, none of President Mugabe's ministers are about to put their necks on the line to help, at least not for long. I have no faith anymore, and no hope. What's more, I'm feeling emotionally battered and disloyal to myself. As much as I adore my elephant friends and am anxious about their welfare, I'm no longer even sure of who I can trust. Is it finally time to walk away?

I force myself to take more time to think this through. Just like after Lady's death, I take to my bed and curl up in a ball. Tears flow. It's not like me, to crumble like this, and the answer comes to me. I know—for certain this time—that this is finally it. I have to leave. I fear that I'm becoming hardened to much that is awful and wrong. Worse, I risk becoming complicit. As desperately sad as it is, my mind does not waiver. I simply can't do this anymore. I remember my litmus test: 'You have six months to live and can do anything you wish with your remaining time on earth. Where will you spend your time?' I know it would not be here. Anywhere but here.

After speaking with friends, I decide to take the nuclear option and post about the situation openly on the elephants' Facebook page. This is not the sort of thing that you do in Zimbabwe. But I'd tried dealing with this privately and quietly. It hadn't worked.

The consequences of going public are predictable. Revenge is one thing you can always count on in this country. The land grabbers, the hunters and a few others, including Minister Saviour Kasukuwere himself, at least temporarily, are now out to jointly discredit me.

But my work with these elephants has been widely celebrated for more than a decade. The support I receive both locally and internationally is overwhelming, even more so after an interview I give to *National Geographic*. It's the only one that I agree to do.

'Sharon is to elephants what Dian Fossey and Jane Goodall are to gorillas and chimps,' Don Pinnock, a respected South African investigative journalist, is later quoted as saying. 'She's put up a heroic fight for so, so long and in giving up in the face of such poaching and brutal opposition is a real danger signal for elephants in Zimbabwe and, really, in Africa.'

Zimbabwean author and conservationist Bookey Peek writes to me: 'Your leaving is a tragedy . . . You have done everything a person could possibly do, and so much more . . . You must be proud, so very proud, of that . . . There is no stronger testimony to love, dedication and absolute trust than that picture of you leaning out of your cruiser and giving your girl a kiss . . . They will never forget you.'

Craig Rix, the publisher of *Travel Africa* magazine, echoes Bookey's sentiments from the United Kingdom. 'You selflessly battled away, in a way that most of us wouldn't have the courage to do. Take heart that you did everything you could.'

Ever-supportive Ayesha in South Africa sends me a little online plaque that reads, 'Sometimes you have to chuck it in the fuck-it bucket, and move on.'

I hear nothing from Minister Kasukuwere until two weeks before my 52nd birthday, and then I don't hear directly from him: he sends a Parks Authority person to my door on Easter Sunday night to tell me that I must report to him in Harare, on Tuesday, for an 8 a.m. meeting.

'He can't talk to me himself?' I ask. 'Has he all of a sudden lost my phone number?' I'm as cranky as a snared buffalo about this, and not careful with my words. 'Do you guys honestly expect me to just get up in the morning and drive more than eight hours to Harare, on the last day of a busy public holiday? Are you serious?' I know that scores of people will likely die tomorrow on the awful Zimbabwe roads—which makes me wonder, fleetingly, if the plan is to simply add one more.

And then he tells me something that he's probably not supposed to. 'That one who took Kanondo,' he says, 'you will be there together. You have to go.'

I simply shake my head, close my door and email ministers Kasuku-were, Mutasa and Nhema. I write that I am absolutely not interested, at this late stage, in entertaining any land grabber who they may have now decided I should work alongside. I know what I believe to be right and wrong with all of this. I have compromised enough over the years, more often than I should have. I simply cannot compromise myself further now.

I need to stand in my own truth. I make it clear that I will not be trav-elling to Harare to be a part of this sham.

I know that attempts to discredit me will now intensify.

The next day I can't even bring myself to risk going back out on the estate to try to find my elephant friends, who by now number over five hundred.

I just can't face it. It will be easier not to say goodbye. I still need to figure out the logistics of leaving. What do I try to take with me, and what do I leave behind? Should I attempt to ship anything? What about my 4x4?

I learn that in Australia, activist Jude Price, under the banner 'For Elephants International', has created an online petition protesting the Presidential Elephant land grabs. These days it seems there are a million online petitions about a million different issues, most of which go nowhere. Activists come in all shapes and forms, not all of them necessarily helpful and skilled. A good advocate is one who is focused, diplomatic and knowledgeable; someone who doesn't run on emotion and ego and who follows through. Jude is one of these. And she does more than just advocate. From her home in Adelaide, she actively raises funds. 'I know that your mind is made up, and I understand your decision to leave,' Jude tells me. 'We're proceeding regardless.'

She's been working with another committed online group called 'March For Elephants' and the petition is live. A few Zimbos concerned with animal welfare are involved too. I'm grateful for their interest and concern, but I am feeling completely drained. I leave them to it. In a country like Zimbabwe, where the government cares little about public opinion, and where so many suspicious deals are done, I don't hold out much hope that their efforts will change anything for the elephants.

My friend Reason, who I've known for many years by now, unexpectedly arrives on my doorstep, unaware of everything going on. We sit together on my sofa.

'*Mandlo*, your sofa is broken,' he exclaims, clearly startled by how he has sunk down almost to the floor. 'Broken like Zimbabwe,' he adds without even a hint of a smile.

I fill him in on all of the latest.

'You must be angry,' he declares.

'Angry?' I think about this for a moment. 'No, I'm not angry,' I say. 'I'm just really very *disappointed.*'

'Arrhhh but that is much worse than angry,' he says. 'You're leaving, yes?'

'Yes,' I say. 'This time I really am.'

'Having to step away from these *ndlovus*, is like stepping away from an overcrowded kombi [Zimbabwe's notoriously dangerous minibuses]. It might save your life,' he says.

We sit in silence.

'Do you know what the worst part is?' he asks me.

I say nothing.

'Arrhhh, but there are too many worst parts,' he decides, shaking his head. 'It is best to leave now now,' he tells me. This is the Zimbabwean way of saying *right now*. 'Nothing will change. This government, they always want to send hyenas to investigate other hyenas over what has happened to the missing goats. It never works.'

'You're right,' I say, 'it doesn't.'

'It matters, no, if a goat or a cow or a cat is black or white. You, *Mandlo*, are white, it does not matter, you and me are the same. Stand up proud that you caught many mice. You are not hungry now. You can leave happy. I will be seeing you back one day.'

Reason's words are comforting in a way that only those from a black African can be. He puts the back of one hand into the palm of the other and pats his heart. He wishes me well as he walks away.

I've lived in Hwange longer than I've ever lived anywhere in my life, including my childhood home, which I left when I was twelve for boarding school. This is my home. It will not be easy to leave.

Johnny Rodrigues has become aware of further plans to rip young elephants from their families inside Hwange National Park to send to Chinese zoos. He fears this could involve hundreds of young elephants this time around. My mind and stomach reel from this news. None of this would be happening without Minister Kasukuwere's approval and support.

Just as concerning, Minister Kasukuwere has been urging Zimbabwe-ans to 'lobby the world' so that more of its stockpiled ivory can be legally sold to China and other Asian countries. One elephant is being poached in Africa every fifteen minutes and this is how Zimbabwe responds to the crisis, despite the Parks Director General recently acknowledging that 'poaching will remain a threat in the country's vast game parks as long as there is a ready market for ivory and rhino horn'.

On the evening of my birthday I sigh wearily when I once again hear repeated gunfire from my cottage, and I make one final report. I'm disgusted now, not just disappointed, that shots continue to be heard from photographic lodges. I email Minister Kasukuwere one last time and don't mince my words. 'You surely need to clean this sport-hunting industry up, or you need to shut it down,' I tell him.

Unsurprisingly, he doesn't reply. He knows as well as I do how many well-connected people operate in this industry. Right now, Zimbabwe is ranked among the most corrupt nations in the world. A failed state. And Minister Kasukuwere knows that I am leaving. He no longer has to pretend to be listening.

There's another brutal attack on a white farmer and his daughter. While taking their dogs for an afternoon walk on their own land, they had been bound with wire and attacked with axes. Both subsequently die from their horrific injuries.

I can't bear to think about any of this anymore. I once believed that watching a sunset and a moonrise alongside my elephant friends in this Hwange wilderness could repair anything. But it has gotten so bad, so mad, that not even this can now ease my pain. I arrived in Zimbabwe 21 years after the War of Independence ended. It's now 34 years on, yet I frequently feel as if that war is still being waged.

I take another look around at all of my books and photos and files and thirteen years of possessions and mementos. I lost it all once before, in the Grantham floods. Does any of this really matter now? I can live without it all, I decide, too many strange phone calls and unusual noises now disturbing my dark nights.

I can't face one more day of it. I need to make myself get out of here.

# GODSPEED

# 2014

The next morning, I throw what is most important into my 4x4 and I leave. Just like that. I don't plan to ever come back. Shaynie will deal with the rest of my things, carting everything away, distributing what my friends can use and discarding the rest.

Barbara is waiting for me in Bulawayo, relieved that I'm safe and out of that place. I am shattered, but I also share her sense of relief. She looks at me with eyes filled with pain and sadness. 'I should have taken your advice about the green bananas,' I say to her, trying to smile.

Later, I realise that in my haste, I've left a folder of important documents behind, locked in a tin trunk. 'You're not going back there by yourself,' Barbara declares. 'If you go back, I'll have to go with you.'

We don't go immediately. I am tired and need to sleep—which I do for days on end. Then, I begin making enquiries about selling my 4x4 and booking my flight out.

A one-way flight.

A week later an article appears in the Bulawayo *Chronicle*. It quotes the provincial Minister of State for Matabeleland North (previously known as the governor; the same office that had previously caused so much trouble). His name is Cain Mathema, a man who I have never met. 'We are under siege,' he says. 'They want us to be seen as failures because they don't want us to benefit from our resources and some Western agents in our midst influence that. One of them is an Australian woman . . .'

Although it is hilariously ridiculous, this time I don't laugh. Shaynie is quick to remind me that 'they target only those they fear': 'It's a mark of how well you've done your job with the elephants, that these deceitful people even bother to be concerned with you.' They're not worth losing sleep over, I know. But I do lose sleep—over their pitiful lies and deception.

I'm indescribably tired. I stay off the internet. I change my phone number and put an automatic response on my email. My friends know how to contact me, including Mandy. 'So this little girl from country Queensland is still managing to unsettle those who run Zimbabwe,' she writes. 'I'm so glad you're out of there.'

Meanwhile I hear that interest in the petition is building all over the world. It's now clear to even more people that private claims on this land should never have been allowed. Predictably, the ministers targeted by the petition (including those from both Lands and Tourism) are passing the buck among themselves, which is, surprisingly, even reported in the government press. Minister Kasukuwere is being bombarded with correspondence, urging him to enforce the Cabinet directive. I'm pretty much staying out of it all, still declining to speak to journalists and wanting the whole thing to end.

Eventually, I travel with Barbara back to Hwange. All I feel is a desperate need to be away from this place, and a deep sadness that it's come to this. We are back at my cottage for no more than twenty minutes, grabbing my documents and some extra things that Barbara and Dee can use, and then we are out of there for good.

Just down the road, we come upon two elephants by the roadside, the last Presidential Elephants that I will likely see. It's Louise from Lady's family, and her eighteen-month-old daughter Layla. Behind them are Louise's older two offspring, Laurie and Louie. There is no one else in sight. The L family is still split up, following Lady's tragic death. This is still so sad for me.

All of the elephants have, however, enriched my life in ways that I will never forget. They're my family. I can't bear to think I won't be seeing them again. 'I need to keep going,' I say to Barbara, choking back my distress. And we do, stopping for only a few seconds to wish all of my elephant family godspeed.

'I wish we had taken your *Thandeka Mandlovu* signs,' Barbara says to me sadly as we drive along. 'I would have liked to keep them.'

Shaynie is once again working hours away from Bulawayo, but she returns for a couple of days and joins me in her home, where I've been spending more time than she has. It's an emotional time for both of us. We enjoy a chat and an Amarula before bed.

There are all sorts of rumours flying, including one that I've gone off to study penguins in Antarctica! 'Shaynie,' I probe, 'did you have anything to do with that one?'

'So, what about the bateleurs?' she asks, keen to change the subject. 'Did they stop looking down on you?'

'You know, I haven't seen one all year. In fact I haven't felt Andy's presence through any of this. Maybe he's gone away too.'

The next morning I drag myself out of bed and decide to check my emails. My heart skips a beat when the first thing I see is a story about the reclusive creator of the cartoon strip, Calvin and Hobbes. It was one of Andy's most favourite things in the world. His obsession had me searching far and wide in Australia for books missing from his treasured collection. 'I'm not sure that I believe in coincidences anymore,' I smile over my hot chocolate. 'Perhaps it's a sign? Maybe Andy's not gone after all.'

'Maybe like all of us, he just wanted you out of there too,' Shaynie says.

After having not heard from him for two months, I decide to email Saviour. Because my professional relationship with him is over, I no longer feel a need to call him Minister Kasukuwere. The amount of activity generated from the elephants' Facebook page is often staggering now, despite no new posts. He needs to know that this issue is not going away quickly and that many potential tourists are fast losing all confidence in Zimbabwe. My tone is one of disappointment. I ask him to at least fix up game-drive access and monitoring restrictions now in the grabbed areas. I tell him that nobody in the Parks Authority or the Wildlife Ministry has requested any information from me—none of my thirteen years of notes, reports, files, schematics and identification photographs—so there is no point in me leaving anything behind. I ask him, yet again, to think about these Presidential Elephants as a flagship herd to benefit the *nation*. Then, I say goodbye and wish him well.

He replies, simply saying that my email is 'appreciated' and that he has 'noted all' that I said.

I decide that I will travel on to Harare and spend some final time with Carol. I'll take with me two trunks of useful bits and pieces to store with Keith and Raynel, in case I return one day to work with elephants somewhere else. They're urging me to think hard about opportunities in the more peaceful, sane Botswana. I'm thinking about my previous offer in South Africa.

More frequently though, I'm just focused on getting out of here. I can't help but feel that I've had my fill of Africa for a while, although I know I'll never give up the battle for elephants entirely. Attempting to sell my 4x4 in the capital makes good sense, since there's more activity there and I need to find somebody with ready cash. I'll book my flight once it's sold.

First though, I try to enjoy some 'last times' in Bulawayo. 'Last time' walking the city streets with no other whites in sight; 'last time' searching for designer labels at the street markets; 'last time' buying fruit from the ladies with their pyramids of produce; 'last time' ordering pizzas from the friendly attendant at Pizza Inn who always ensures there's extra sauce on the base; 'last time' in the peaceful Matobo Hills.

In Matobo, Shaynie and I lie on our backs on a huge rocky boulder, gazing up at the fish eagles. It's been nearly eight years since she first told me that 'an eagle flies further when in a turbulent wind'. 'Even eagles get unbearably tired, Shaynie,' I sigh. 'I'll miss coming here.'

We share texts and photos with Dinks in South Africa. 'Oh, what a sadness,' Dinks wails. 'Do you know how these photos tear at my heart-strings? I could just curl up and commit harikari. Love and miss you both to the moon and back.' And then, a few minutes later: 'If longing could cause me to sprout wings, I would tell you to pour coffee. I'm coming.'

Barbara and Dee join me as I say some goodbyes around town. We keep our sunglasses on to hide our tears. I give Dee my baby names book, from which I chose names for the elephants, which breaks our hearts a little more. Every day, I wonder if the elephant families I named and came to love are still intact.

It didn't work out for CJ and Herbie in South Africa. Now they're back, and I'm the one who is leaving. There are hugs all around, long and tight.

Shaynie is being forced to give up her home, unable now to afford the rent in this crazy country.

'I hope you find another home soon, Shaynie,' I say, as we tackle our sad goodbyes.

'You too . . .' she whispers.

I drive through the city centre before turning towards Harare. Last time, last time. Everything is as run-down and filthy as ever. But still my heart is torn in two. I know that I'm unlikely to ever be back.

# ANOTHER PATH

## 2014

I am relieved to finally be across the country in Harare, with Carol. Now, at last, I can start trying to disentangle myself from it all. After the winter sun disappears, we sit gazing into the flames of a log fire, sipping Amarula.

'You no longer had a choice,' Carol tells me.

'I know.'

'What will you do now?' she asks.

'I will . . . I still don't know what I will do,' I confess.

'You would've had to keep compromising yourself year after year,' she says. 'You need to keep remembering that. And when you forget, you just need to ask your friends why you left. They won't have forgotten . . . You gave those elephants thirteen years, and you shared them with the world. That's a victory in itself. Now there's other elephants needing your help.'

I stare into the glowing coals, desperately hoping that all of my elephant friends will be okay. And we toast to times that we will never forget.

Zimbabwe is in meltdown, the economy once again teetering on the brink of total collapse. Sanctions are still being blamed for most things, although the new farmers' lack of productivity is now the fault of climate change! Forget that agricultural fields aren't being irrigated, there's not even any water in Carol's classy suburb unless you sink a borehole or truck it in. The electricity outages are increasingly outrageous. We've had no power for twelve, thirteen, sometimes fourteen hours a day, day after day. The pot holes are deeper than ever and could just about swallow a giraffe. There is litter everywhere. Indigenous trees are still being felled at alarming rates. It's said that 70 per cent of the population of 14 million live on less than US$2 a day. Unemployment now sits at around 85 per cent, agriculture is in ruins and the government is broke, barely even able to pay its civil servants. Broke and broken. Except for the ever-increasing number of ostentatious houses and top-of-the-range vehicles belonging to the obscenely wealthy politically connected elite.

'Zimbabwe will never be a colony again,' is President Mugabe's most well-known chant. At every opportunity he reminds the whites of their place in this country. Now he declares that they 'can stay in apartments in our towns, but they cannot own land'.

Hundreds of unemployed youths are given t-shirts and food and are bussed to the airport to greet the president on his return from frequent trips away. They carry placards, often professionally printed, that proclaim such things as WHITES, OUT, as they hail their president with rapturous applause.

In his Hero's Day speech (a day that honours the fallen heroes of the liberation war), while we struggle to cope with no power and no water, President Mugabe announces: 'Zimbabwe has made tremendous progress in the provision and rehabilitation of infrastructure. In the energy sector, government has committed financial resources towards the rehabilitation and maintenance of existing power infrastructure in order to achieve optimal performance . . . Government is committed to the proper management of our environment, water . . .'

I swear, for the past thirteen years, I must have been living somewhere else, on a whole other planet. Carol reminds me that the ZANU-PF headquarters in downtown Harare is located on a street named Rotten Row.

This is a country just about ready to implode.

There's talk of Saviour becoming a future president. I decide to email him once more. 'Saviour,' I write, 'I swear to God, if it turns out that one day *you* become president—after all that you *didn't* do for the Presidential Elephants—I'm going to come back and shoot you myself.'

Which, he tells me in reply, makes him laugh.

I think about Keith and Raynel urging me to consider Botswana for future elephant work, and decide to keep my options open. I take a chance and ask Saviour if he'd mind passing to me the contact details of his counterpart there. Somewhat surprisingly, he tells me that he thinks Botswana would be 'a very good idea'. Whether he's taking the opportunity to make certain that I leave Zimbabwe, or whether he genuinely wants to help me, I'm not sure. But he forwards me these details, and I tuck them away safely for now.

I sell my 4x4. Everything has become painfully real. Tears well up in my eyes as I watch it being driven away, laden with a million of my memories, to its own new life. Once again I feel my life crashing down around me.

A hundred kilometres away, Lol and Drew are packing up their lives too, in preparation for a move to South Africa. When Andy died, Drew was just a toddler. Today he is a wise young man of eighteen, but there's no way he's going to leave behind the big soft-toy horse that I gave to him the day before Andy's funeral. There were other similar gifts over the years. 'Those furry things from his past, he guards fiercely,' Lol tells me.

This lifts my heart. This special family will forever be intrinsically entwined in my life.

'Hold your head up our darling and keep walking,' Lol urges.

I wander around craft shops and outdoor markets one last time and buy myself a little wooden elephant with wings, to fly with me across the ocean. And to fly me back safely, when my mind feels a need to return.

Carol drives me to the airport with my pathetic couple of suitcases in tow; all that I have of thirteen years and seven months spent in this country.

'I'll be seeing you in Hawaii,' Carol says to me. She plans to live there for a while, in a house she already owns, once she finally gets around to leaving Zimbabwe. We all need to be somewhere else; anywhere but here. I hug her goodbye, not knowing if I'll ever really see her again.

I'm holding it together, feeling ready to finally leave. That is, until I allow myself to think once more about my elephant family. I decide to give it one last try. For them. I sit in the departures lounge, one of the few white faces in a sea of black travellers, and text Saviour. He wouldn't expect anything less from me. He once said to me, 'Nobody loves these elephants more than you.'

'Please,' I beg him, 'for the elephants that I loved so much, won't you at least fix . . .'

Saviour reads my message and replies without delay. 'It pains me that it has come to this,' he says. And that, for me, sums up all that is so ludicrous, so implausible, so wrong, in this crazy country. *Why, then, didn't he do more for the Presidential Elephants?* He could have done so much more. I simply can't hold it together any longer. Tears stream from my eyes and over my cheeks like water spilling over the Victoria Falls. I don't want to be having this meltdown in public, and I try hard to pull myself together. But still the tears flow.

A black woman takes a seat beside me. 'Are you leaving special ones behind?' she asks me gently. And I lose it all over again, unable to speak.

From the window of the plane I look down on Harare and across the troubled land that is Zimbabwe, feeling so desperately sad over how it all turned out. But also comforted, knowing that for so many years, I gave it my all.

By the time I touch down in Queensland, more than 24 hours later, I'm feeling completely exhausted. And unexpectedly liberated. Huge tidal waves of immense relief are washing over me. I embrace the country of my birth with open arms.

Everything looks so fresh and neat and thriving. I'm strangely comforted by bright, shiny shopping malls, and the polished hustle and bustle. It all seems so splendidly functional, rational and safe. For a while at least, I need a place of certainty—and here it is, all around me. From the Grantham home where I grew up, the Milky Way looks just like it does in the African bush; a dazzling path that you might skip and dance along. The immensely wide daytime skies are familiar too, vivid blue and filled with birds. It is the ocean that I've longed for most of all. After spending time with my family, I travel on to the Sunshine Coast to write and revive. And to reflect.

The dry winds of Africa have shaped me. I've been bent and twisted, like the velvety pods of the *Acacia erioloba*. I've emerged wiser now, stronger and proud. My giant Hwange friends, I know, will live with me forever. As I gaze out over the vastness of the Pacific Ocean, at the golden path of moonshine on its surface, I see elephants ambling towards me, huge ears flapping in the stillness of the night. I feel their warmth and friendship, and hear their rumbles. I breathe deeply and pat my heart, in the African way. I am one with them. Still. And I know that I had a remarkable ride, with them by my side. Despite everything that happened, I relished it.

This is where it all begins. Another path. Another place. Another new adventure, with my Hwange elephant family alive, inside of me.

# POSTSCRIPT

## OCTOBER 2014—JANUARY 2016

The day after I arrived back in Australia in October 2014, Barbara died. She fell in her Bulawayo flat after suffering a debilitating migraine, but her injuries should never have claimed her life. Zimbabwe's hospital system had let young Dee down once more. Her emails to me were heart-wrenching as she tried to come to terms with it all. She opted to scatter her mother's ashes in the Matobo Hills. Dee has since left Zimbabwe, and moved to the United Kingdom. She, like so many others, needed to be somewhere else.

I found it impossible to walk away from Zimbabwe's elephants completely. On the surface I may have appeared silent, but I was never inactive. In late November, just six weeks after I left Zimbabwe, Johnny Rodrigues reported that 34 young elephants, some believed to be as young as two years old, had been ripped from their mothers in Hwange National Park to meet demand from Chinese zoos. They were being held in *bomas* inside the park. It was feared that up to 200 would ultimately be caught and transported. I began liaising with Minister Saviour Kasukuwere from afar, pleading with him to rethink his country's policy on this. The idea of us still being in contact was perhaps absurd, but I had a direct line of communication with him so I needed to try. At one stage it sounded possible that the captures might actually cease, and an Australian television crew began preparing to cover the story of the elephants' plight. But, once again, Minister Kasukuwere's story changed, time and time again.

In February 2015, it was reported that several elephants had been shot to feed guests at President Mugabe's 91st birthday celebrations. Again there was international outrage, although it is little known how common this sort of thing is in Zimbabwe. Unexpectedly, on the day of President Mugabe's birthday, Zimbabwe's *NewsDay* republished some of my interview with *National Geographic* about the private land claims in Presidential Elephant areas. Even so, nothing changed on the Hwange Estate. Tourists continued to complain bitterly about decent game-drive access, while others were being told they were viewing elephants from the Presidential herd, even if they were not. (As the years pass and populations grow, increasing numbers of elephant families regularly wander out of the national park and onto the estate, so there's often a 'mix' of elephants on this land, and indeed inside the national park as well. Now, some people simply generalise about what they're seeing.) The waterholes that I'd scooped were once again filled only with neglect. But at least there were people still watching, and applying pressure to fix the problem areas.

A month later, Minister Kasukuwere took a vicious public swipe at Johnny Rodrigues. The *Bulawayo Chronicle* quoted the minister as saying: 'What does Rodrigues know about animals, a Rhodesian Selous Scout who wants to tell us how to run our animals in this country. He used to kill our people during the war of liberation. That's what he only knows and we are saying this to him: mind your own business chief, the days when you used to kill Africans are over. Shut up, we're now fed up with you.'

The tragedies in Hwange didn't stop. One night in April, Australian wildlife conservationist Greg Gibbard from Perth (affectionately known as Gibby)—who worked inhouse for the Painted Dog Conservation project—was brutally murdered with an axe at the project base, by a disgruntled black Zimbabwean ex-employee. Gibby was 61. I didn't know

Gibby all that well but we'd shared a few drinks over the years and always stopped for a chat whenever we met on the roads. I could only wonder what causes such deep-seated hatred and rage. This sort of brutality was shocking, but nothing in Hwange surprised me anymore.

Despite stories that more than 80 young elephants were now in *bomas* ready to be exported, the Parks Authority had captured no more than the 34 youngsters that Johnny initially reported. Those that didn't die or escape were still being held in cramped *bomas* inside Hwange National Park. Through all of the early months of 2015, I'd kept up frequent communications directly with Minister Kasukuwere. He'd retained enough respect for my work and knowledge of elephants to at least keep tolerating me, even if he was now standing firm. Once it became clear that the export was definitely proceeding despite global concern, my focus switched to encouraging Minister Kasukuwere to at least leave the weaker elephants behind. I knew that Roxy Danckwerts, who recently founded the Zimbabwe Elephant Nursery (an extension of 'Wild is Life' on the outskirts of Harare), would take on the care of any left behind. She, too, was liaising directly with Minister Kasukuwere and we had begun liaising with one another.

In early July, 24 of the young elephants were airlifted to China. Photographs later revealed their distressing plight: a life of captivity, with no adult bonds or parental guidance, ahead of them all. Three luckier ones remained in Zimbabwe. At least one of these three was of an age where it still would have been suckling frequently from its mother at the time of capture. Named Annabelle, Matabele and Kukurakura, these elephants are in the care of Roxy and her team and could do with your support. Please look them up and follow their progress. One day, when they're old enough, we all hope it will be possible for them to be returned to the wild.

Meanwhile, Johnny reported that Cecil the lion had been killed by an American sport-hunter, and there was unprecedented world outrage. While the American dentist who carried out the despicable deed was the focus of international anger, it was the Zimbabwean professional hunter who escorted this client who was always more to blame. The American was under his control and guidance, after all. Although Cecil certainly wasn't the first majestic lion to be shot in Hwange, his death struck a chord, particularly over the way he had been hunted.

Finally, unethical sport-hunting in Zimbabwe, and particularly in Hwange, was in the international spotlight. A second Zimbabwean hunter was subsequently reported to have been arrested after also presiding over the wrongful hunt of a lion. The Parks Authority publicly named him as Headman Sibanda, who had threatened me. Men like Sibanda though, are far too well connected. Despite all of the talk, nothing much is likely to change, at least not for long, in Hwange while so many unethical hunters are around. Following Cecil's death, some international airlines changed their policies and now refuse to carry the remains of sport-hunted animals.

When a photographic safari guide was subsequently tragically killed by a male lion inside Hwange National Park in late August while escorting a group on foot, Zimbabwean journalists wrote of the spirits being angry and of 'Cecil's revenge'. The guide's name was Quinn Swales. He was the nephew of my friends Keith and Raynel.

Then in September *All the President's Elephants* screened on television in Hungary, bringing my life and work with these extraordinary elephants back to the fore. People always ask about the decree reaffirmation and Lady in particular after watching this documentary. Sad memories flooded back as I answered a torrent of emails.

As if all of this wasn't enough, by late September another series of horrendous cyanide poisonings in Hwange and around the country led to more elephant deaths. Once again, the poachers were after ivory. More than 70 elephants were reported to have been killed by cyanide in just one month, and that number kept rising. At the same time, some rotten cogs in the wheels of the Parks Authority were arrested for ivory smuggling. The Hwange Main Camp ecologist, one of the most senior of the Parks people on the ground, was among them. Thefts from Hwange's ivory strongroom had also been discovered. Corrupt Parks staff, and some policemen, were finally being exposed as ivory smugglers, and I for one was not even a little surprised.

During October, Zimbabwe was again in the spotlight over another appalling hunting incident. This one didn't occur in Hwange, although it certainly could have had the magnificent elephant bull found his way there. In a legal, escorted hunt in the south of Zimbabwe, a German sport-hunter killed an elephant with tusks that almost reached the ground. This elephant bull had wandered into the wrong country. A CNN reporter described the elephant as looking 'prehistoric, almost like a woolly mammoth'. In fact, he was said to be the largest elephant bull found in Zimbabwe for decades, perhaps more than 30 years. All hunters know how rare such a specimen is these days. And they blew him away. To put his head on a wall.

To top all of this off, Zimbabwe confirmed that it will continue to rip young elephants from their families to meet demand from zoos. And it plans to continue lobbying to sell its ivory stockpiles.

During 2015 all of my Cabinet contacts, except for Saviour Kasukuwere, were among those who were either expelled or suspended from the Ruling Party for allegedly plotting a coup to oust President Mugabe. Even Didymus Mutasa, once one of Mugabe's closest confidantes and the man who'd helped arrange for the initial and subsequent decrees for the Presidential Elephants, was expelled and described by the president as a 'stupid fool'. Francis Nhema, who appears in *All the President's Elephants* on behalf of the president, was suspended for five years, losing his ministerial and Cabinet seats although, bizarrely, he's been allowed to remain as a ZANU-PF member of parliament.

Minister Kasukuwere has since been promoted. He no longer has anything to do with wildlife, having been handed the higher-ranking ministry of Local Government. He also currently holds the powerful Ruling Party position of National Political Commissar, the person expected to ensure that ZANU-PF wins elections. It is now more clear to me than ever that during my last year in Hwange, and especially during my last few months, all of my high-level contacts were too preoccupied with internal politics, jostling for power and positions, to do the right thing by elephants.

Minister Kasukuwere has since thanked me and acknowledged my work and commitment to Zimbabwe's elephants. Several times over this past year he has declared, 'You will be back.' He will probably think differently after he reads this book.

Wilderness Safaris' guide Lewis Mangaba, who introduced me to Cecil the lion, has also told me that I'll be back. 'Thank you for all you have done for our beloved Zimbabwe,' he wrote in an email. 'You at least did something, and that energy no one can destroy. Hope you will soon pack your bags and be on a flight to Zim to be among the elephants that you love. I strongly believe you will be back. Peace and love be multiplied to you.' Like so many ordinary Zimbabweans he cares little for black–white hatred.

Roxy from Zimbabwe Elephant Nursery wrote to me about the lucky three elephants who weren't sent to China, encouraging me to visit. 'Can't wait for you to meet this trio Sharon. You have helped both them and me so much over the past few months . . . Elephant hugs to you!'

Others still want to see me elsewhere. My long-distance friend, Ayesha, who lives near Addo Elephant National Park in South Africa, urged, 'Hurry up and finish that book so you can come and have ellie time in Addo. There's ocean AND ellies here. Perfect for you!'

Carol emailed (still promising to leave Zimbabwe any time now) to say, 'I am just glad you are not still here in the country, facing it all on the ground.' And she had good news too. 'Tim Tams are back on the shelves in Harare!'

Shaynie really wants me to be missing it all, but I can't give her that assurance. My Zimbabwe friends though—both elephant and human— are in my thoughts, every day.

Lol and Drew didn't end up moving to South Africa after all. Lol met back up with a Dutch friend, Jacques, who grew up in Zimbabwe and who she first met when she was ten years old. They married in Harare in December 2015 and are making plans to live in the UK, and later in the Netherlands.

Very soon after in December, my dad died. I'm thankful to have had fourteen months living close by him. The day before he passed away in his high-care nursing home in Toowoomba, he asked me, as he had on previous occasions, to read to him from my manuscript for this book. I told him with a smile that he must be '*verruckt in the kopf*'! He squeezed my hand as I told him too that Andy would be waiting to meet up with him, just as they had on my dad's beloved Fraser Island in 1999 (the year before Andy died). My dad is buried in cattle grazing country, in the grounds of a quaint little white, wooden church where I once went to Sunday school. When, shortly after his funeral, Australia's weather forecasters began reporting a monsoon trough in the Gulf of Carpentaria moving towards Queensland and likely to develop into Cyclone Stan (my dad's name), family and friends all smiled.

Tragically, by January 2016, poachers with cyanide had infiltrated the key home-range of the Presidential Elephants. One carcass was confirmed poisoned, but I fear the number of dead could be much higher. Bodies, as I know only too well, are not always found. Just as disturbingly, a new orphan arrived at the Zimbabwe Elephant Nursery. He was found covered in blood (probably his mother's blood), roaming terrified through the township of Dete, just down the road from where I used to live. Three female elephants had reportedly been shot in the area, and this little elephant was certain not to be the only orphan roaming around. These are horrifying developments. Some people in Zimbabwe like to say that all is okay with the Presidential Elephants. But the only way to know what has *really* happened to them over the past few years is for me to one day—if sanity ever returns to the country—try to carry out a detailed survey of the seventeen extended families in order to determine who is now missing from each one.

Later, it was very encouraging to see *All the President's Elephants* as a finalist in the International Elephant Film Festival—'the best of the best' elephant films in the world from the past nine years—an event that involved both the United Nations and CITES. As a finalist, it will now be showcased extensively throughout the world, with specifically targeted areas to include the African nations, China, the United States, Vietnam and Thailand, where ivory trade is high. It's also hoped that screenings to school children in African nations where poaching is high, will help them fall in love with elephants.

If you'd like to support anti-poaching efforts in Zimbabwe, please go to the Perth-based SAVE Foundation website www.savefoundation.org.au and select 'Donate Now'. If you specify 'Presidential Elephants' as your reason for giving, president Nicholas Duncan will ensure that 100 per cent of your donation (converted into needed equipment) reaches reputable anti-poaching teams on the ground. Donations made in Australia are tax-deductible. You can also make contact with me directly via www.sharonpincott.com and Facebook.

Some experts predict, based on current trends, that elephants could be extinct in the wild within the next couple of decades; potentially within my lifetime. When you see great numbers of elephants in countries such as Zimbabwe and Botswana, this seems impossible. But elephant poaching has reached unsustainable levels. If there are some 400,000 African elephants left in the wild today and 30,000 continue to be killed annually for their tusks, their future certainly doesn't look bright. Elephants live a whole decade and more before they give birth. And then they give birth only every three to four years on average. Recovery, therefore, is not rapid. Raw ivory is reported to be bought from poachers for less than US$100 per kilogram—and sold to Asian countries, where demand remains high, for more than twenty times this amount. The future actions of countries like China are key to the survival of elephants in the wild.

People frequently ask me what they can do to help the plight of the world's elephants. Not everyone is ready or able to fully immerse themselves in their own dedicated journey on the ground. If you are, prepare yourself for the roller-coaster ride of hope and heartbreak. If you aren't, you'll find plenty of conservationists around the world who could do with your moral, and if possible your financial support.

The photographic tourism industry is so important to Africa's wildlife, so long as it is properly controlled. Before you book anywhere on the African continent do check that you're supporting reputable lodges that are, in turn, putting a percentage of their profits back into supporting the wildlife, and also the impoverished communities who live among these wild animals.

Those activist and advocacy groups around the world who professionally lobby governments and decision-making bodies rely on you, the concerned public, to add voices to their campaigns.

While it is easy to heap *all* blame on African countries such as Zimbabwe, it must always be remembered that if there is no demand for the likes of ivory, elephant hunts and live young ones, there is no market. We must also remember that governments have to somehow find the money to support the running and protection of wildlife areas. There is no single simple solution, especially in places where corruption abounds. But unless we all take time to do just a little for our threatened and endangered species, their end could certainly be near.

My own journey with elephants is set to continue.

# ACKNOWLEDGEMENTS

Without the presence of these people in my Hwange life, my years with the elephants would have been so much harder—Dinks (Deline) Adlam, Shaynie (Charmain) Beswick, Ayesha Cantor, Val De Montille, Bobby Dempsey, Ernie and Carmen Deysel, Eileen Duffy, John and Del Foster, Craig Haskins, Mandy Keating, Miriam Litchfield, Gladys Mbomba, Carol McCammon, Andrea McKain, Busi Ncube, Caleb Nel, Henry and Natalia Nel, Jabulani Ngwenya, Karen Paolillo, Greg Rasmussen, Julia Salnicki, Lol (Laurette) Searle and her son Drew, the late Barbara Strydom, Dee (Desree) Strydom, Keith and Raynel Swales, Marion Valeix, CJ (Cynthia) and Herbie van den Berg, and Esther van der Meer and husband Hans Dullemont. Your part in my story will be remembered always. To those who have become dear friends, I'm forever thankful. Also to Corinne Carthy (nee Doneux), Susan Grady (nee Heming), Sue McMurchy, Christine Turner and Anne Waldie (nee Dobson) for support and friendship spanning 30 years.

Extra special thanks must go to Shaynie Beswick, who provided me with a Bulawayo base, even during the years when she was barely there (and really should have cancelled her lease), from where I shopped for supplies and recovered my spirit. Special thanks, too, to Carol McCammon, who also opened her home to me whenever I managed to get to Harare. To those in Hwange who helped ensure that I at least had a roof over my head, I'm grateful. And to all who lent a hand over the years, including Nicholas Duncan and those associated with the SAVE Foundation of Australia (these days known as the SAVE African Rhino Foundation), and others associated with the Matabeleland branch of Wildlife Environment Zimbabwe, you made a difference in my Hwange life. To Mandy Keating, endless thanks for Facebook assistance when my internet access was so poor, and for your ongoing website contributions.

To all of the elephant-lovers and advocates around the globe, the world would be a much poorer place without you. To the many hundreds who provided moral support, frequently taking time to drop me a note of encouragement, I thank you. To those who found their way to the Hwange bush carrying a little something to warm my heart, I will always be grateful for your thoughtfulness and laughter. Small things really did help to make some of the big things bearable. To the Button-Voorn family, the Green family and the Strachan family in particular, I will never forget our days together with the elephants.

Without placing you at further risk, I put my hand on my heart and remember those, especially in the Wildlife Ministry, Parks Authority, Forestry Commission, police and photographic safari circles, who were supportive and understood well the difference between right and wrong, even when others beside you did not and it wasn't wise for you to say so. To you I say—*Ngiyabonga. Wazvita.*

I take this opportunity to make special mention of a stranger who was kind to me beyond measure. Roberto Sabatino stepped up to the mark in South Africa when the thoughtful Ayesha Cantor secretly put out a plea for laptop assistance for me after a power surge destroyed mine. I'd never had any prior dealings with Roby and had no idea who this generous, unassuming man was. The laptop was only six months old when I realised that I had to leave Hwange, and Zimbabwe. I contacted Roby before leaving, to make a plan. His gracious words touched my heart at a time when my faith in humanity was wavering: 'The laptop was a gift, it is yours to keep. It was the least I could do for all the amazing work you have done with elephants . . . I expect nothing in return . . . [A] smile is priceless for me. I believe a little kindness and compassion can go a long way in this world.' I have cherished Roby's words, as much as I have his laptop (on which I wrote this book).

My sincere thanks to Deb Fleming, ex-*Australian Story* executive producer, and my publisher Rebecca Kaiser from Allen & Unwin for help and enthusiasm in making this book a reality. It was my Zimbabwean friend Val De Montille, still living in Brisbane, who helped these introductions along. To Bobby Dempsey, who rode with me through all the months of oftentimes difficult writing. Further deep gratitude to Rebecca and Bobby, and also to Aziza Kuypers and Andrea McKain for gentle guidance and wisdom while editing. Many thanks to Allen & Unwin publicist Sarah Haines for enthusiastically embracing this book, and to Angela Handley for kind assistance.

I'll always be grateful to the late Andy Searle, whose memory continues to inspire me. To my dad, Stan Schulz, I know you would have been proud to hold this book in your hands. And a special thank you to other family members who helped me over the years from afar, and whenever I returned to Australia.

My deepest gratitude must go to my beloved Hwange elephant family, and to the mystifying continent that is Africa, for golden days and all that you've taught me about life, love, loss. And resilience.